THEOLOGICAL F
COLLABORAT

This book examines the theological fou ... to Christian ministry. The discovery that C ... 'one of another' creates energy and joy in ministry and empowers the Church in an age of mission.

Outlining the present challenges for ministry, Stephen Pickard offers an historical perspective on ministry over the last century; develops a theory of collaborative ministry based on a dialogue between theology and science; and explores some implications of collaborative ministry for lay and ordained people of the Church.

This book breaks new ground in its theory of collaborative ministry through a dialogue with the sciences of emergence. It also offers fresh insights on important texts in ministry; relationships between Christology, Pneumatology and ministry; a relational ontology of ministry; episcopacy, ecumenism, ordination vows and wisdom for team ministry.

Explorations in Practical, Pastoral and Empirical Theology

Series Editors: Leslie J. Francis, University of Warwick, UK
and Jeff Astley, Director of the North of England
Institute for Christian Education, UK
Martyn Percy, Ripon College Cuddesdon and
The Oxford Ministry Course, Oxford, UK

Theological reflection on the church's practice is now recognised as a significant element in theological studies in the academy and seminary. Ashgate's new series in practical, pastoral and empirical theology seeks to foster this resurgence of interest and encourage new developments in practical and applied aspects of theology worldwide. This timely series draws together a wide range of disciplinary approaches and empirical studies to embrace contemporary developments including: the expansion of research in empirical theology, psychological theology, ministry studies, public theology, Christian education and faith development; key issues of contemporary society such as health, ethics and the environment; and more traditional areas of concern such as pastoral care and counselling.

Other titles in the series include:

Theology without Words
Theology in the Deaf Community
Wayne Morris
978-0-7546-6222-8

Entering the New Theological Space
Blurred Encounters of Faith, Politics and Community
Edited by John Reader and Christopher R. Baker
978-0-7546-6339-3

Hospital Chaplaincy in the Twenty-first Century
The Crisis of Spiritual Care on the NHS
Christopher Swift
978-0-7546-6416-1

Evangelicalism and the Emerging Church
A Congregational Study of a Vineyard Church
Cory E. Labanow
978-0-7546-6450-5

Theological Foundations for Collaborative Ministry

STEPHEN PICKARD
Diocese of Adelaide, Australia

ASHGATE

Published by
Ashgate Publishing Limited
Wey Court East
Union Road
Farnham
Surrey, GU9 7PT
England

Ashgate Publishing Company
Suite 420
101 Cherry Street
Burlington
VT 05401-4405
USA

www.ashgate.com

British Library Cataloguing in Publication Data
Pickard, Stephen K.
Theological foundations for collaborative ministry. – (Explorations in practical, pastoral and empirical theology)
1. Cooperative ministry. 2. Pastoral theology.
I. Title II. Series
253–dc22

Library of Congress Cataloging-in-Publication Data
Pickard, Stephen K.
Theological foundations for collaborative ministry/ Stephen Pickard.
p. cm. – (Explorations in practical, pastoral, and empirical theology)
ISBN 978-0-7546-6829-9 (hardcover : alk. paper) – ISBN 978-0-7546-6835-0 (pbk. : alk. paper)
1. Cooperative ministry. 2. Group ministry. 3. Church management. 4. Pastoral theology. 5. Christian leadership. I. Title.

BV675.5.P53 2009
253–dc22

2009013492

ISBN 9780754668299 (hbk)
ISBN 9780754668350 (pbk)
ISBN 9780754697282 (ebk)

Printed and bound in Great Britain by
MPG Books Group, UK

Contents

Part V Recovering Orientations

Preface

Wherein lies the joy of Christian ministry? My own conviction is that the joy of Christian ministry arises out of collaborative practice where team-work, shared ministry and common purpose combine together to further the mission of God in the world.

In this book I draw upon my experience in ministries of various kinds and in different contexts. As priest in a team ministry in a large rural town in a new housing area in Australia, in the pit-village daughter-church of a city parish in the United Kingdom, in university chaplaincy in the UK, in theological education and ministerial formation in the Uniting Church and Anglican Churches in Australia, in the school of theology of an Australian university and more recently as an assistant bishop in the Diocese of Adelaide. For over a quarter of a century I have ministered in these different environments as an Anglican priest, professional theologian, leader of academic and ministerial institutions and bishop in the Church. For quite a number of those years I have also been a member of a local church in which I have 'sat in the pew' so to speak. The reality of being 'of the baptised', deacon, priest, bishop and theologian has been woven together in surprising and life-giving ways. It has alerted me to the remarkable capacity of the people of God to exercise discipleship and ministry in the world.

I know from experience that the joy of 'ministry for all' resides in collaborative practices wherein all play a part and regard the ministry as a truly shared task rather than the preserve of one particular group. I also know that this approach and attitude is not automatic: it has to be worked at and often encounters resistance from clergy and laity alike. The joy of ministry is costly but the outcomes are an expansion of all the ministries of the people of God. Traditional orders of ministry, far from being usurped, are enhanced and blessed through collaboration. The newer ministries are freed and energised. This reciprocity in ministry generates deep joy; something that gave the apostle Paul remarkable energy for new mission and faithful witness (e.g., Phil. 4:1; 1 Thess. 2:20). I experienced this same dynamic in ministry in my early years as a deacon and priest. In this case the parish's traditional 'harvest festival' was transformed into a celebration of the harvest of the ministries of the baptised. The work and ministry of the whole people were blessed and released for mission in the world. This liturgical act proved a remarkable confirmation of the responsibilities of the baptised and the esteem in which the ordained leaders were held. The joy of the gospel overflowed.

The present book is an opportunity to stand back from such experiences to reflect on the inner secret of ministry that is truly collaborative. In this sense the book delves into the theological and ecclesiological matrix of Christian ministries, in particular their relation to each other and how and why collaborative ministry makes sense in the light of the gospel. It is implicit in the nature of the gospel that the ministries of the Church are intertwined in the gospel – as the title of the book says 'one of another' in the service of the kingdom of God (Rom. 12:5). The springboard for these reflections is my experience and theological work as an Anglican. This is reflected in some of the material in the historical sections of the book. However the dynamics of ministry uncovered in this exploration hopefully resonate with Christians across the ecumenical spectrum. Indeed one of the key intentions of the book is to provide a fresh basis for ecumenical conversation in that most intractable of areas, ministry.

I have not written a practical guide to collaborative ministry: how to, what works, what doesn't. There is quite a lot useful material in this area. Rather I have tried to write a book for the practitioner who wants to draw a little deeper from the theological well that nourishes good practice. As a result the book is an extended inquiry into a theory of collaborative practice. If it encourages a more principled and intelligent practice it will have served some useful purpose.

The book has a variety of readers in mind and has a number of entry and exit points. The historical chapters of Part II will have more immediate appeal to those familiar with the history of the Anglican tradition. Those interested in engaging with the theological nerve centre of the book can go directly to Chapter 3 then Part III. The latter parts of the book (Parts IV and V) will hopefully stimulate those with a more practical bent in ministry. The relevant chapters offer ecclesial, practical and vocational approaches to a theology of collaborative ministry.

Acknowledgements

This book is the fruit of many years of Christian ministry in various contexts. I am deeply grateful to those colleagues and friends who have helped shape my own ministerial practice and theological reflection over many decades.

The leading ideas in this book took shape through the years I was Director at St Mark's National Theological Centre in Canberra Australia. I owe a debt of gratitude to the remarkable faculty I had the privilege of leading throughout that period of ministry. In particular, I thank my colleagues in the ministry formation program, Graeme Garrett, Elaine Farmer, Richard Bowie and the late Owen Dowling for their wisdom and insight into the nature of Christian ministry. I also thank my colleagues in the Public and Contextual Theology Strategic Research Centre (PACT) of Charles Sturt University, of which I am a member, for their friendship and support and in particular those colleagues who have commented on various chapters in this book.

I am also grateful to St Mark's for sabbatical leave in 2004 which enabled me to write the main chapters of this book; the hospitality of Wesley House Cambridge; and Professor Stephen Sykes for a Visiting Fellowship at St John's College Durham. This book would not have seen the light of day had it not been for a months leave from Adelaide Diocese in May 2008; a visiting fellowship at Cuddesdon College Oxford and the encouragement of its Principal, Canon Professor Martyn Percy; and to Sarah Lloyd of Ashgate Publishing who made it all finally possible. As ever my wife Jennifer has taught me most about the calling and joy of being a collaborator in all things great and small.

This book is dedicated to the faculty of the School of Theology of Charles Sturt University at St Mark's, partners in the Gospel of Christ.

Chapter 1
Collaborative Ministry: An Introduction

Collaborative Ministry and Spiritual Maturity

'To exercise ministry in a collaborative manner requires spiritual maturity.' This was a comment made to me by a colleague when I told him I had completed a manuscript on the topic. My first thought was, 'Why, of course'. The more I pondered this the more I came to see that the matter of being spiritually mature rarely emerges in discussion of ministry. There is an important sense in which we are always learning, always finding new dimensions and depths to the ministerial calling, always being challenged to move beyond the known into new regions. To be spiritually mature in ministry is not something one attains one day and then ceases growing. Maturity in Christ is a lifelong project.

This seems all well and good. I have discovered more about being a preacher in the last ten years and become as a result a better preacher – I hope – than I was when I first began over 35 years ago. I have matured and I trust that this maturity has been a multifaceted thing and as a result I stand in a different place as a preacher today than a decade ago; that I have a greater appreciation of the task of the preacher and am able to draw from deeper wells of spiritual wisdom in my preaching. If nothing has changed then something has gone wrong: the ordination vows I undertook have not issued forth in the fruit promised. Yet my colleague's response haunted me. Collaborative ministry is not rocket science – at least so I thought. It ought to come naturally for the Christian disciple. Ought not a collaborative approach be one of the first things we learn in ministry whether lay or ordained? Ought not this way of ministering together be second nature in the body of Christ? Instead of belonging to the weightier matters of ministry ought not collaborative ministry belong to the milk and first things; to be counted among the basic doctrines about Christ, repentance, faith, baptism laying on of hands, resurrection and judgement (Heb. 5:12–6:2)? Is it not conceivable that tucked away in this list of the basics might be something about working together in ministry?

The problem with the above assumption is that it is precisely that, an assumption. In my experience this assumption is repeatedly negated by the actual practices of the Christian community. It is remarkable how poorly formed are the habits for collaborative practices among clergy and lay people. Indeed I would go so far as to say that clergy generally evidence minimal aptitude for such a way of ministry, perhaps even less than lay people. Otherwise apparently spiritually mature, wise and able leaders show little understanding of what it means to be 'working with others' in ministry and leadership. A truly collaborative approach to ministry seems to require something of us that we lack the spiritual capacity and will to deliver. Working in teams and working as a team in a cooperative manner was precisely the way Jesus engaged in ministry. It gave power and was truly transformative. Even those who emulate this gospel pattern often still evidence all the traits of a controlling leader.

I have come to the conclusion that collaborative ministry ought to be located within a theology of Christian baptism. To be a true collaborator requires multiple deaths and burials. This applies to churches and their ethos as much as to individuals. Collaborative ministry is a ministry that requires resurrection of a new self with others. And this seems to be an exceedingly painful and often tortuous process. Many of the church have been victims of a ministry that has been the very antithesis of a collaborative venture. Unreconstructed Christian leaders often exercising extremely successful ministries can remain blind to the collaborative way.

Why is this so? The reasons are many and varied. Certainly a key issue in the above is the matter of power. Life in relation to others involves the exercise of power. Contrary to popular rhetoric these days power per se is not a bad thing, nor is it a necessary evil. The fact is that power is everywhere: human life, society, the earth and the cosmos are fields of power. The *dunamis* of the Spirit gives life and breath to all things. Furthermore human development and maturation requires an emerging sense of personal power and those who for various reasons grow up without a sense of empowerment or acquire it in dysfunctional and unhealthy ways can easily misuse it. And of course human beings, no matter what their background or make up, are quite capable of the misuse and abuse of power. A collaborative approach to ministry requires both sharing of power and a generous bestowal of power. This is a deeply regenerative action and increases the power available. However this dynamic is counterintuitive and something most of us resist out of fear of our own diminution. We are more used to 'grabs for power' or inappropriate relinquishing of power. So at a basic level of human life collaboration is challenging to say the least and more usually resisted.

What we more often observe is reversion to either autocratic or unhealthy, submissive forms of relation. The autocratic way in ministry deals with fear and anxiety about loss of control by the exercise of power over others. Power may be released and authority delegated but this is more often not true delegation but task assignment. This kind of leadership knows little about true collaboration or collegiality. However, for many, such an autocratic leadership can be extremely appealing for it offers certainty and sureness. It is a style of leadership that often masks itself as collegial but at heart others only ever work *for* such a leader and rarely *with*. The autocratic leader uses the gifts of others but creativity, where it is allowed, is carefully managed.

The alternative to autocratic leadership is often an unhealthy submissiveness in which a person's gifts and creativity for ministry are continually suppressed; the voice is lost, vision wanes, stasis sets in, energy levels diminish, creativity dies. In this scenario collaboration is thwarted due to the lack of confidence that a person has anything to contribute to shared life and ministry. Obediential following rather than truly shared ministry is the mark of such an approach. Both of these defaults feed off an isolationist and individualist approach to ministry. There is little or no understanding of what it means to be members 'one of another' (Rom. 12:5), orientated towards the other as the ontological foundation of life and ministry.

A collaborative approach to ministry in the body of Christ requires the capacity to move beyond the defaults we commonly observe in leadership – of autocratic or submissive behaviour. But this presumes cooperation. This seems to be innate though human beings also seem disposed to opposite behaviours.[1] The result is that we live in constant tension between these two elemental drives. However within contemporary Western societies there seems to be an overriding emphasis upon competition. Human society is geared to a market economy that thrives on competition. Our political life is combative, particularly in the Westminster parliamentary system. Of course this is not all loss for it is manifestly much more preferable to debate and win an argument than to engage in military action to win the day. However the two may be more closely linked than we would wish. Nonetheless the competitive spirit is deeply encoded into our way of life economically, socially, politically and alas religiously. Where competition rather than cooperation dominate the scene it is axiomatic that power will be skewed in unhealthy ways.

In the life of the Church we see all too clearly the influence of the competitive spirit between churches, within churches, and among leaders and the ministries of the body of Christ. The prevailing cultural values have a far greater impact on our religious life and forms of ministry than most of us either realise or care to know. Even more troubling is the remarkable ways in which competition and misuse of power can acquire religious legitimation. Divine sanction of competition is the final seal and establishes the conditions for unfettered misuse of power in the supposed interests of a higher good. Needless to say collaboration between churches and within churches and their various ministries will always struggle for recognition.

The Appeal to Relationality

The collaborative spirit is an alien experience within the competitive environment of modernity. Even in circumstances where people work together in a collaborative manner the motivations for such behaviour are inevitably skewed in self-serving ways. This generates a softer form of 'I-mode cooperation' nonetheless.[2] However, to move in a genuinely different direction – 'we-mode cooperation' – requires in

---

[1] See Raimo Tuomela, *The Philosophy of Sociality: The Shared Point of View* (Oxford: Oxford University Press, 2007), pp. 149–81. Tuomela states: 'Cooperation seems to be innate, a coevolutionary adaptation based on group selection, the basic reason for this being that human beings have evolved in a group context.' He also notes the fact that people seem disposed to 'defect, act competitively, or even act aggressively' (p. 150).

[2] Ibid., pp. 151–7.

the first instance nothing less than a conversion of self towards the other; to the 'one God and Father of all, who is above all and through all and in all' (Eph. 4:6). To be orientated towards God is the natural response to one who has decisively turned towards the world in Jesus Christ. The 'mode of togetherness' of the life of the Holy Trinity is emblematic of the inclination of such a God towards the world and the human being. Rublev's icon captures the collaborative spirit so well.[3] Each of the members of the Trinity is inclined towards the others in a deferential posture of respect and acknowledgement of shared life; each is constituted as person by virtue of their relation to the other. The persons of the divine Trinity are pre-eminently 'members one of another'. However the movement is a double gesture, the inclination to the other is at the same time directed to the holy table. It is an invitational gesture of hospitality to the world to gather. God's collaborative character is by nature outwardly directed, open, invitational and hospitable. This is mirrored in the economy of God's love which is fundamentally a sending forth (John 3:16). The Eastern emphasis on the divine procession of the Son and Spirit embodies this movement of God towards the world as a mirror of God's eternal being. The apostolic God's sending forth is not something alien to God's inner being but rather the appropriate manner of the eternal orientation to the other within the life of God.

The perichoretic (lit.: 'dancing around') life of God is the deepest foundation for a collaborative ministry. Recognition of this fact has provided the springboard in contemporary theology of ministry for so-called relational understandings of ministry.[4] Such language abounds today and is part and parcel of notions of the interconnectedness of all ministries and the priority of shared 'every-member ministry'. This is well and good, at least as far as it goes. But an appeal to relational ministry and concomitant critique, if not rejection of any hierarchical form of ministry makes life too easy. It often trades on a simple correspondence between the life of the triune God as community of interconnected persons and the shape and form of Christian ministry and leadership. The discourse of relationality is underdeveloped in dealing with issues of conflict and difficulty in ministry and it

[3] Rublev's Icon of the Trinity, or the Icon of the Old Testament Trinity, was painted by Andrei Rublev around 1410 and now hangs in the Tretyakov Gallery in Moscow. Based upon an earlier icon, the 'Hospitality of Abraham', it depicts the three angels who visited Abraham at the Oak of Mamre (Gen. 18). Rublev changed the subject to focus on the Mystery of the Trinity.

[4] For example, Robin Greenwood, *Transforming Priesthood: A New Theology of Mission and Ministry* (London: SPCK, 1994), ch. 4 'A Relational Theology of Ministry'; Edward Hahnenberg, *Ministries: A Relational Approach*, (New York: Crossroad, 2003). Compare the discussion of perichoresis by Graham Buxton in *The Trinity, Creation and Pastoral Ministry: Imaging the Perichoretic God* (Milton Keynes: Paternoster Press, 2005), pp. 129–42, 149–76. Buxton offers a more general application of the concept of perichoresis to pastoral ministry.

tends to set up idealisations about the way ministry ought to work. Disappointment will be close at hand.

A relational approach to ministry that takes its cue from the doctrine of the Trinity has, as yet, not been able to give a rich account of collaborative ministry operating within a structured and hierarchically ordered system of ecclesial ministries. Relational discourse seems to be the provenance of Spirit-led ministries and flat hierarchies. Collaborative ministry discourse seems more at home in various forms of Protestant and Pentecostal churches where 'every-member ministry' has a familiar appeal and congregational forms of church life predominate with little or no organic connection to wider circles of the ecclesia. On the other hand episcopally ordered churches – which accounts for the major part of global Christianity – seem far less sympathetic, structurally at least, to collaborative ministry. The supposition here is that overly ordered churches, which embody significant levels of ministerial authority cannot, by nature, generate genuine collaborative ministry. It will always be trumped by top-down decision-making and the more collaborative impulses are too easily dispensed with. But is this necessarily the case? Anecdotal evidence suggests that local independent congregational churches in the Protestant and Pentecostal traditions seem as susceptible as episcopally ordered churches to dysfunctional ministry patterns and autocratic and/or overly submissive forms of ministry which are anything but collaborative. Things are not as simple as they seem and part of the intention of this book is to show why this is so and how a collaborative approach to Christian ministry ought to be a real possibility in churches with highly differentiated and hierarchically ordered ministries as much as Pentecostal and Independent churches with flat hierarchies of authority. Indeed a case is made to show why highly differentiated orders of ministry, when understood and operating as they ought, provide ideal conditions for collaborative ministry.

One thing is clear from the recent deployment of Trinitarian categories to ministry. That is, that the move from reflection on the doctrine of the Holy Trinity to a theology of ministry appears to be deficient. As yet we lack a theory that recognises (a) the deeper Trinitarian wells from which genuine collaboration in ministry arises and (b) at the same time recognises the significance of highly structured and ordered forms of ministry that trace their emergence to the earliest period of Christian ministry and mission. What we need is a theory to account for both theological and historical features of the Christian tradition. Collaborative ministry within a structured and ordered ecclesial set of ministries – either episcopal or non-episcopal – may not only be a real possibility but an implicate of the gospel of God. But the reasons for this need to be more adequately displayed than hitherto. The logic of collaborative ministry and the way it actually works within the ecclesia of God requires clear specification. A good theory will be one that can show why and how the ministries of the church are interconnected and what kind of connectedness this entails. In this way the inner logic of collaboration becomes manifest.

As its title suggests this book examines the kinds of theological and ecclesiological foundations required for a ministry of the people of God that is genuinely and richly collaborative. Whilst the notion of 'collaborative' ministry is familiar enough, the Church's rhetoric rarely matches its best practice in this regard. I have touched on some of the reasons for this above though it is not the intent of this book to examine the whole compass of issues involved. More particularly, the present book focuses upon the distinctly theological and ecclesial foundations that justify a collaborative ministry. Such an approach seems to be precisely what is required at a time when the Church is engaged in a significant refocusing of its energies towards mission, is blessed with an abundance of new ministries of the people of God, yet remains anxious about the resourcing of its mission and often uncertain concerning the purpose of ordained ministry.

Although, as mentioned above, the idea of collaborative ministry is familiar enough, exactly what this means and how it operates within the body of Christ deserves at least some preliminary specification. To collaborate means to work with another. The accent is on 'with' rather than 'for' or 'under'. It is a cooperative activity that requires trust in others, humility concerning one's own wisdom and competences and a desire to release the creativity and gifts of those with whom one works. This kind of collaborative way generates an ethos and mode of engagement even as it directs certain kinds of work practices. Such an approach to ministry is described in terms of partnership in the writings of the apostle Paul.

From the above depiction of collaborative ministry it is clear that it is relevant to all ministry. We might say Christian ministry has a collaborative character. It arises out of a baptismal theology of death to self and new life in Christ. This is the litmus test for all ministry that bears the name of Christ. The whole people of God are called, by virtue of their baptism, to collaborate, working together for the coming kingdom of God.

In this sense it is as true to speak of a collaborative ecclesia as it is to speak of collaborative ministry. The people of God do not decide of their own accord to operate in a collaborative manner. The ecclesia is, by virtue of being the body of Christ, a collaborative entity. As a creature of the Word and Spirit the ecclesia of God is a new community in relation to God and the world. It has emerged as a miracle of grace from the work of the Spirit of the God and Father of our Lord Jesus Christ. And this grace is not something alien from creation as such. Rather the social and cooperative form of life belongs to creation. Collaboration is encoded into the way God creates and acts. It is more than an interesting fact of cultural and social anthropology. The theological roots lead to cooperative and collaborative life founded in creation and orientated towards redemptive existence.[5] As a result when the Church acts in a collaborative manner it actualises its own deepest reality.

---

[5] See Daniel Hardy, 'Created and Redeemed Sociality' in Colin Gunton and Daniel Hardy (eds.), *On Being the Church*: *Essays on the Christian Community* (Edinburgh: T&T Clark, 1989), pp. 21–47.

It can do no other. Collaborative ministry is not an optional extra but the manner in which the ministry of the gospel is a gospel ministry.

As the biblical tradition and early history of the Church indicates there are a variety of differentiated ministries within the ecclesia of God. Within this mix there are specific representative ministries and various orders that have developed over time – for example, the most common: deacons, presbyters, bishops. In this context it is appropriate to talk about a collaborative leadership. Such leadership has a double reference both in relation to the wider corporate ministries of the Church and also in relation to other forms of leadership. In this latter case collaborative ministry has a collegial character. From the above brief discussion it is clear that collaborative ministry is a layered and rich concept that includes ethos and character of life as much as the specifics of cooperative ventures with others.

Precisely because the collaborative venture involves a measure of self-forgetfulness and desire to see others develop their gifts and potentialities, the way of collaboration is also a delicate and fragile mode of togetherness. Its strength is its weakness; trust can be betrayed, competition can appear in subtle ways, creativity can be denied or thwarted, an ethos can be weakened and disappear. The way of collaboration is the way of the cross through brokenness and glimpses of ministry raised together in Christ. The spirit of collaboration is nothing less than the Spirit of Love that connects and inclines every member of the body of Christ towards the other. This is the work of the perichoretic Spirit who gathers, directs and energises the ministries that serve the gospel of God. I will have more to say on this in the chapters that follow. A collaborative approach to ministry is, like the gospel itself, a treasure to be valued and cherished. In like manner collaboration is a matter deserving of an appropriate agonizing over, just like the gospel (Jude 1:3).

One of the most obvious and problematic areas for collaborative ministry is between clergy and laity. Tensions here have often been resolved by one dominating the other or one simply cutting itself adrift from the other. There are myriad scenarios here. Yet it is curious how little attention has been paid to the question of the relation between the ministries, particularly the basic relation between ordained and the corporate ministry of the Church. It is no exaggeration to say that the lack of inner coherence among the ministries is a major cause of conflict and dissipation of energies within churches and continually thwarts progress on the reconciliation of ministries across divided communions. An account of the theological and ecclesiological foundations for collaborative ministry could be of significant value for ecumenism and mission at the micro and macro levels of the Church.

Questions on the Agenda, Theoretical and Practical

The book is concerned with a range of questions that can be broadly divided into two groups:

Theoretical: What understanding of ministry is necessary for a fully collaborative practice to emerge? What are the inner relations between the ministries that justify a collaborative venture in ministry? How might the relations between the ministries enhance and enable each ministry to realise its full potential and purpose? Is there an understanding of God's dynamic ordering of life that offers clues for a dynamically ordered understanding of ministry? How might more recent explorations of Trinitarian and relational categories be properly transposed into a doctrine of ministry to justify collaborative ministry? What is the reciprocal relation between collaborative ministry and the form and structure of the Church? How might theological and ministerial formation be reconceived for a truly collaborative ministry? How might such ministry contribute to a missionary shaped ecclesiology? What has such a ministry to do with the gospel?

Practical: Wherein lies the joy of Christian ministry? Is it in doing a job well? But what would this look like and who is to judge? Is the joy and satisfaction of ministry a function of success, growing a new church, seeing others catch a vision? Maybe as a pastor it consists in the quality of face-to-face encounters, a sermon that plays a part in human transformation, or maybe the more mundane but urgent issue of balancing the parish books! For the myriad of new ministries of the people of God wherein lies the joy of ministry? Is it the very fact of being trusted and released to do the work of the kingdom? And how do such ministries contribute to the joy of the ministry of priests, pastors and ministers? At different stages in the book each of the above questions comes to the fore. However, the connecting thread throughout is a concern for the foundations required for an ecclesially responsible and faithful ministry consonant with God's remarkable and surprising collaboration with the world in Jesus Christ through the Spirit.

The present book is written on the premise that the joy of ministry is rooted in the capacity for collaborative practices that draw the gifts of the body of Christ together and orientate them towards the world. This seems simple enough but it is quite difficult to achieve in practice. There are a number of reasons for this. Perhaps the major problem is the deeply entrenched divide between laity and clergy. This fracture runs through the many traditions of Christianity and can be traced to the formative period of the Christian Church. It is not too much of an exaggeration to speak of a continual conflict between clergy and laity. This has many forms and can be discerned beneath the surface of much contemporary rhetoric to the contrary and some good examples of successful collaborative ministry. The secret of joy in ministry is located in collaborative practice (2 Cor. 1:24) wherein ministries are intertwined and orientated towards each other for the sake of the kingdom. The apostle Paul refers to this in terms of the members of the body of Christ being 'one of another' (Rom. 12:5). The conception is remarkable and profound in its simplicity. Indeed, as I will argue in Chapter 9, understanding ministries 'one of another' is foundational for collaborative practice. The key here is cooperation rather than competition. But the price is high. It means risking personal claims to power and authority in order to work together for the common good. This does not do away with representative ministries but they work differently together with the whole people of God. How and why this is the case is the purpose for writing this book.

Structure and Approach: An Overview

The book is divided into five parts:

Part I, 'Ministry and the Ministries' (Chapters 2 and 3), examines the nature and dynamic of the relationships between the ministries. A schematic outline is provided of the theological and ecclesial issues involved. It will provide a background map for a critical appraisal of a number of issues in the ministry today.

Part II, 'Theological Trends in Ministry: Historical Perspectives' (Chapters 4, 5 and 6), offers connected accounts of developments in ministry in the twentieth century using the Anglican Church as the focus for the inquiry. The intention in such an approach is to uncover trends and tensions in ministry – especially in the ways the ministries are related to one another – that have relevance beyond Anglicanism for the wider ecumenical Church. These case studies provide raw material for uncovering the dynamic between the ministries and prepare the ground for Part III.

Part III, 'Towards a Theory of Collaborative Ministry' (Chapters 7, 8 and 9), develops a theory of collaborative ministry in dialogue with the science of emergence, applies this to a Scripture text and explores the implications for the relations between the ministries and ecumenism. In Chapter 7 the interrelationship between ministries identified in the previous chapters is analysed in terms of the ideal of integration. The chapter identifies problems in the contemporary appeal to Trinitarian and relational categories for ministry. Chapter 8 develops the foundations for a theory of collaborative ministry. It does this via a dialogue between theology and theories of emergence and complexity current in the sciences. The dialogue between theology and science is taken up into an ecclesial framework in Chapter 9 and tested against a case study in Scripture. This chapter suggests an approach to the ministries that could enable the churches to move beyond many of the current obstacles and inherited problems. The collaborative theory proposed is a way of preserving what is held to be valuable for Catholic, Protestant and Pentecostal traditions. The intention is to provide a fresh platform for conversation through a new understanding of the relations between the ministries of the Church.

Part IV, 'Reforming Orders' (Chapters 10, 11 and 12), explores issues relevant to priesthood, deaconate and episcopate. Whilst the springboard for this section is the orders of the Anglican Church the discussion of orders has relevance beyond this communion. These chapters do not pretend to offer a full coverage of the issues concerning the threefold orders. The focus throughout is on aspects of the relationship of these ministries to the wider ministries, difficulties and possible ways in which to reconceive the operation of these orders in the light of a more thoroughgoing relational approach to ministry and church. To that end Chapter 10 builds on a dynamic understanding of order (Part III) in discussing a relational ontology of orders. It explores the implications of this for a number of current issues with priesthood; lay presidency, ordination, indelibility of orders, ordination of women to the threefold order. Chapter 11 examines the significance of ecclesiology and its distortions as the background to the reform of the episcopate. The attraction and illusion of current management theory for episcopal practice is discussed, systemic ecclesiological problems are identified and proposals for recovery of catholicity from 'below' are developed. Chapter 12 continues the focus on the episcopate. On this occasion the question of reform and renewal is developed in relation to the ecumenical movement. Recovery of episcopal identity is interpreted as an ecumenical gift. The chapters of Part IV serve the interests of more grounded and interpersonal ministries with an accent upon common engagement and shared ministry at the local level. The marks of the Church have to be crafted from below through ministries that bear the marks of the gospel.

Part V, 'Recovering Orientations' (Chapters 13, 14 and 15), rounds out the inquiry with three chapters considering ordination vows, collaborative ministry for mission and a brief final chapter drawing together the various themes and threads of the book. Chapter 13 examines the virtues of ordination vows and the significance of promise as a category for personal and communal identity, the implications of vows for the relations between the ministries, their significance for preparation for ordination and their ongoing importance for theological education and formation. Chapter 14 examines the practical nature of collaborative ministry. It does this through a sermon preached at the induction of a team leader of a new mission development in a country parish. Chapter 15 explores the theme of friendship as the glue for genuine collaborative ministry.

PART I
Ministry and the Ministries

Chapter 2
Rediscovering the Ministries of the People of God: Mapping the Territory

Christian ministry is in a stage of transition and subject to severe turmoil. The range of issues on the agenda are significant and diverse. Indeed ministry matters cover a wide territory in the Church and theology. Maps are essential for journeys and the more complicated and important the journey the more important it is to have a good map. This chapter provides a brief map of the territory covered by ministry. Critical issues are flagged, tensions and trends are identified, warning notes are sounded, new possibilities for exploration are signalled. Hopefully such a map will provide a reference point as we journey through the theological territory of Christian ministry in the chapters that follow.

Ministry of the Whole People of God

Baptism, Community and Ministry

There is no doubt that the last half of the twentieth century has witnessed a remarkable and important development in the ministry of the whole people of God. This development is one of the great achievements of the ecumenical movement of the past century. 'Gone are the days when the ordained priest was a one man band [*sic*] who led an otherwise passive community. The whole community is now clearly seen to have a role.'[1] The critical move theologically is the clear nexus established between baptism and Christian ministry. Luther's doctrine of the priesthood of all believers has taken firm root in the consciousness of the wider Church. The ministry of the laity is foundational for the life and witness of the people of God. The biblical roots are strong and the grounding in baptism in the death and resurrection of Christ as the pattern for all Christian ministry is exciting not to mention sound theologically. Baptism is thus the sacrament of initiation into the community of faith for a life of service (*diakonia*) and witness (*marturia*). Baptism, community and ministry are thus inextricably linked.

This development received its clearest and most significant expression ecumenically in the 1983 *Baptism, Eucharist and Ministry* document of the

---

1 Peter Carnley, *Reflections in Glass* (Sydney: HarperCollins, 2004), p. 157.

World Council of Churches. The document was the fruit of many decades of patient conversation between the churches and has become the reference point for subsequent discussions of ministry. Thus in the context of the 'calling of the whole people of God' it is stated that:

> The Holy Spirit bestows on the community diverse and complementary gifts … for the common good of the whole people…. All members are called to discover, with the help of the community, the gifts they have received and to use them for the building up of the Church and for service of the world to which the Church is sent.[2]

The focus on the gifts of the Spirit for ministry and mission in the world is unmistakable in the opening section of the report. This pneumatological emphasis is in keeping with the earlier sections of the report on baptism.

However, as many commentators have noted, the reflection on ministry quickly turns to disagreements amongst the churches about how the life of the Church is to be ordered. Differences over the 'place and forms' of ordained ministry prompt the critical missional question: 'How, according to the will of God and under the guidance of the Holy Spirit, is the life of the Church to be understood and ordered, so that the Gospel may be spread and the community built up in love?' The promising start on the ministries of the Christian community soon becomes focussed on orders per se. At this point the more familiar tradition is reasserted; the ministry of those ordained 'is constitutive for the life and witness of the Church'.[3]

Yet within this context there is the reminder that 'all members of the believing community, ordained and lay, are interrelated'.[4] The nature of the interrelation is specified; the community requires the presence of the 'ordained' to remind the community of their reliance upon Christ, to build the community in Christ, to strengthen its witness and to be an example of holiness for the community; the ordained 'can fulfil their calling only in and for the community' and 'cannot dispense with the recognition, the support and the encouragement of the community'.[5]

The fact that a strong relationship between ordained and laity is proposed is a positive. However the nature of this relationship begins to look somewhat unidirectional with a focus on what the ordained are and do *for the community*. Moreover the earlier emphasis on the 'diverse and complimentary' gifts of the Spirit upon the whole community for its strength, witness and service is muted at best. The discussion of ministry appears somewhat skewed in the direction of ordained ministry. What is not clear is how the corporate and ordained ministry 'animate each other, each focusing the activity of God – in each other; each

---

[2] *Baptism, Eucharist and Ministry*. Faith and Order Paper No. 111 (Geneva: World Council of Churches, 1982), p. 20, par. 5.

[3] Ibid., p. 21, par. 8.

[4] Ibid., p. 21, par. 12.

[5] Ibid.

therefore "brings the other to be" in the way which God's mission in the world requires'.[6] This lack of clarity obtains even where the emphasis is on *collaborative* leadership.[7]

Beyond Baptism, Eucharist and Ministry*: Some Problems and Promise*

Baptism, Eucharist and Ministry was produced over 25 years ago and since that time the growth of the ministry of the whole people of God has continued throughout the churches. The new ecclesial ministries of the Roman communion are a case in point.[8] An accompanying discourse refers to 'collaborative ministry', 'total ministry' or 'every-member ministry'.[9] This is an encouraging development however such discourse and its link to baptism is not without its problems. First, the term ministry can easily become a catch-all term to include ordained ministry, other ministries and many aspects of discipleship common to all Christians, for example, prayer and activities of care-giving. The same word 'does service both for what is common to all Christians and for what differentiates within the Christian community'.[10] Thus Helen Oppenheimer states: 'Unless ministry can be distinguished from everything else which is not ministry, it hardly seems worth talking about.'[11]

A second more critical issue has been raised by John Collin's study of *diakonia*.[12] Collins offers a powerful challenge to the traditional ethical slant on the notion *diakonia* (i.e., of humble service) arguing that *diakonia* has to do with a 'duty imposed by divine authority'. Given the strong link between *diakonia* and ministry, Collin's calls into question the tendency to reduce ministry to all acts of lowly service in the Christian community. His controversial argument suggests a

---

6 *Education for the Church's Ministry*. Report of the Working Party on Assessment of the Committee for Theological Education. ACCM Occasional Paper no. 22 (London: Advisory Council for the Church's Ministry, 1987), p. 29, par. 29.

7 For example, see the recent discussion of collaborative leadership (in contradistinction from collaborative ministry) by Andrew Dawswell, 'A Biblical and Theological Basis for Collaborative Ministry and Leadership', *Anvil* 21/3 (2004): 165–78. Dawswell, distinguishes between collaborative ministry and collaborative leadership. However, he confuses two related issues; the collaborative character of *all* ministry and *particular* representative ministries associated with leadership of the Christian community.

8 Zeni Fox, *New Ecclesial Ministries: Lay Professionals Serving the Church* (Franklin: Sheed and Ward, 2002).

9 For a recent example see David Robertson, *Collaborative Ministry* (Oxford: Bible Reading Fellowship, 2007).

10 Robert Hannaford, 'Foundations for an Ecclesiology of Ministry', in Christina Hall and Robert Hannaford (eds.), *Ministry and Order* (Leominster: Gracewing, 1996), p. 21.

11 Ibid., p. 23.

12 John Collins, *Diakonia: Re-interpreting the Ancient Sources* (Oxford: Oxford University Press, 1990); John Collins, *Deacons and the Church: Making Connections between Old and New* (Leominster: Gracewing, 2002).

much stronger association between deacon and messenger or ambassador. Collin's corrective opens up possibilities for *diakonia* as 'servant–ambassador' embracing a ministry of both word and deed. Certainly the term 'ministry' may be capable of much sharper specification and freed from the individualism of much that goes by the name of ministry and associations with 'general service or benevolence'. As Hannaford notes, where this has occurred the 'axis of thinking on ministry has shifted from the collective life of the community to the life and duty of Christian individuals'.[13]

A third issue concerns the nature of the relationship of ministry to baptism, and is implicit in *Baptism, Eucharist and Ministry*. It is usual in contemporary discussion to regard baptism as a sacramental sign for a vocation to Christian ministry in whatever form this may take. In a general sense this has validity; indeed it remains an important insight. It suggests that baptism can operate as the generic source for all ministries, including ordained ministry. The danger in this popular understanding is alluded to by John Zizioulas, who argues that baptism represents the first order – chronologically and ontologically – of the Church. For this Orthodox theologian 'there is no such thing as "non-ordained" persons in the Church'. The rites of baptism and confirmation (which involve 'laying on of hands') are 'essentially an ordination'. In this act the person 'does not simply become a "Christian", as we tend to think, but he [*sic*] becomes a member of a particular "ordo" in the eucharistic community. When this is forgotten the laity become the "non-ordained" – unnecessary in the eucharistic community – and clericalism appears.' The other alternative is to make the baptised person 'the basis for all other "orders", as if he [*sic*] were not himself a specifically defined order but a generic source or principle'.[14] The former move associated with clericalism is more common in Catholicism. However the latter development explains much of the contemporary confusion within Protestantism concerning the purpose of orders. Thus it is not uncommon for Protestant theologians to view the development of a 'specialised priesthood' as necessarily entailing a diminishment of the general priesthood.[15] Whilst Zizioulas's approach is an improvement on those ecclesiologies that diminish the importance of the lay baptised it also raises questions about the significance of the order of the baptised for those who subsequently enter another order of the Church.[16] In recent years Roman Catholic theologians have developed a notion of the *charism* of leadership being one of the

13 Hannaford, 'Foundations for an Ecclesiology of Ministry', p. 25.

14 See, John Zizioulas, *Being as Communion: Studies in Personhood and the Church* (London: Darton, Longman and Todd, 1985), p. 216.

15 Colin Bulley, *The Priesthood of Some Believers* (Carlisle: Paternoster Press, 2000), p. 319. Associated with this view is a failure to understand the full significance of a 'non-sacerdotal' and 'representative' understanding of priesthood (pp. 323, 325). Bulley, in the forward to his book, oversimplifies thus: if general priesthood is to increase, special priesthood must decrease.

16 See Hannaford, 'Foundations for an Ecclesiology of Ministry', p. 42.

gifts of baptism.[17] I will have occasion to return to this later however, for the moment, I note the fine nuance of Hannaford: 'Baptism does not, then, so much bestow a ministerial calling as call someone into the ministerial community of the Church'.[18]

The above problems associated with the expansion of the common ministries ought not obscure the development of ministry as a phenomenon of the whole church. The theological foundation of this can be located in a renewed emphasis on the work of Christ through the agency of the Spirit. This recovery of the dynamic relation between Christology and Pneumatology constitutes the theological promise at the heart of recent developments in the understanding and practice of ministry. An example of this in modern ecclesiology is the work of the Roman Catholic theologian, Edward Schillebeeckx. His doctrine of ministry is undergirded by an appeal to an originative pre-Pauline (Antiochene-Christian, Jewish-Christian) Christianity in which the critical factor was the role played by the baptism in the Spirit; 'baptism in the name of Jesus'. Christians baptised into Christ were therefore *pneumatici*. This was the 'foundation of all church life' and the energy driving the early missionary movement.[19] The apostle Paul's encounter with this early tradition was often conflictual. Though, as Schillebeeckx notes, Paul's concerns arose out of a pastoral mission; the emphasis was thus 'contextual pastoral strategy, not kerygma or dogma'.[20] Schillebeeckx's challenge to traditional Roman Catholic approaches to ministry is clear:

> This early egalitarian ecclesiology in no way excludes leadership and authority; but in that case authority must be one filled with the Spirit, from which no Christian, man or woman, is excluded in principle on the basis of the baptism of the Spirit.[21]

Schillebeeckx's recovery of the primacy of charisma over institution – an approach that links him with the late nineteenth-century work of the Protestant Rudolph Sohm – is neither unfamiliar nor uncontroversial in Roman Catholic circles.[22]

---

[17] Hahnenberg, *Ministries*, p. 74. Compare Hannaford, 'Foundations for an Ecclesiology of Ministry', pp. 50–51.

[18] Hannaford, 'Foundations for an Ecclesiology of Ministry', p. 43.

[19] Edward Schillebeeckx, *The Church with a Human Face: A New and Expanded Theology of Ministry* (London: SCM, 1985), p. 35.

[20] Ibid., p. 37.

[21] Ibid., p. 39.

[22] The Sohm tradition is discussed further in Chapter 7 of this book. The Roman Catholic scholar Francis Martin identifies the 'fundamental lines' of Schillebeeckx's approach with Sohm's. Martin argues that Schillebeeckx minimises the ministerial life of the church represented in office (Francis Martin, *The Feminist Question* [Grand Rapids, Michigan: Eerdmans, 1994], pp. 93–4). For more on the Sohm tradition see Alistair Campbell, *The Elders: Seniority within Earliest*

His emphasis on *charism* finds a natural sympathy with those from the Pentecostal traditions of Christianity.[23]

A Continuing Tension: Baptism and Orders

The growth and development of the ministries of the people of God has been a renewing force in the churches. However, the course of Christian ecumenism suggests an uneasy alliance between the emergence of a baptismal paradigm for ministries and the traditional orders of ministry. Unresolved tensions appear in the reflections of successive Faith and Order reports of the World Council of Churches and in the numerous ecumenical dialogues of the late twentieth century.[24] The Anglican–Roman Catholic International Commission (ARCIC) is instructive. The new context sets the backdrop for the 1973 statement: 'The ordained ministry can only be rightly understood within this broader context of various ministries, all of which are the work of one and the same Spirit.'[25] Ordained ministry shares in the 'priesthood of the people of God'. 'Nevertheless their ministry is not an extension of the common Christian priesthood but belongs to another realm of the gifts of the Spirit.'[26] The subsequent 'Elucidations' in 1979 referred to two priesthoods as 'two distinct realities',[27] ministry becoming 'an umbrella word for two priesthoods only analogously related'.[28] As John Collins notes, this elucidation effectively nullifies the force of the opening statements regarding the common context for the ministries. Any residual anxiety that the sacrament of orders might be 'a simple ecclesiastical institution' rather than 'from Christ', is dispelled in the 1993 'Clarifications' of ARCIC 1.[29] Gifts of the Spirit for such ministry may be *in* and *through* the Church but a certain distance in relation to the Church is maintained. ARCIC's approach

Christianity (Edinburgh: T&T Clark, 1994), ch. 1. For other Roman Catholic critics on Schillebeeckx see Martin, *Feminist Question*, p. 94; Aidan Nichols, *Holy Order: Apostolic Priesthood from the New Testament to the Second Vatican Council* (Dublin: Veritas, 1990), p. 181.

23 See, e.g., James D.G. Dunn, 'Ministry and the Ministry: The Charismatic Renewal's Challenge to Traditional Ecclesiology', in James D.G. Dunn (ed.), *The Christ and The Spirit*, vol. 2, *Pneumatology* (Edinburgh: T&T Clark, 1998), pp. 291–310. The paper was originally given in 1982.

24 See the critical discussion in Collins, *Diakonia*, pp. 26–40.

25 Anglican–Roman Catholic International Commission, *The Final Report* (London: SPCK, 1982), p. 30, par. 2.

26 Ibid., p. 36, par. 13.

27 Ibid., p. 41, par. 2.

28 Collins, *Diakonia*, p. 33.

29 *Clarifications of Certain Aspects of the Agreed Statements on Eucharist and Ministry of the First Anglican-Roman Catholic International Commission: Together with a Letter from Cardinal Edward Idris Cassidy, President, Pontifical Council for Promoting Christian Unity* (London: Church House and Catholic Truth Society for the Anglican Consultative Council and the Pontifical Council for Promoting Christian Unity, 1994), p. 9.

to ministry leads to what Alan Brent has called an 'unsynthesised antinomy'[30] expressed in the following terms: the priesthood of Christ and the priesthood of the community are 'two distinct realities'; priestly ministry is 'not an extension of the common Christian priesthood but belongs to another realm of the Spirit'. The tacit assumption here is that a strong doctrine of catholic orders requires such a sharp differentiation. The price is a lack of integration of ecclesial ministries. The ministries of those in orders and the ministries of the rest of the baptised represent parallel tracks.

Collins locates the general problem in what he refers to as 'the modern fixation on a churchwide ministry'.[31] This problem becomes evident in 'an attempt to fit a new evaluation of ministry into an older theology of priesthood'.[32] Perhaps 'new wine in old wineskins' is a doomed enterprise, though Collins notes the inventiveness of numerous Roman Catholic theologians in searching 'for a way to balance out roles within "every-member ministry" without thereby necessarily making of Christianity "a one-caste religion"'.[33] Anglicans have not shown a similar critical reflection though its many dialogues over the last two decades are certainly evidence of significant energy being given to the matter of ministry, in particular ordained ministry.[34]

Development of ministries has not only generated some unresolved tensions within and between the churches. It has also signalled a challenge to prevailing traditions of clericalism that have tended to keep the form and function of Christian ministry locked up within certain offices in the Church. To be sure there has existed a strong counter tradition to clericalism in the Church which is exemplified in the modern era with the Quakers, and some other Protestant churches, for example, Brethren. However, the clerical paradigm has displayed remarkable tenacity in the mainstream churches of modernity. The Roman Catholic scholar, Aidan Kavanagh, has drawn attention to the gradual distancing of the ordained Christian ministries from the *plebs Dei* from the high Middle Ages to the twentieth century. He notes that the 'effects are all around us. The other Christian ministries, where they survived, have been presbyteralized, and the rest of the church has been

---

30 Alan Brent, *Cultural Episcopacy and Ecumenism: Representative Ministry in Church History from the Age of Ignatius of Antioch to the Reformation with special reference to Contemporary Ecumenism* (Leiden: E.J. Brill, 1992), p. 61.

31 Collins, *Diakonia*, p. 34.

32 Ibid.

33 Ibid. Collins' detailed word study of *diakonia* may be successful in narrowing the meaning of ministry but this does not provide a basis for disregarding the fact of the explosion of the 'ministries' of the whole Church.

34 This is evident in the key international dialogues over the past 20 years with the Reformed, Evangelical and Lutheran Churches where ministry has been a major topic though not the interrelations between the ministries.

deministerialized.'[35] The assimilation of ministries to traditional orders continues the clericalisation of the laity and also points to the need for a theology of lay vocation in the world, a matter central to Luther's insight.[36]

The development of ministries and their challenge to clericalism is one thing. But a deeper issue is hinted at by the former primate of the Anglican Church of Australia, Peter Carnley who notes that:

> Whilst this emphasis on the collaborative ministry of the whole people of God is undoubtedly a good thing, its downside is that we have tended, perhaps unintentionally, to devalue the importance of the ordained ministry, and even to blur the boundaries between the respective roles of ordained and lay people.[37]

Valuing the distinctiveness of ordained ministries and calls for clarifying boundaries may be useful and needful. However it also may conceal an anxiety concerning the identity and purpose of those in Holy Orders. To what extent such identity issues are the result of the explosion of the ministries of the baptised is an interesting yet extremely difficult matter to determine. Peter Carnley's instincts may be quite right; today the question of Holy Orders is very much a puzzle for many in the Church, not least those ordained to ministries that have such a valued and ancient pedigree in the Church. At an anecdotal level there is certainly plenty of evidence to suggest significant confusion amongst clergy regarding their role and authority within the modern church. Drop-out rates among clergy are high, stress and overload is common and the prevailing culture of economic rationalism and unrelenting ministerial activity provides a worrying relief from the burden of internal confusion (too busy to think about it) and a partial rationale for one's existence. The more articulate and able do a reasonably good job of developing new job descriptions that give energy and purpose but often with little reference to their own ordination vows and brief.

These problems are not the preserve of one particular denomination but affect those charged with specific ministerial responsibility in the orders tradition whatever their ecclesial affiliation. Within the churches there are further tensions that make orders controversial or at least problematic. The main issue here concerns recognition of ministries among the different churches. In the view of the Roman Catholic theologians Karl Rahner and Heinrich Fries this subject 'is one of the most difficult problems discussed in ecumenical dialogues; the mutual recognition

---

35 Aidan Kavanagh, 'Christian Ministry and Ministries', *Anglican Theological Review* 66, Supplementary Series no. 9 (1964): 38.

36 For a contemporary discussion see Charles Miller, 'The Theology of the Laity: Description and Construction with Reference to the American Book of Common Prayer', *Anglican Theological Review* 84/2 (2002): 219–38. His article offers a rationale for the renewal of the 'lay apostolate'.

37 Carnley, *Reflections*, p. 157.

of ministerial offices'.[38] *Baptism, Eucharist and Ministry* indicated where work still needed to be done. Thus not only are orders under fire vis-à-vis the wider ministry of the whole people of God, orders remain a source of contention between churches. In this context it is relevant to note that the nineteenth-century papal letter of Leo XIII, *Apostolicae Curae* (1896), pronouncing ordinations performed according to the Anglican rite 'completely null and void' still stands. As a result the Anglican Church has the somewhat dubious distinction of being the only communion of Christendom upon which the Roman Church has made an official pronouncement regarding the invalidity of its orders.[39]

Problems to do with identity, boundaries, purpose and function are exacerbated by continued reference to 'the ordained ministry'. This phrase belongs to the common currency of discussion of the theme of ministry. No doubt the terminology is a useful and efficient short-hand phrase to specify certain ministries. However it harbours significant dangers and easily distorts perceptions of the relations between the ministries of the Church. Primarily the notion of 'the ordained ministry' suggests an ontologically distinct order within the ecclesia into which certain persons are inducted. This generates the entirely fictitious idea that those whom the Church call to the office and work of deacons, priests and bishops are, in the first instance, being relocated to a different metaphysical realm, that is, the ordained ministry. Thus one is ordained into 'the ordained ministry'.[40]

Where such a view prevails the relationship between those of the 'ordained ministry' and other non-ordained ministries will be one of obediential following for the latter. There can be no genuine interrelationship which values mutuality and collaboration. Indeed, it is possible to entirely overlook the fact that the question of the relation between general ministries and 'ordained ministry' may be a topic worthy of consideration. This is evident in the work of two Anglican theologians, Anthony Hanson and Richard Hanson. When they turn their minds to the subject of the 'Theology of the Ordained Ministry' the question of the relationship between such theology and other ministries of the Church does not appear on the radar screen.[41]

How might we better understand the dynamic relation between the ministries of the baptised and the ministry of those in Holy Orders? We may say that the Church, through its ecclesial processes and rites, so orders its life that among the

---

38 H. Fries and K. Rahner, *Unity of the Churches: An Actual Possibility* (Philadelphia: Fortress Press, 1983), p. 115.

39 For the full text of the papal letter with contemporary discussion, see R. William Franklin (ed.), *Anglican Orders: Essays on the Centenary of Apostolicae Curae 1896–1996* (London: Mowbray, 1996).

40 See the helpful discussion in *Ordination and Ministry in the Uniting Church*. Report from the Assembly Commission on Doctrine for study and comment, Uniting Church in Australia (Sydney: National Assembly, 1994), p. 27.

41 Anthony T. Hanson and Richard P.C. Hanson, *The Identity of the Church* (London: SCM, 1987), pp. 144–60.

multiplicity of its ministries it ensures that the offices of deacon, priest and bishop will continue. Yet the Church does not have an 'ordained ministry' as such, in the same way that it does not have a 'non-ordained ministry'. What it does have are certain ministries – traditionally 'major orders'[42] – for which the liturgical rite of ordination is deemed appropriate. Thus whilst there are important differentiations among the ministries this does not resolve itself into a simple and absolute divide between 'the ordained ministry' and 'the non-ordained ministry'. Unfortunately, the prevailing terminology only reinforces suspicions among the 'non-ordained' of being undervalued and increases confusion among 'the ordained' as to the true nature of their ministry in times of rapid change and concomitant developments in 'lay ministries'.[43]

To speak of rites for the ordering of ministries opens up another important but more often ignored area these days. The rite of ordination is an instance of a powerful rite of passage. Things are different on the 'other side' of the rite. The person initiated into the new order has a different status from before. They stand in a different place and this new status (lit.: 'standing place') alters who they are in relation to others.[44] The anthropological dimension of such a rite of passage deserves greater attention.[45] It is necessarily intertwined with the theology of ordination rites. The weight given to such ecclesial boundary rites has a significant impact on the nature of the relations between those in Holy Orders and the ministries of the baptised. Insofar as ecclesiastical rites of passage have suffered diminishment in the modern period so too has the significance of ordination as a life changing rite for both individuals and the community of faith.

---

[42] In the Western Church there has long existed 'major orders' – traditionally bishop, priest/presbyter, deacon. It is the major orders that have commonly been described as 'Holy Orders', thereby attributing a degree of importance or significance to such orders of Christian ministry (*sacri ordines*). In the West, the subdeacon has also been included (from the thirteenth century) as one of the 'major orders', although this is not so today. In the East, the subdeacon has always been regarded as belonging to the 'minor orders'. In the sixteenth century, Protestantism reworked the threefold orders in varying ways; by changing names (e.g., priest to pastor), adding new ministries (e.g., elder) or by dispensing with the episcopal order or all orders as such. In the West, 'minor orders' have included porter, lectors, exorcists and acolytes. In the wake of Vatican II, these were renamed '*ministeria*' and reduced to two (i.e., lectors and acolytes). In the East, since the seventh century, lectors and cantors have survived though porters, exorcists and acolytes have been merged in the subdeaconate. For further see *The Oxford Dictionary of the Christian Church*, ed. F.L. Cross (Oxford: Oxford University Press, 1974). One result of this is that orders per se evidence a degree of fluidity over time.

[43] For a discussion of the emergence of the notion of laity relation to the clergy see Chapter 8.

[44] See the discussion in Chapter 10.

[45] See the early twentieth-century catalyst for this perspective, Arnold van Gennep, *The Rites of Passage*, trans. M.B. Vizdom and G.L. Caffee (Chicago: University of Chicago Press, 1960).

As a result of the above developments and tensions it is not an exaggeration to speak of the fate of 'Holy Orders' in the modern Church.[46] It can appear as the poor victim lying at the side of the road waiting for a kind Samaritan to come by, tend its wounds and restore it to life. Alas none such has arrived though there have been many that have passed by and noted the sorry state of affairs.

Clarifying the Relations between the Ministries

An Urgent Theological Task

If it is the case, as stated in *Baptism, Eucharist and Ministry*, that the ministries of the Church are interrelated, that ministries for which the Church ordains and the wider ministries of the baptised are shaped and energised by Christ and the Spirit, then a number of things follow. First, it is clear that one of the most pressing and fundamental tasks will be to clarify the nature of the relationship between the ministries. This clarification cannot occur apart from consideration of the ministries in their particularity. Yet it is a distinct task that requires particular attention in order to properly develop an understanding of *any* ministry. Problems associated with ordained ministry cannot be solved or even unravelled over against, or without regard to, challenges and opportunities presented by the growth of wider ministries of the Church. As Werner Jeanrond notes in relation to issues of community and authority what is 'most urgently needed is a reassessment of the relationship between the ordained minister and the ordained community'.[47] Is it the case that corporate and ordained ministry 'are interanimative in the Church's performance of its task, and therefore of its being'?[48] In what sense might this be understood and how might such a proposal be developed to better display the true interrelationship between the ministries of the people of God? How might this

---

[46] Of course the notion of the 'modern' Church is highly problematic. The cultural assimilation of the Church to modern secularism creates conditions in which the notion of 'holy' is already rendered impotent if not superfluous, not only beyond the Church but *within*. For a discussion of the recovery of the concept of 'holy' as a term carrying meaning for the modern person see Graham Hughes, *Worship as Meaning: Liturgical Theology for Late-Modernity* (Cambridge: Cambridge University Press, 2003). Hughes's approach is very different from John Webster's (*Holiness* [London: SCM, 2003]), who develops a 'Trinitarian dogmatics of holiness' based on an *intensive* engagement with the Christian tradition. Only at the end of the book does Webster acknowledge the 'incommensurable' relation between his unfolding of holiness and the modern displacement or dissolution of any notion of holiness. The problem with this approach is that the dogmatics operates within an enclosed circle of meaning.

[47] Werner Jeanrond, 'Community and Authority: The Nature and Implications of the Authority of the Christian Community', in Gunton and Hardy (eds.), *On Being the Church*, p. 98.

[48] *Education for the Church's Ministry*, p. 29, par. 29.

understanding serve the *missio Dei*? Such questions are central for the ensuing chapters of this book.

A genuine mutuality and accountability in ministries, both within particular churches and between churches, is a critical issue for the inner life of the Church. The issue is not simply a matter for the internal life of the Church. The reason is clear: the purpose and tasks of ministry concern the Church's purpose and mission. A present challenge is how to recognise and honour both the remarkable growth and diversification of corporate ministries and those ministries for which the Church has historically ordained people. A recent attempt by the Jesuit theologian Philip Rosato, inquires into the complimentary relations between the priesthood of the baptised and the ordained. However, this important piece of analysis remains confined within a traditional Roman Catholic frame; 'the ordained represent his [Christ's] transcendent headship of, and the baptised his immanent presence to the Church, and through it, his headship of and presence to humanity'.[49] These two separate modalities of Christian priesthood are 'orientated to each other'. Yet in Rosato's account they seem to move in two different directions, that is, from above (ordained) and from below (baptised) corresponding to the divinity and humanity of Christ. The interrelation between the two priesthoods and their concomitant ministries harbours within it significant unreconciled tensions related to the problems of a two-nature Christology.[50] It is a problem that will surface repeatedly in our examination of the development of ministry in the following chapters.

Charism, Ministry and Office: A Question of Nomenclature?

Opening up a conversation on the interrelatedness of the ministries has proven quite difficult. There are a number of reasons for this. At one level it is a problem of nomenclature. There are a host of terms: *charis*, *charism*, *charismata*, ministry, ministries, *ordo*, order, orders, office. Within the earliest communities of faith, as seen in Paul's Corinthian correspondence, the *charismata* became contentious with tendencies to rank, weigh and assess their relative importance. Some questions arise. For example, does *charis* have theological priority over *charisma*? Does *the* ministry have similar priority over ministries?[51] Often *charism* and *charismata* have been considered to be in tension with those expressions of *charismata* that

---

49 Philip Rosato, 'Priesthood of the Baptised and Priesthood of the Ordained: Complimentary Approaches to their Relation', *Gregorianum* 68/1–2 (1987): 260.

50 The derivation of the ministries by analogy with the two-nature doctrine of Christ is not uncommon but not for that reason any less problematic. For further discussion see Chapter 7.

51 This was the view of Karl Barth. See Bernard Wannenwetsch, '"Members of One Another": *Charis*, Ministry and Representation: A Politic-Ecclesial Reading of Romans 12', in C. Bartholomew et al (eds.), *A Royal Priesthood: The Use of the Bible Ethically and Politically: A Dialogue with Oliver O'Donovan*, vol. 3 (Carlisle: Paternoster Press; Grand Rapids: Zondervan, 2002), p. 214.

have been regularised into orders and a particular office. And in popular usage *charisma* is more often applied to a particular persons' general leadership appeal.

Order can have narrower or wider meanings; the former pertaining to particular *orders* of ministry, though even here the history of the discussion indicates tension and fluidity.[52] Certainly since Vatican II there has been a recognition that *charism* and order 'are operative in the ministries of the laity',[53] although this suggests that the notion of order ought not be made unduly restrictive in its ambit. Certainly a danger persists that ordering might ignore some *charisms*.

Is 'ministry' a generic term for all ministries or does it specify those who have been ordained to a particular *ordo*?[54] To what extent are the ministries a more regularised and public recognition of particular *charismata*? In answering this question it may be more helpful to understand *charisms* less as 'sparks of supernatural power and energy erupting against the stream of communal life' and more as gifts of the Spirit 'that has ministry as its goal'.[55] On this account *charisms* 'are expressions of the Spirit-filled life of the ministerial community of the Church'.[56] This approach presumes that ministry 'is the proper and normal expression of *charism* in the life of the Church'.[57] This also has the merit of linking ministry to an activity of the Spirit rather than a creation of the Church. 'Ministry is the public and communally recognised form of *charism*'.[58] This also suggests that the familiar contrast between '*charism*' and institution is overly simplistic and does not do justice to the dynamic that obtains between the two.

The contemporary discussion of the nomenclature, particularly among catholic scholars, indicates an attempt to reconnect gifts, ministry and office. Francis Martin refers to a '*charism of service*' – special endowments of the Spirit for service, for example, prophecy, teaching, words of wisdom, preaching, healing, interpretation

---

52 For example, see the discussion by Nichols, *Holy Order*, ch. 3, 'The Medieval Theology of Order'. Nichols traces the discussion in the medieval Church over the nature of order, disputes over its sevenfold structure, differentiation and rationale for the ordering within the sacrament of order, tensions between 'papal presbyterianism' and apostolic episcopacy.

53 Fox, *New Ecclesial Ministries*, p. 317.

54 Nichols notes that *ordinatio* 'was a term used at Rome for appointing civil functionaries to their office: Jerome uses it as a synonym for the Greek *cheirotonia*, the laying on of hands.... Those so inducted into office, or otherwise distinguished from the general body of the populace, were, in ancient Rome, an *ordo* – which thus became, at Christian hands, the proper term for the clergy's special place within the people of God' (*Holy Order*, p. 52), and that this practice was officially sanctioned by the Theodosian Code, promulgated in 438/39 (*Codex Theodosius* 16.5.26) (ibid., p. 169 n. 38).

55 Hannaford, 'Foundations for an Ecclesiology of Ministry', p. 51, quoting the Roman Catholic scholar Thomas O'Meara.

56 Ibid.

57 Ibid.

58 Ibid.

of tongues, care of others.[59] He distinguishes these from other manifestations of the Spirit whose purpose may not include service, for example, the gift of tongues, the single state (1 Cor. 7:7). *Charisms* of service 'can be conferred and exercised sporadically for the good of the community'.[60] The move from occasional to a more permanent exercise of *charism* is signalled by the term 'ministry' though, as Martin notes, a number of gifts in the New Testament 'imply a more permanent type of exercise'.

Martin proposes that the term 'office' indicates 'a stable ministry' which secures the 'permanence of apostolic teaching' 'by giving it a genuinely historical dimension, a consistent existence extending over both space and time'.[61] For this Catholic scholar the structuring reflects the dynamic between occasional and more permanent expressions of the *charis* of God. He notes that whilst *charisms* and ministry express 'the aspect of "otherness" inherent in the source of the Church's life', office 'adds' to this in two ways: first, by adding an aspect of otherness 'that works within the corporeal and thus historical nature of the church'; and second, the authority of office 'adds' to the dimension of authority inherent in *charism* and ministry, 'the dimension of objectivity – office is transmitted through some form of human historical activity'.[62] In this way office functions both '*within* the church' and '*over against* the church'. Apparently for Martin the 'otherness' of *charisms* and ministry is not of the same order as that belonging to office, which alone is singled out as functioning 'over against the church'.

Martin's approach is not unfamiliar in both Catholic and Protestant traditions.[63] But is it sustainable? Are not all activities of the Spirit both *within* and *over against* the church? Might it not be more accurate to understand office as providing an enduring ecclesial symbol of the dialectic intrinsic to the operation of God's *charis* (through *charism* and ministry) in and beyond the community of faith. This would make it unambiguously clear that the real issue underlying discussion concerning nomenclature is the importance and indispensability of *differentiated representation*. In other words, it has to do with an *ecclesiology* of ministry. Luther saw this clearly when he noted that the selection of particular people to be ordained into an office did not contradict either the principle of faith or the 'universal priesthood'. 'Just because we are all priests of equal standing, no one must push himself forward and, without the consent and choice of the rest, presume to do that for which we all have equal authority.'[64] The understanding of

---

[59] Martin, *The Feminist Question*, pp. 90–91.

[60] Ibid., p. 91.

[61] Ibid., p. 92.

[62] Ibid., pp. 92–3.

[63] See further in this chapter for discussion of the Reformed Tradition on this point. In Chapter 3 I will examine the relationship between ministry 'over against' the Church and a strong Christological emphasis on ministry.

[64] Martin Luther, 'An Appeal to the Ruling Class of German Nationality as to the Amelioration of the State of Christendom' [1520] in *Martin Luther: Selections from*

ministerial representation implicit in Luther's approach was, as we shall see in Chapter 4, critical for the Anglo-Catholic Moberly writing in the late nineteenth century. The issue of differentiated representation has been clearly expressed by a contemporary Lutheran scholar:

> Every charisma represents the one *charis* just as every special ministry (e.g., teaching) represents the one ministry (of witnessing God's *charis*) of the church by representing one charisma (e.g., understanding doctrine) in particular.... Every office (e.g., teacher) represents the ministry (of teaching) in a (publicly ordered) way which differs from the way in which the ministry is represented by every other member.[65]

This reflection on the operation of the gifts in Romans 12 offers a helpful insight into the dynamic of the ministries. In respect to this Pauline structure of representation 'office' is a later development in response to increasing organizational complexity. In the early period of Christianity ministerial differentiations and terminology (charisma, ministry and office) is quite fluid.[66] I will to return to this matter in Part III. For the moment we note that the discussion of the relations between such terms and their referents, is neither settled nor entirely clear and is symptomatic of more fundamental issues relating to the rationale for the ministries, their relations and their representative functions within the Church. In particular the relations between *charism*, ministry and office remain unresolved and contested.

Problem of a Clerical Focus

Another reason for the difficulty in examining the interrelations between the ministries arises from the fact that the unresolved nature of ministries *between* the churches has occupied the centre ground. In particular this concerns the mutual recognition of ministries as an urgent and intractable problem. One consequence of this has been to further entrench a clerical view of ministry given the emphasis on ordained ministry. A cursory nod is given, either as brief introductory or concluding comments on wider ministries of the Church. As Hannaford states; 'The problem is that the doctrine of ministry has customarily proceeded from hierarchology rather than ecclesiology. The net effect is a narrowly one-sided and distorted view of ministry which is divorced from the collective life of the

---

his Writings, ed. John Dillenberger (New York: Doubleday and Co., 1961), p. 409.

[65] Ibid., p. 215.

[66] See discussions in Martin, *The Feminist Question*, p. 95, who also considers office pertaining to the gifts of ministry (p. 108); Arthur G. Patzia, *The Emergence of the Church* (Downers Grove: InterVarsity Press, 2001), pp. 180–83, who refers to the relation between the ministries as a 'series of interlocking and overlapping circles rather than a row of separate entities'.

whole Church.'[67] Modern ecumenical dialogues on ministry do not conform exactly to this pattern. Typically the question of ministry is set within the wider context of Church, followed by reflection on ordained ministries (*Baptism, Eucharist and Ministry* is somewhat of a prototype of such forms). *Baptism, Eucharist and Ministry* is not atypical of ecumenical approaches to ministry where the ecclesial context and wider ministries quickly gives way to concerns for ordered ministry.

Hannaford argues that to overcome hierarchology 'we need to show that a theology of ministry, understood as action on behalf of the Church, is consistent with an understanding of the Church as an organic community, where ministerial differentiation contributes to and does not diminish the unity and coherence of the whole body'.[68] Evidently the question of the ministries cannot be resolved without reference to the ecclesia, its calling and purpose in the world. The way forward on the interrelation and reconciliation of the ministries within and between churches will be best served by attention to an ecclesiology of ministry.[69] It is certainly the case that the doctrine of the Church has been a major theme of the second half of the twentieth century. We thus turn briefly to the emergence of ecclesiology and consider its relevance for the issue of ministry.

Ministry and the Emergence of Ecclesiology

Some years ago the well-known Lutheran scholar, Jaroslav Pelikan, stated that 'the doctrine of the church became, as it had never quite been before, the bearer of the whole of the Christian message for the twentieth century, as well as the recapitulation of the entire doctrinal tradition from preceding centuries'.[70] Pelikan was pointing to the emergence of ecclesiology as the principle of coherence for the central themes of Christianity. Was this a sign of the failure of Christianity – a retreat into its religious 'enclave'[71] – at least in the West? Or was it indicative of an intuition about community and sociality: something quite central and creative in the life of faith in the world? In defence of Pelikan's proposal I would point to the emergence of ecclesiology as one result of the remarkable missionary movement of the nineteenth century. The mission experience raised critical issues concerning the relations between the divided churches and proved a major impetus for the modern ecumenical movement. Mission generated reflection and 'soul searching' concerning ecclesial identity and inter-church relations. Ecclesiology, a theme that

---

67 Hannaford, 'Foundations for an Ecclesiology of Ministry', p. 26.

68 Ibid.

69 From the Catholic perspective Kavanagh, 'Christian Ministry', p. 42, refers to the pressing need for a restored 'ministerial ecclesiology'.

70 Jaroslav Pelikan, *Christian Doctrine and Modern Culture (since 1700)* (Chicago: University of Chicago Press, 1989), p. 282.

71 Robert Bellah et al., *Habits of the Heart: Individualism and Commitment in American Life* (New York: Harper & Row, 1985), pp. 71–5 refers to 'lifestyle enclaves' which point to societal retreat from the public to the private domains of life.

historically has attracted little interest theologically, became increasingly important both practically and theoretically. Behind this lay the gospel imperative enshrined in the high priestly prayer of Jesus, 'May they be brought to complete unity to let the world know that you sent me and have loved them even as you have loved me' (John 17: 23). Ecumenism was not an optional extra. The Church was called to embody the oneness of the divine life; gospel and church were inextricably related.

But to speak of gospel is to call attention to God. Over the last two-hundred years the God question has been a site of considerable conflict in the light of the rise of more virulent forms of secular atheism and serious questions from within the Christian community about the character of God in the wake of the First World War. A theology of protest emerged which argued that the God of the gospel was not to be simply identified with the values and aspirations of European culture clothed in religious garments. Other theologians worked hard to resist the marginalization of the divine from the affairs of the world, the sciences, humanities and so on. The twentieth century thus bore witness to a remarkable flowering of Trinitarian theology under the impetus of Karl Barth, among others. The re-emergence of a Trinitarian consciousness in Christian theology provided the foundations for a truly ecumenical ecclesiology whose key element has focussed on *koinonia* (communion) and the life of the Spirit. Ecclesiology has thus become a critical, if not *the* lens through which the central themes of Christian faith are interpreted. All roads may not lead to the Church (heaven forbid) but they may lead through it.

How fairs the Anglican church in this? Do Anglicans have a doctrine of the Church? The Anglican bishop and theologian Stephen Sykes has pointed to the relative paucity of Anglican reflection on the church as such. He has exposed the flaws in the 'no special doctrines' doctrine; that Anglicans adhere to what was believed by the undivided Church of antiquity.[72] Whilst this has been appealing for many Anglicans, especially in ecumenical circles, it actually undermines Anglican reflection on its own identity and mission and could easily foster an unfounded pride.[73] On the other hand Anglicanism has been one of the leaders in the ecumenical movement over its history which suggests that there is a powerful though implicit ecclesiology that generates openness to the wider ecclesia and society.[74]

---

[72] Stephen Sykes, *Unashamed Anglicanism* (London: Darton, Longman and Todd, 1995), ch. 6, 'Anglicanism and the Anglican Doctrine of the Church'.

[73] The 'no special doctrines' appeal continues at a popular level. See Richard Giles, *Always Open: Being an Anglican Today* (Cambridge, MA: Cowley, 2004), p. 39, quoting Stephen Neill.

[74] Certainly the traditional Anglican emphasis on the doctrine of the incarnation has been an important basis for a positive engagement of Anglicanism in the world. In a theologian like F.D. Maurice this developed into an ecclesiology centred on God in society and the particular vocation of the Church to embody the form of God's presence in the world. The Maurice tradition has continued to exert a strong influence on Anglican understandings

What has this all got to do with questions of Church polity and ministry? Lack of Anglican reflection on the nature of its own life and calling has meant that Anglicanism harbours significant tensions arising from unreconciled internal diversity. Positively it commends itself as a comprehensive church, though internal tensions regarding this self-understanding can emerge in the ecumenical world where tensions *within* Anglicanism become manifest. This can be observed in questions of ministry and order among the churches.[75]

It is quite clear from ecumenical conversations in the latter half of the twentieth century that it is the doctrine of ministry that represents the most difficult and intractable area to make progress on in the ecumenical world.[76] However, it has become equally clear that ministry and Church are inextricably linked and reasons

---

of the Church as an open, hospitable community. For discussion of Maurice's ecclesiology see Torben Christensen, *The Divine Order: A Study in F.D. Mauice's Theology* (Leiden: E.J. Brill, 1973).

75 Porvoo, Meissen and the recent Church of England/Methodist Covenant are well-known examples. See *The Porvoo Common Statement*. Conversations between the British and Irish Anglican Churches and Nordic and Baltic Lutheran Churches. The Council for Christian Unity of the General Synod of the Church of England Occasional Paper no. 3 (London: Church House, 1993); *On the Way to Visible Unity* [The Meissen Common Statement]. Board for Mission and Unity, GS 843 (London: Church House, 1988); *An Anglican-Methodist Covenant*. Common Statement of the Formal Conversations between the Methodist Church of Great Britain and the Church of England, GS 1409 (London: Church House, 2001). An example from my own context in Australia also bears testimony to this. Dialogue between the Anglican and Uniting Church has run into serious difficulties on the question of ministry and order. See the account of the various dialogues by Duncan Reid, 'Are Bishops an Ecumenical Problem? Episcopacy and Episcope in Two Bilateral Conversation', in Alan Cadwallader (ed.), *Episcopacy: Views from the Antipode*, (Adelaide: Anglican Board of Christian Education, 1994), pp. 291–9. Anglican response to successive dialogue reports at diocesan and particularly general synod level indicate that within Anglicanism significant diversity obtains on issues to do with ecclesiology, Eucharist and ministry. The persistence of unresolved internal conflict can thwart progress in inter-church dialogue. The report of the Anglican and Uniting Church National Dialogue, Australia, *For the Sake of the Gospel: Mutual Recognition of Ordained Ministries in the Anglican and Uniting Churches in Australia* (Sydney: General Synod of the Anglican Church of Australia, 2001), has already generated debate and critique from a variety of sources, in particular bishops (including the Anglican primate as chair of the Doctrine Commission). Archbishop Peter Carnley's paper in response to the report – reprinted in Carnley, *Reflections*, pp. 156–80, illustrates the theological differences and confusions within Anglicanism over the doctrine of orders and ministry. His main protagonist in the paper is not, in fact, the Uniting Church, but an Anglican priest and theologian from the Church of England, Robin Greenwood.

76 See *Baptism, Eucharist and Ministry* on ministry, in particular pars. 21, 23, 26, 53 and accompanying commentary. See the incisive reflections of the Australian Roman Catholic theologian, Gerard Kelly, 'The Recognition of Ministries: A Shift in Ecumenical Thinking', *One in Christ*, 30 (1994): 10–21.

for difficulty in ministry can usually be traced to differing understandings of the Church or different construals of the relationship between Church and ministry. An emerging consensus is that the life of the body of Christ provides the frame and form for ministry. But what kind of relation are we talking about? Is it a simple linear one? If not what is the nature of its dynamism? Getting this relation right is fundamental for it bears on many of the traditional difficulties Anglicans and others have when it comes to questions of ministry such as relations between laity and those in orders, recognition of ministries in other churches, validity of ministries, relation of orders to each other and to the inner life of the Church, Eucharist and mission.

A number of questions arise from the above: How are questions of ministry related to Church and gospel? What weight ought to be given to ministry and orders, including bishops within the life of the churches? What does it mean for a church to be in the apostolic succession? Such questions can only be flagged at this point. My starting point is simple: reflection upon ministry ought not detour around the reality of the ecclesia but be undertaken in consciousness of the strong relation that obtains between church and ministry. Examining the nature of that relationship opens up some deeper issues for a theology of ministry. This is the task of the next chapter. In this way Chapters 2 and 3 provide the basis for the exploration of the dynamics of ministry in the rest of the book.

Chapter 3
On Knowing One's Relations: Church, Ministry and Theology

Church and Ministry in Dynamic Relation

The rediscovery of the ministries of the whole people of God has occurred at the same time as ecclesiology has emerged as a major theme in contemporary theology in the last century. As indicated in Chapter 2 the history of mission and ecumenism has been the field on which these twin developments have flourished. Undergirding and informing this has been a renewal in Trinitarian theology in which the theme of communion has been strong. The literature on these developments is significant. A persistent and unresolved issue in these developments has been the nature of the relationship between Church and ministry. Lack of attention to and clarity about the nature of this relationship continues and is the reason for many of the present difficulties the Church faces in ordering its ministries for worship, service and mission.

Identifying the dynamic relation between the Church and its ministries is a critical step in understanding how the ministries work together to bear witness to the gospel. Not surprisingly neither the Church nor its ministries operate in a freewheeling manner but rather are heavily influenced by different theological emphases. How this dynamic relation between church, ministry and theology operates is the focus for this chapter. The rediscovery of the ministries of the people of God and the relations between the ministries will be found to be the result of the way in which church, ministry and theology operate. The nature of this dynamic needs uncovering in order to clarify the interrelatedness of the ministries and their place within the purposes of God in creation and redemption. This is the purpose of the present chapter. This will be particularly important as background analysis for the theory of collaborative ministry developed in Part III.

The Priority of Ministry and Christology

One powerful stream of thought usually associated with the more Catholic wing of the Church, but not entirely so, has given priority to ministry over Church. On this account the Church is constituted by a validly and divinely instituted ministerial office that has its origins in Christ's authority and institution. The more Catholic version appeals to an apostolic succession in the ministry either in a 'harder' form – through tactile succession from Christ and the first apostles – or a 'softer' version that locates the succession in office as such but still appeals to the antiquity of this succession.[1] This theory of continuity of ministry is associated with a view that ministry is constitutive of the ecclesia. It is a view well attested in Roman Catholicism and became particularly important in nineteenth-century Tractarianism in Anglicanism. The Anglican theologian Paul Avis, refers to this as the 'apostolic paradigm' and links it in Anglicanism with the movement for the Church's autonomy in relation to the state.[2] However its lineage goes back much further and continues to exert considerable influence upon Anglican scholars.

Thus when the former Anglican primate of Australia, Peter Carnley, considered the matter he noted, somewhat cautiously at first, that 'there is a sense in which this apostolic ministry is logically prior to the Church itself, insofar as the Church *comes to be* around the ministry of word and sacrament' (my emphasis).[3] However, the correlation between Christ and the ministry, and its constitutive force for the being of the Church is unambiguous for Carnley: 'The starting point for our understanding of ministry is the mission and ministry of God who calls the Church into being; the ministry of word and sacrament is a share in, and an instrument of, this ministry, which is constitutive of the Church'.[4]

There is a Protestant version of this approach to ministry and Church. It is familiar in Reformed theology and polity and has traces in Calvin's doctrine of ministry. In this case the appeal is not to an apostolic succession stretching back into the earliest period of Christianity. Rather the accent is on the preservation of the apostolic succession in faith through the divinely instituted office of those called by God to exercise the ministry of preaching the Word in the Church. The supposition is that Christ has instituted this office in the Church in order that the Church will be continually called to new obedience to Christ and be reformed. This approach is the basis for the reformation notion of *ecclesia semper reformanda*. It is the logical result of a doctrine of the Church as a *creatura verbi divini*.[5] If the Church is the creation of the divine and eternal Word then that ministerial office which is charged with preaching the authoritative word is absolutely pivotal in the re-constituting of the ecclesia at any point in time and space. Thus in a recent restatement of the Reformed position on the integrity and authority of ministry

---

[1] See Richard Norris, 'Bishops, Succession and the Apostolicity of the Church', in J. Robert Wright (ed.), *On Being a Bishop*. Papers on Episcopacy from the Moscow Consultation, 1992 (New York: Church Hymnal, 1992), pp. 61–2.

[2] Paul Avis, *Anglicanism and the Christian Church* (Edinburgh: T&T Clark, 1988), pp. 167–72.

[3] Carnley, *Reflections*, p. 173.

[4] Ibid. However, having argued for the logical priority of ministry over Church, Carnley then asserts, contrary to the position of Robin Greenwood, 'that the Church is not a community gathered around a minister but a ministering community … in fact it is both'. For this to be the case a more nuanced account is required than Carnley has offered for the nature of the relationship proposed between Church and ministry.

[5] Christoph Schwobel, 'The Creature of the Word: Recovering the Ecclesiology of the Reformers', in Gunton and Hardy (eds.), *On Being the Church*, pp. 110–55.

James Haire and Gordon Watson expound Calvin's emphasis on Christ's rule in the Church through proclamation of the Word and administration of the sacraments.[6] The designated agents for this rule of Christ are the teachers and pastors through whom the body of Christ is 'built up'. In ordination the Church recognises 'that its Lord through the means He has chosen mediates its life to it'.[7] In this context it is clear that being 'built up' and 'mediates its life to it' point to a fundamental constitutive activity for the office of the ministry.

Calvin's own position may not be entirely clear. On the one hand he was in no doubt that the ministry was essential for the Church and authority for ministry was from Christ not from the Church. On the other hand he did not really examine in detail to relationship between Church and ministry. He was clear that the Church is founded on the doctrine of the apostles and prophets. When the Anglican Anthony Hanson considered the matter he concluded that Calvin 'was a supporter of the traditional view: our Lord instituted a ministry to which he committed all rule and authority (or nearly all rule and authority) in the church'.[8] The ministry may not be constitutive of the Church without qualification but it is clear in which direction Calvin was pointing. This approach finds strong and continuing support among theologians in the Reformed tradition and is implicit in the restriction of 'ministry' to those ordained for the building of the body of Christ.[9] Hanson's main complaint with the Reformed view was that it had not given sufficient attention to the relationship between church and ministry.

However, fundamental to this stream of thinking is its strong Christological foundation for ministry. In both Catholic and Protestant forms the ministry, as the mode through which the presence of the living Christ is actualised (in sacrament and/or word) is formative and reformative of the Church. There is a certain inner logic to this position and it has exercised considerable power in the history of the Church.

The priority of ministry in relation to the Church (certainly practically and implicitly theoretically) is operative across the Protestant/Catholic divide, though in different ways. This can be observed in the well-known depiction of Catholicism and Protestantism stated so sharply by Friedrich Schleiermacher in the early nineteenth century: 'The antithesis between Protestantism and Catholicism may be provisionally conceived thus: the former makes the individual's relation to

[6] See James Haire and Gordon Watson, 'Authority and Integrity in the Ministry of the Church', *Phronema* 18 (2003): 32.

[7] Ibid., p. 45.

[8] Anthony Hanson, *The Pioneer Ministry* (London: SPCK, 1975 [1961]), p. 127.

[9] See Collins, *Diakonia*, p. 35, for reference to the distinction in the Second Helvetic Confession of 1566 between the common priesthood and 'the ministry', and much later in Edinburgh in 1937 the determination of ministry (ordained) for the building up of the body of Christ.

the Church dependent on his relation to Christ, while the latter contrariwise makes the individual's relation to Christ dependent on his relation to the Church.'[10]

The divinely instituted ministry was fundamental for both communions. For Protestantism it was the office for instruction and preaching of Christ's doctrine as foundational for a person being of the Church. In Catholicism the ecclesial world of the Christian is actualised through the ministration of the Eucharistic celebrant who offers the sacrifice of Christ. In both cases the ministry is pivotal for being in relation to Christ in the Church.

However, it is also true that in a more self-consciously ecumenical age the ecclesial dimension of ministry has received a much stronger emphasis in both Reformed and Catholic churches. The major ecumenical dialogues of the twentieth century bear ample testimony to this. From the Reformed wing the Scottish theologian, Thomas Torrance, developed a notion of the royal priesthood in which ministry is understood as the priesthood of the Church and an associated emphasis upon the corporate episcopate.[11] In the wake of Vatican II, Roman Catholic theologians have tended to discuss ministry within a richer ecclesial setting, though tensions remain. However the recent assessment of Roman Catholic developments in ministry by Edward Hahnenberg is as relevant to Reformed and other Protestant churches as to the Catholic Church: 'The concern is that, despite qualifications to the contrary, granting priority to the christological representation weakens the ecclesial and relational nature of the priest's ministry.'[12]

The Priority of Church and Pneumatology

In recent years there has been a rediscovery of another quite different approach to ministry that significantly reconfigures the relationship between ministry and Church. In this approach ministry is an emergent *charism*-generated activity of the whole Church. The community of faith, under the guidance and inspiration of the Holy Spirit receives and exercises the gifts of God for the common good, witness and service: the mission of the Church. In this case the relation between ministry and Church places the accent clearly on the Church as the community of faith in which and for which ministries arise. The ordering of ministries is thus an ecclesial activity.

There is no doubt that this approach to ministry has become an increasingly important feature of ecclesial self-understanding over the course of the last 50 years. A good example of this way of interpreting the relationship between Church and ministry is offered by the New Testament theologian, James Dunn. In an important paper in 1982, 'Ministry and the Ministry: The Charismatic Renewal's Challenge to Traditional Ecclesiology', Dunn drew attention to the connection between the

---

[10] Friedrich Schleiermacher, *The Christian Faith* (Edinburgh: T&T Clark, 1968), p. 103.

[11] Hanson, *Pioneer Ministry*, pp. 153–4.

[12] Hahnenberg, *Ministries*, p. 56.

work of the Holy Spirit, the nature of the Spirit's *charisms* and the ministry of the whole Christian community.[13] He noted that the Pauline conception of the Church (esp. 1 Cor. 12; Rom. 12), in which 'Paul envisages the local church as the body of Christ, as a charismatic community, where each member, by definition, has a function within the body, a role within the community of faith' has been a key element in Charismatic renewal and classical Pentecostalism. Dunn explains that in Paul's vision of the body of Christ – the charismatic community:

> *Charisma* cannot be restricted in terms either of the 'who' or the 'what'. Charisma is not given to a select few; 'to *each* is given the manifestation of the spirit' (1 Cor. 12:7). And *charisma* is not reserved for a particular set of clearly defined gifts; whatever word or act mediates grace to the believing community is *charisma*.[14]

Dunn goes on to note that for Paul, '*charisma* is synonymous with *diakonia*, ministry (1 Cor. 12:4-5) and concludes: ' "Ministry" is not given only to a few, but to each; "ministry" is not confined to a particular set of clearly defined functions but describes every word or act of grace to the believing community.'[15]

The purpose of Dunn's argument at this point was to highlight the Pentecostal and Charismatic contribution to a theology of ministry that recognised 'its proper range and diversity' following the Pauline concept of '*all*-member ministry, of ministry as *every* expression of grace'. Over against this Dunn referred to the traditional concept of *the* ministry in which 'the ministry' 'reflects the long established presumption that when Christians talk of 'ministry' they are to all intents and purposes talking about the role of the 'ordained ministry', the clergy'.[16] In Dunn's view even the important reformation appeal to the priesthood of all believers had become 'confined, in effect, to the realm of personal piety, the right of the head of the household to conduct family prayers as its highest expression'.[17]

Dunn recognised advances amongst the churches in respect to the ministry belonging to the whole people of God. However, he argued that this had merely created two classes: the ministry of the ordained and the ministry of the laity 'with only the sketchiest or rather incoherent attempts to explain their relationship to each other'.[18] The concept of *charism* 'has been drawn in, but only as a kind of sop to the laity, not as an alternative concept of ministry which might actually call in question the axiomatic structure between clergy and laity and the hierarchical

---

13 Dunn, 'Ministry and the Ministry'.

14 Ibid., pp. 292–3.

15 Ibid.

16 Ibid. Of course it was precisely the dangers of rather loose conceptions and ministerial practices that was one of the motivating factors for the development in later canonical documents of more stabilised notions of 'the ministry', i.e. the clergy.

17 Ibid.

18 Ibid, p. 294.

structure built upon it'.[19] Furthermore, the term 'laity' remained an embarrassment since it denoted the whole people of God.

The burden of Dunn's paper was to assess the challenge of Pentecostalism to the traditional doctrines of ministry. However, his discussion highlights the impact of pneumatology in finding an approach to ministry and church in which the body of Christ is the ministering community of faith. Ministry does not precede nor constitute the Church but arises out of and for the life of the community. In this approach the ecclesia has a practical (and perhaps ontological) priority in relation to ministry. Such a conception is not unproblematic as the experience of Pentecostalism has shown, where charismatic leaders have exercised excessive authority over the community and\or communities of faith simply fail to heed wise counsel. Nor does this approach necessarily resolve the matter of the relationship between the ministries within the organizational life of the presently constituted Christian churches.

What this construal of the relation between church and ministry draws attention to is the agency of the Spirit as the giver of *charisms* for ministry. It contributes to what has been termed the 'laicizing of Christianity'.[20] It is an emphasis recognised across the ecclesial spectrum. In Hahnenberg's recent theology of the ministries he recognises the impact of this Pauline emphasis on *charism* of the Spirit for ministry. But he notes that: 'Unfortunately, Paul's vision of broadly available *charisms* did not last. In the Christian West, the rise of christological approaches to ministry pushed pneumatological approaches aside.'[21] He notes the division that emerged between *charism* and institution, the loss of *charism*'s ecclesial and hence relational context and the resultant marginalisation of *charism*s. He might also have noted the tendency for such *charism* to be assimilated into the traditional ministerial orders. In the wake of Vatican II there has been a recovery of *charism* as the dynamic underlying the Church's ministries. How this emphasis on *charism* funding both traditional offices and newer ministries will be developed remains to be seen.[22]

The significance of the Spirit and *charism* for the recovery of a more ecclesial approach to ministries is not simply the preserve of Pentecostalism and the Charismatic renewal. There is an emerging ecumenical consensus that the ecclesia is foundational reality for all ministry. The debt to pneumatology may be less

---

[19] Ibid. This is an interesting and important point given the major examination of *diakonia* by John Collins that gave scant and unsatisfactory attention to the relationship between *diakonia* and *charism*, see *Diakonia*, pp. 255–6.

[20] David F. Wright, 'The Charismatic Movement: The Laicizing of Christianity?', in Deryck W. Lovegrove (ed.), *The Rise of the Laity in Evangelical Protestantism* (London & New York: Routledge, 2002), pp. 253–63.

[21] Hahnenberg, *Ministries*, p. 61.

[22] Hahnenberg discuses Küng's notion of 'temporary' and 'permanent' *charisms* and the *charism* of leadership as a way of singling out certain central ministries in the community. See ibid., pp. 72–3.

clear. However, what is clear is that there is a powerful pneumatological stream feeding into the understanding of the relationship between Church and ministry that destabilises traditional conceptions of the relation which have tended to give priority to the authority of ministry.

Church and Ministry: Towards a Trinitarian Integration

Problems remain where the emphasis is on either Christology or Pneumatology. Where ministry is developed in relation to Christology the differentiation and authority of ministerial office is accentuated. This is the strength of this approach. But the danger is over-differentiation and closure in relation to other ministries. The effect is to leave little opportunity for a satisfactory specification of the scope, legitimacy and authority of other ministries. Ministry tends to be sucked up into a Christologically determined ministerial office focused on the clergy. Where the emphasis is on pneumatology the field of ministries is significantly expanded and remains relatively open. Whilst this has many benefits it also generates an inability to achieve properly differentiated ministries. This may lead to significant confusion in the effort of the ecclesia to fulfil its calling.

It is possible to recognise a correlation between capacity for differentiation and relative openness or closure.[23] It seems that high degrees of differentiation generate relatively strong closure and make it difficult to give a sufficiently rich account of the relations between the ministries. It is not the fact of differentiation per se but the strength it exerts in creating sharp boundaries that easily operate as barriers. The supposition here is that the well-being of the entity – in this case a particular ministry or office in the Church – is more firmly secured by 'standing alone'. Often in the history of the tradition this separateness and over-againstness from the Church has been associated with an appeal to an originative event that has 'fixed the boundary'. Such over-differentiation bestows an undue self-importance upon the ministry. From this perspective it is almost inevitable that attempts at relating this ministry to other ministries inevitably diminish the latter. One result of this dynamic is that the system (in this case officially instituted ministry) is over-stabilised leading it to ossify and stagnate.

Where differentiation of ministries is relatively fluid there is an associated openness for innovation in ministry but it becomes difficult to give an account of the diversity of forms of ministry and their inner relations. The reason being that there are no longer any stable forms in view. This danger arises from an over idealised notion of 'absolute openness', 'an infinity which overflows every thought

23 The conceptual frame offered here is indebted to the important discussion of the issues of relative closure/openness and differentiation in the human sciences in relation to the nature of human beings in Daniel Hardy, *God's Ways with the World: Thinking and Practising Christian Faith* (Edinburgh: T&T Clark,1996), pp. 23–4, 93–7, 103–13.

and differentiation'.[24] This 'converts openness into a closure, but one which is beyond understanding'.[25] Whilst this approach presents a fundamental challenge to the former view it struggles to generate enduring forms through time and space. The system is constantly in danger of dissipation. Relative closure and openness and degree of differentiation and boundedness, are important conceptual heuristic tools for understanding both the history of ministry and the interrelationships between the ministries of the Church. The above difficulties are associated in different ways with an essentially static ontology of order. How this might be overcome through a reconception of order is addressed in Chapter 7.

For the moment we note that the relationship between ministry and Church is clearly not simple; it cannot be stated as a simple one-way dynamic. The best insights of modern ecclesiology recognise this and attempt to describe the dynamic in richer and more satisfactory ways that do justice to the reality of a Church and ministry informed by the life of the triune God. As a result the appeal to Trinitarian relations and communion as a clue to the form and function of the ecclesia and its ministries is widespread.[26] However, it is questionable how successful the discourse has been in uncovering the proper relations between the ministries.[27] There are a number of reasons for this. First, to some extent reflection on ministry continues to be driven by either strongly Christological or Pneumatological emphases and this ensures that the attempt to specify the relations between the ministries will succumb to the problems noted above. Second, the current appeal to Trinitarian and relational modes of understanding often fails to generate insight at more particular levels, such as relations between the ministries.[28] The discourse tends to remain abstract and uninformative. This problem has been noted by Daniel Hardy:

> That is the reason why the recovery of relational thinking in theology, which has been so much stressed in modern times, is only a first step in the development of adequate conceptualities for theology. What is required is more attention not only to the fact that relations are intrinsic (or internal) to their terms but also to their variety and dynamics – how they operate in differing situations. Without this, when used either for God and for God's relation to the universe, relational thinking will remain an abstract idea.[29]

---

[24] Hardy, *God's Ways with the World*, p. 109. The result is yet another form of 'transcendental monism'.

[25] Ibid.

[26] See, e.g., Greenwood, *Transforming Priesthood* (Anglican); Colin Gunton, 'The Church on Earth: the Roots of Community', in Gunton and Hardy (eds.), *On Being the Church*, pp. 48–80 (Reformed); Hahnenberg, *Ministries* (Roman Catholic); Zizoulas, *Being as Communion* (Orthodox).

[27] The recent attempt by the Roman Catholic theologian, Edward Hahnenberg, is the most sophisticated and ground-breaking in this respect.

[28] This is a problem with Robin Greenwood's *Transforming Priesthood.*

[29] Hardy, *God's Ways with the World*, p. 138.

Hardy's comments are apposite for the present enquiry. Notwithstanding increasing attention to issues of church and ministry it is far from self-evident how relational approaches to ecclesiology and ministry have advanced our understanding about the ways the ministries of the Church operate in a genuinely collaborative manner. In other words, whilst the trends in Trinitarian thinking in relation to ecclesiology and ministry are evident, the work of transposition and interweaving of Trinitarian and relational categories into an ecclesiology of ministry remains significantly underdeveloped.

A simple one-way relationship between church and ministry is not sustainable. Most commentators would recognise this, at least to some extent. Yet the dynamic relationship between church and ministry is often missed or not grasped. The deeper and more intractable problems that arise from faulty construals of the church–ministry relation remain embedded within the familiar affirmations concerning ministry and church. For example, it is not unusual for churches to reach agreement on a range of ministry matters: the ministry of the whole people of God; the nature of the Church as a community in which there are a variety of gifts and graces; the importance of ministerial offices amidst a growing diversity of other ministries. Furthermore, there is often a consensus on problems to do with ministry, for example, rampant Western individualism, the democratic spirit of the age and the loss of a sense of authority in communities of faith, and conflicts between clergy and laity.

However, notwithstanding consensus reached, both formal, and informal, regarding the above matters, the unresolved tensions between the ministries remains embedded in the discourse. For example, doctrines of ministry that have traditionally appealed to a strong Christological basis for the legitimation of office and exercise of authority often simply reassert the tradition as a means of securing the *communio* of the Church in a fragmented world. Those doctrines of ministry that look to the gifts of the Spirit in the body of Christ appear to have an easier time of it. Spirit, ministry and community seem more organically related. This pneumatological approach can function reasonably well at the 'local church' but is unable to provide a wider ecclesial vision of the Church. It does not generate structures of continuity and forms of ministry to enable the endurance of the community of faith. One result is that energy for ministry is too easily dissipated and looses coherence. This spirit led ecclesiology often ends up appealing to an overarching authoritative office such as 'apostle'.[30] Yet problems inherent in either a strong Christological or Pneumatological emphasis in ministry are rarely interrogated. The result is that for all the consensus achieved concerning the nature of Christian ministry little genuine advance is made in understanding (a) why the doctrine and practice of ministry is such an intractable and divisive issue for the churches and (b) how ministry and church are dynamically related.

---

[30] See David Cannistraci, *Apostles and the Emerging Apostolic Movement* (Ventura: Renew Books, 1996) for a discussion of the place of 'apostle' in contemporary Pentecostalism.

How then might church and ministry be related? Robert Hannaford suggests a more organic conception as a way to overcome a view of ministry 'divorced from the collective life of the Church'.[31] In overcoming this we need to show that a theology of ministry, understood as action for and on behalf of the Church, is consistent with an understanding of the Church as an organic community, where ministerial differentiation contributes to and does not diminish the unity and coherence of the whole body.

It is a sentiment few would disagree with no matter what their church affiliation. Hannaford is pointing to a relationship between church and ministry which is highly integrative. It may be possible to extend this further. A fully integrative relation would point to an essential interweaving of ministry and Church. On this account the Christian community would not have priority over its ministries. Nor would the ministries of the Church have priority over the Church. Neither would be the sole constitutive power of the other. 'Rather there is a reciprocal relationship such that to be an apostolic community is to be a ministering community in which there are particular ministries. Church and ministry are given in and with each other.'[32] This important insight from a report of the Uniting Church in Australia has much to commend it. It indicates both a genuine complimentarity and co-inherence between church and ministry. The same report finds this essential link between community and ministry embedded in baptism. This is a sacramental sign of incorporation into the life of the triune God and the apostolic community of the gospel; a ministering community for the sake of the gospel. Thus in baptism community and ministry 'are given in and with each other'. Under such conditions neither one nor the other has ontological priority; neither one nor the other are the constituting power of the other. Ministry arises in and is given with the reality of the Church. The Church arises in and is given with the reality of ministry. Some such relation would seem to be necessary in order to develop a rich ecumenical ecclesiology of ministry.

The challenge in such a fundamental conception is to allow the force of this interpenetrative relation to inform a theology of ministries and their relations. However this conception remains too general and requires further specification. For example, what might we expect such a reciprocal relation as envisaged here, to achieve in relation to the question of the ministries? We have already observed a number of problems associated with less integrative accounts of the relation between church and ministry. The problems were twofold. One failed to maintain an appropriate openness due to an over-differentiation of certain ministries (Christological model). This necessarily impoverished its account of the variety of ministries and their complimentary forms. The other approach was under-differentiated and lacked the stable structuring necessary for the endurance of ministries (Pneumatological). Thus it could not generate an appropriate closure regarding the forms of ministry. In both cases the interrelationship between the

[31] Hannaford, 'Foundations for an Ecclesiology of Ministry', p. 26.

[32] *Ordination and Ministry in the Uniting Church*, p. 11, par. 19.

ministries was defective; the former too sharply delineating between traditional offices and newer ministries; the latter unable to generate sustainable boundaries.

But how might one test for the existence of a genuine reciprocity between Church and ministry? Its manifestation in the actual forms of life of ministering communities would be an important litmus test of its operation. One place where this feature of the life of the Church could be tested would be in the area of ministries of the Church. Where a reciprocity obtained between Church and ministry the relations between the ministries would manifest both appropriate closure through enduring specifications and at the same time exhibit a relative openness to new forms of differentiation. In such a dynamic ministries would have both fluidity and yet perdurable forms.

Ministry and its Multiple Horizons

God with the World: The Ultimate Horizon

Certainly a great deal of contemporary reflection on the nature of the Church and the ministries suggests a genuine striving after a dynamic between the ministries that is both integrative and reciprocal. And there does seem to be a consensus that the clues, if not the answers, to some of the most intractable issues to do with the ministries of the Church lie buried in the riches of a dynamic Christian Trinitarianism. This suggests that the ultimate horizon for a theology of ministry and the relations between the ministries will have to find ways of tracking and specifying the dynamic presence and action of God in the world and therefore the Church. This should not be surprising given that the point of the ministries of the ecclesia of God is to enhance the Church's witness through word and deed to the ways of God in the world. The ministries which exist to serve this purpose do not exist at a distance from such divine action but rather ought to exemplify the actual form and life of the triune God in the way they perform their task and relate to each other. Ministry and its ministries are called to follow God's own mission in the world. This suggests two inter-related horizons for ministry; creation and the *missio Dei*.

The Horizon of Creation: Ministry as Work

To the extent that the locus for ministry transcends the boundaries of the institutional Church and is directed to the *work* of God in the world the language of 'ministry' is correlated to God's work and creativity in the world. Ministry is rooted in creation even as it is redemptive in its orientation. This matter has significant bearing upon the issues of ministry, vocation and work in the 'secular' world. It is worth pausing for a moment to consider this matter. There is a close theological link between *diakonia* ('service'/'ministry') and *ergon* ('work'). It breaks open the usual categories within which the question of ministry and the ministries is discussed. For the most part the discourse of ministry operates within the frame of redemption and it is not difficult to see why, in the light of Paul's letters to the emerging post-Easter church, the ministry of reconciliation is the critical focus. However, such a ministry is grounded in the work of God.

The Johannine tradition of 'God the worker' is particularly rich and illuminating in this regard.[33] The work of God is manifest in the Word made flesh, the signs of God's glory are manifest in the works of Jesus, and the disciples are empowered to continue the work of God through the Spirit of God, the Paraclete (one who comes alongside to support another) who collaborates with them. The theme is present in the Pauline notion of 'fellow worker' with others (2 Cor. 1:24) and with God (1 Cor. 3:9).[34] For Paul there is a common work done in a collaborative manner, that is, in a way that befits those who are called to cooperate in the work of the triune God. As is clear from the text, for the apostle Paul, a cooperative approach to ministry is closely linked to a life of joy. Foundations for a ministry of reconciliation can thus be traced to the work of the reconciling God whose work in creation is doubled and renewed in the work of redemption. Behind the Johannine prologue lies Genesis; the light coming into the world is the light that gave light to the world and created all things (John 1:1–3). God's work and the incarnate work of Christ are bound together and the latter recapitulates the former. The primary reference to work is thus to God as the creator whose work is testimony to the divine creativity and energy.

To link the work of God to ministry is a particular instance of the larger issue of the relation between creation and redemption. The problem of the bifurcation of creation and redemption in the history of the Christian tradition is reflected, at least to some extent, in the problems encountered in relating ministry to the wider ministries of the baptised and indeed to the vocation and work of the people of God in the world. For the most part the discourse of ministry and the ministries has been somewhat narrowly construed and given a churchy reference. Ministry is something that takes place 'in the Church' or 'for the Church' and this has generated significant difficulties in giving an adequate account of the ministries and vocations of the whole people of God in the world. For this reason a theology of lay vocation and work has remained relatively underdeveloped and tangential to the concerns of the Church.[35] To this extent the bifurcation between work and ministry is an instance of the unreconciled tension between creation and redemption.

---

33 See the discussion of work (*ergon*) in John's Gospel and elsewhere in the Scriptures in *The New International Dictionary of New Testament Theology*, ed. Colin Brown, 3 vols. (Exeter: Paternoster Press, 1978), 3:1150 and, more generally, pp. 1147–59.

34 See for example the discussion of *synergoi* (fellow workers) in 2 Cor. 1:24 by Margaret Thrall, *The Second Epistle to the Corinthians*, 2 vols., ICC (Edinburgh: T&T Clark, 1994), 1:160–61

35 See the remarkable recent book by Armand Larive, *After Sunday: A Theology of Work* (New York: Continuum, 2004) and the earlier book by Miroslav Volf, *Work in the Spirit: Toward a Theology of Work* (New York: Oxford University Press, 1991).

However, if the ministries of the people of God were rooted in a doctrine of creation – related to God the creator and worker – and followed the creating and redeeming work of God *in the world* this would give a particular orientation to the work of the baptised and their diverse ministries.[36] Far from undermining the particularity of ecclesial ministries (for example, those in orders) such an approach widens the reach for which such orders have responsibility. It also makes it abundantly clear that the creative and redeeming work of God is much wider than a narrow churchy focus. The baptised are called, in their life, vocation and work, to follow the creative and reconciling work of God and offer their gifts and talents accordingly. Ministry rooted in a creation/redemption paradigm is thus ministry founded in God the worker.

The distinction between 'ministry' and 'work' clearly requires more careful consideration for it draws attention to an underlying dynamic between creation and redemption. A strong correlation between these two themes gives renewed significance to a theology of work and vocation in the world. It also raises the stakes considerably concerning the purpose of 'orders'. Their domain of responsibility is much wider than traditionally thought. But this also makes it even more urgent to determine exactly how such responsibilities are properly undertaken. The specific ministries of the ecclesial redemptive order cannot be construed as antithetical to the wider ministries of the baptised expressed liturgically and dispersed in society. The dynamics of the reciprocity between the ministry and the ministries, between orders and the laity, between the ecclesial world and the wider society, between creation and redemption all belong to a similar field of inquiry. This is critical for our present purposes because it highlights the importance of uncovering the collaborative nature of all work and ministry. In this way reflection on the nature of ministry becomes a litmus test of our understandings of the relation between creation and redemption as well as our doctrine of the Church.

A second matter that necessarily follows from the above concerns the *missio Dei* as a critical horizon for consideration of the ministries of the Church. Here the economy of God's own life – that is, God's appropriate openness to the world and rich modes of self-differentiation – provides the resources and wisdom for understanding both the purpose and interrelations of the ministries of the ecclesia of Christ. This theme will run like a thread throughout this book and receive particular attention in Part III.

---

[36] Larive, *After Sunday*, locates work within a theology of creation and creativity but distances it from the redemptive and reconciling work of God. This is unfortunate for in trying to recover the creation perspective he has not attended to the dialectical relationship between creation and redemption and its implications for a well-rounded theology of work that incorporates this dynamic relation.

Conclusion

Chapters 2 and 3 have begun a discussion of the rediscovery of the ministries of the people of God, the emergence of ecclesiology and the different kinds of relationships that obtain between ministry and Church. It is a preliminary discussion in an area that has surprisingly received little treatment in an ecumenical and missionary period. I have observed the impact of both Christological and Pneumatological concerns on the nature of the relation between ministry and church. In this context I have proposed an understanding of the relationship between church and ministry that is genuinely reciprocal. Church and ministry are given in and with each other, neither have ontological or practical priority over the other. I argued that this reciprocity could be tested in the area of the relations between the ministries of the Church. In this respect I noted the fundamental challenge in exploring the interrelationship between the ministries, traditional and new. The challenge was how to develop a relational view of ministries that (a) recognised the importance of properly differentiated representative ministries to enable the Church to fulfil its mission and at the same time (b) protected a natural openness for the continued development and eruption of ministerial *charism*s. This is an ecumenical task of the highest order given the problems between the churches over the recognition of ministries and the difficulties faced within churches in relation to ministry.

This chapter has also drawn attention to the wider horizons for the consideration of ministry. The ultimate horizon was identified as the *missio Dei* and the dynamic of God's presence and action in the world (horizon of creation). A reciprocity was proposed between the way ministries were interrelated and the dynamic of God's own openness and differentiation in the world. What this means is that whilst our foreground concern is the ministries of the Church and their proper relations, the background informing the discussion reaches into the nature and form of God's manner of participating in the world and human affairs. Thus, although the theme of ministries is a properly ecclesial matter its resource is not purely ecclesiastical nor historical but theological. Moreover, the link between divine presence and action and ecclesial ministries is not a simple and direct one. For this reason the discussion ought never to fall into the trap of assuming to read off from the doctrine of the Trinity in a simple and direct manner an understanding of the ministries. Rather, the triune dynamic remains as background and is mediated through creation and the wider ecclesial world. The interrelations between the ministries of ecclesia ought to be able to show forth, or at least offer clues as to the ways, work and ministries of human beings in the world with God. Consideration of the ministries is thus fully ecclesial and precisely for this reason offers wisdom for the way in which human society might be ordered for creative and redemptive purposes in the world.

The chapters that follow will explore a variety of issues relevant to the understanding of the ministries and their relations. It is admittedly a selective approach but is undergirded by the schematic outline of the present chapter.

It will provide a background map for a critical appraisal of a number of issues in the ministry today.

PART II
Theological Trends in Ministry: Historical Perspectives

Chapter 4
The Question of Origins: The Legacy of R.C. Moberly's *Ministerial Priesthood*

Introduction

This chapter (and the two which follow) do not offer a comprehensive account of the development of ministry in the Church through the twentieth century. That is a project well worth the undertaking, however it is not to the purpose of this present inquiry. Rather, what is offered is a sketch of trends and tensions in ministry. Within this general theme a particular issue is the relationship between the diversity of ministries that has been so much a feature of the twentieth century and the traditional ministerial orders. Because ministry is an ecclesial activity particular attention will be given to the way in which Church and ministry have been conceived, and the implications of this for the relationship between the ministries of the Church and the possibilities that arise for a truly collaborative ministry.

The present chapter traces an particular understanding of ministry in the modern period through examination of the Anglican scholar R.C. Moberly's influential, *Ministerial Priesthood*.[1] It provides an interesting and important case study into the much debated question of the *origins* of ministry.

In the next chapter the Moberly tradition is traced in relation to Michael Ramsey's *The Gospel and the Catholic Church* and Anthony Hanson's *The Pioneer Ministry*. Both works were influential treatments of ministry by Anglicans in the first 60 years of the twentieth century and open up issues concerning the *purpose* of ministry. The three writers provide a helpful starting point in discerning trends and tensions in contemporary ministry revolving around the relationship between differentiated representative ministry and wider ecclesial ministries. From questions of *origins* and *purpose* of Christian ministry I move to the matter of the *reach* of ministry – who and what is necessarily included in the work of ministry – in Chapter 6. This chapter identifies continuing trends, tensions and new developments in the final decades of the twentieth century.

---

[1] R.C. Moberly, *Ministerial Priesthood: Chapters (Preliminary to a study of the Ordinal) on The Rationale of Ministry and the Meaning of Christian Priesthood* [1897] (London: SPCK, London, 1969).

Although the theologians and texts considered come from the Anglican tradition the kinds of issues discussed and the tensions and trends uncovered are not the preserve of one communion but are indicative of broader ecclesial pressures and developments. This has been highlighted at key points in the argument. The advantages of particular case studies from the stance of one communion outweighs a more broad ranging approach which becomes so general that critical issues and developments are lost sight of. The case studies provide raw material for an analysis of the integrative ideal for ministry in Chapter 7 and constructive proposals in Chapters 8 and 9 for a general theory of collaborative ministry. The practical implications of these proposals are considered in Parts IV and V.

Ministerial Priesthood: The Context

On the eve of the twentieth century, R.C. Moberly, the Oxford Professor of Pastoral Theology, penned these words: 'The basis of a true understanding of Church ministry is a true understanding of the Church.'[2] Moberly appealed to an organic conception of Church in which 'her ministers' were 'specific organs or members of the body'. Moberly's exposition of ministry and priesthood became a classic text of modern Anglicanism and its importance is apparent in its reissue in 1969. Some of Moberly's insights regarding the organic conception of ministry and the nature of the pastoral office have proved quite prophetic becoming part of mainstream ecumenical discourse. Other emphases, such as his appeal to a Tractarian notion of apostolic succession, have not stood the test of time though their influence remains. Moberly's work highlights both the promise and the problems of Anglican approaches to ministry over the course of the last century and also offers a window into broader ecumenical issues concerning the nature of ministry, the relations between the ministries and unresolved tensions between the churches. Accordingly his work is both a useful and appropriate starting point for an examination of ministry in the modern period.

Moberly's significance as an interpreter of ministry in Anglicanism is clear from the literature. In the early years of the twentieth century his work is frequently referred to[3] and a second edition appeared in 1910, minus the long appendix regarding the question of validity of orders originally occasioned by Pope Leo XIII's Bull, *Apostolicae Curae* of 1896. The 1969 reissue of the 1910 edition included an important introduction by Anthony Hanson, Professor of Theology in the University of Hull and producer of another key work on ministry that I shall examine shortly.[4] Hanson drew attention to the enduring significance of Moberly's

---

[2] Ibid., p. 1.

[3] See, e.g., Darwell Stone, *The Church: Its Ministry and Authority* (London: Rivingtons, 1908).

[4] Hanson, *The Pioneer Ministry*.

work, particularly in relation to the concept of 'representative priesthood' and the pastoral emphasis on ministerial orders. These emphases lie not far below the surface of ecumenical dialogues and Anglican self-understanding regarding ministry. Hanson also noted the unsustainability of Moberly's adherence to a nineteenth-century view of apostolic succession. When Robin Greenwood recently turned his attention to the subject of priesthood and ministry Moberly was appraised more critically as an influential exponent of a strand in Anglicanism that, among other things, was guilty of too sharp a distinction between ordained ministry and the laity.[5] On the other hand Moberly's ecclesiology of ministry has struck a somewhat surprising though resonant cord with contemporary evangelical sensibilities.[6]

Ministerial Priesthood appeared in the final years of the nineteenth century against the backdrop of the Oxford Movement's advocacy of 'the apostolic succession' and an associated concern in the Church of England to give an account of its ministry vis-à-vis both the state and the Church of Rome. As Hanson notes, theologians wanted to know: 'How is the Church's ministry authorised?'[7] It is a question that remains an issue for the wider Church. On this score Moberly was clear; authorisation did not rely either upon a legal nexus between the state and the Church (Erastianism), nor upon any pronouncements from Rome. Rather, authorisation for ministry came from Christ *via* the first apostles to the first bishops. In Moberly's view authorisation was a matter settled by examination of the historical origins of ministry. However, this position had to be defended against a more 'liberal' theory of ministry espoused by Edwin Hatch and more cautious assessments of the historical evidence by J.B. Lightfoot and F.J.A. Hort.[8]

---

5 Greenwood, *Transforming Priesthood*, pp. 7–11.

6 See George Carey, prior to becoming Archbishop, 'Reflections upon the Nature of Ministry', *Anvil* 3/1 (1986): 27. See the challenge to Carey on this matter by another Anglican evangelical, David Wright, 'Ministerial Priesthood: Further Reflections', *Anvil* 3/2 (1986): 199–202.

7 Moberly, *Ministerial Priesthood*, p. viii. Hanson points out that whilst the question of ministry was also a point of contention on the Continent the question there was different: 'Is there any justification in the New Testament for having an institutional ministry at all?' This question also remains alive and kicking in the twenty-first century.

8 Moberly, *Ministerial Priesthood*, p. viii. Edwin Hatch, *The Organization of the Early Christian Churches*, Bampton Lectures, 1880 (London: Rivingtons, 1881); J.B. Lightfoot, *The Christian Ministry*, ed. and intro. Philip E. Hughes (London: Morehouse-Barlow, 1983), originally published as an excursus in his commentary on Philippians (The Christian Ministry', in *St Paul's Epistle to the Philippians* [1868] [London: Macmillan, 1986], pp. 181–269); F.J.A. Hort, *The Christian Ecclesia* (New York: Macmillan,1897) (published posthumously). For a recent positive reappraisal of Hatch's position see Norman F. Josaitis, *Edwin Hatch and Early Church Order* (Gembloux: J. Duculot, 1971).

Ministerial Origins: Organic and Mechanistic Accounts

Whilst the defence of the apostolic succession occupied a major portion of the book, Moberly began in a more systematic fashion setting the issue of ministry within the larger question of the relation of the Church to the ministry. He recognised that a true understanding of ministry was based on a true understanding of the Church. Moberly's programmatic statement reads thus:

> The Church is likened to a body; her ministers to certain specific organs or members of the body. If, in the material body, one member differs from, or is related to, another, these mutual differences, or relations, at once serve to explain, and receive explanation from, the unity of the body as single articulated whole. So when we inquire into the rationale of Church ministries, we are inquiring into the principle of the differentiation of functions within a single unity. If there are differences of ministries, if ministry as a whole, is different from laity, these differences at once illustrate, and depend upon, the unity of that whole in which, and for which, they exist. It is a fundamental truth that the differentiation is a differentiation of, and within, unity.[9]

This statement, for the most part, would not be out of place in many contemporary expositions of the Church as a complex, differentiated and interrelated organic entity. Within this relational theology of the body of Christ and its ministries Moberly's own particular orientation shines through: 'her ministers' are *the* 'Church ministries', a matter that is very clear in the differentiation of 'ministry as a whole' from 'laity'. When he begins to expound the unity of the Church Moberly's debt to a late nineteenth-century idealist philosophy becomes apparent.

> [The Church's unity] is not to be understood as a growth which begins from below, and gradually coalesces: her unity is not the crown of an evolution which starts from disunion; the Church is one in idea whether she is one in fact or not; her ideal unity from the first is inherent, transcendental, divine: she is one essentially, as and because God is One.[10]

The Church's fundamental reality is from above, an idea, 'a necessary element in the meaning of the life of the Church'. The underlying transcendental monism is rooted in an uncompromising assertion of divine unity, eschewing any plurality and countering a nascent tri-theism. Moberly's account was swimming against the tide of a more empirical and historical approach that emphasised a unity 'acquired by degrees from below'. In the latter case the movement was from diversity and disunity in history towards a corporate life that led to the idea of unity.[11]

---

9 Moberly, *Ministerial Priesthood*, p. 1.

10 Ibid., p. 6.

11 Ibid., p. 2.

For Moberly it was an argument about ministerial origins. There were, it seems, only two options, divine ('from above') or 'from below', wherein the Church's existence is explained as a sociological phenomenon. A problem arose when the priority of the former account was displaced by the latter. Moberly was committed to the Church's transcendental unity, beyond all differentiations and exigencies of the historical manifestations of ecclesia. This idealist position represents an ecclesial closure to the world; the marks of the Church do not represent a 'statement about the accidents of history, but a profession of essential doctrine'.[12]

How then was the transcendental unity of the Church related to the visible manifestation of the body of Christ? Moberly was no less clear. On the one hand there was a radical difference often observed between the true idea of the ecclesia (the ideal kingdom) and the Church as it practically appears. Yet 'the proper relation between these two is not a relation of contrast, not even a relation of resemblance, but is, in underlying and ultimate reality … the relation of identity'.[13] In keeping with his organic conception of the Church Moberly appealed to the familiar spirit/body relation and proposed that 'the visible Body is the spiritual Church – is so really, even while it most imperfectly is'.[14] It is thus axiomatic that 'the Body is the utterance of the Spirit'. We will find an echo of this four decades later in Michael Ramsey's justification of episcopacy as the 'utterance of the Gospel'. Yet, as I shall note in the following chapter, for Ramsey the emphasis has shifted from philosophical idealism to the theology of the incarnation.

Moberly's argument was in tension with those emerging traditions of an historical empirical bent that offered a more democratic picture of the ecclesia and a naturalistic interpretation of its emergence from 'below'. Bishop Lightfoot's *The Christian Ministry* represented a scholarly Anglican exemplar of this alternative tradition. Lightfoot's extensive and careful analysis of the historical material led him to the view that:

> If bishop was at first used as a synonyme [*sic*] for presbyter and afterwards came to designate the higher officer under whom presbyters served, the episcopate properly so called would seem to have been developed from the subordinate office. In other words, the episcopate was formed not out of the apostolic order by localisation but out of the presbyteral by elevation: and the title, which originally was common to all, came at length to be appropriated to the chief among them.[15]

---

12 Ibid.

13 Ibid., p. 37.

14 Ibid., p. 40.

15 Lightfoot, 'The Christian Ministry', p. 196, cf. p. 227. He continued by stating that the evidence showed that the 'creation [of episcopacy] was not so much an isolated act as a progressive development, not advancing everywhere at an uniform rate but exhibiting at one and the same time different stages of growth in different churches' (p. 227). Lightfoot's

Lightfoot referred to a representative priesthood though he was highly critical of the rise of sacerdotalism on the pastoral and ministerial 'view of the clergy'.[16] Whilst not doubting the divine origins of the threefold order Lightfoot offered a measured assessment tracing it 'to Apostolic direction'.[17]

Moberly's respect for Lightfoot did not prevent him from engaging with some of the key tenets of his work.[18] Sensing the threat to his more organic and idealist ecclesiology posed by Lightfoot's more historicist/theological approach Moberly criticised Lightfoot's more individualistic emphasis – 'Each individual member holds personal communion with the Divine Head'[19] – as evidence of a 'restrained and gentle form' of Montanism. In Moberly's view Lightfoot undervalued the 'outward' and 'bodily' and overemphasised the 'spiritual'. As a result Lightfoot's implied critique of formalism in religion ended up dismissing form per se. Yet, as Moberly knew, 'to get rid of form is of course impossible. The attempt to do so ends really in the substitution of such forms as seem to be least like forms – forms, that is, the most unintelligent and uninspiring – in place of those which are most venerable.'[20] Moberly noted that after a while the initial fire of enthusiasm dies for lack of 'fuel', 'lack of historical continuity, lack of adequate expressiveness or authority of form'.[21] Moberly's counter-proposal was to redirect the animating work of the Spirit to 'whatever belongs to the due and authorised representation or conveyal of that one supreme inward reality, which is God Himself'.[22]

The issue addressed here, as seen in Chapter 2, is remarkably relevant to contemporary conflicts over the ministries and their resourcing from Christological and Pneumatological streams in the tradition. Moberly's idealist ecclesiology leads to a strong correspondence between the '"essentia" of the Church's being' and the 'methods' that are 'indispensable conditions of the essence'. He had in mind those divinely ordained ordinances that were 'part of the essence of God's message to man in the Gospel'.[23] Such ordinances were essential, 'in the sense that, in so far as we are commanded by God to use of them, we have no power of dispensing with the use of them, or of obtaining, otherwise than by the use of them, the gifts which God has bidden us find in and through their use'.[24]

---

inquiries led him to the view that the maturer forms of episcopacy were linked to the latest surviving apostles and their influence, principally St John.

16 Ibid., p. 259.

17 Ibid., p. 267.

18 For a recent discussion of the issue between Lightfoot, Moberly and Charles Gore see Stephen Sykes, '"To the Intent that these Orders may be Continued": An Anglican Theology of Holy Orders', in Franklin (ed.), *Anglican Orders*, pp. 48–63, esp. pp. 50–63.

19 Moberly, *Ministerial Priesthood*, p. 46.

20 Ibid., p. 55.

21 Ibid., p. 55.

22 Ibid., p. 56.

23 Ibid., pp. 58–9.

24 Ibid., p. 60.

Ministry 'Of' but not 'From' the Church

How then are these essential ordinances, that is, 'the ministry', related to the 'laity'? This question is revealing: 'What is the relation that results between this Ministry and either the Body as a whole, or the Laity, if the Laity be regarded apart?'[25] A century later the terms of the discussion have changed. Now it is a question of the relation between the multiplicity of ecclesial ministries, rather than the ministry and laity. But the central problems persist. Moberly distanced his position from Rome; the ministerial order was not a 'sanctified intermediary' of higher status, more holy and able to mediate between 'the mere *plebs Christiana* and their God. Rather, the 'spiritual Body' was the 'whole corporation or Church of Christ', the full spiritual benefits of which – 'Divine citizenship (in a real sense Divine priesthood)' – are given to the whole body in Baptism.[26] Ordained ministers are thus neither intermediaries between the 'Body and its life', nor do they 'confer life on the Body' but 'they are organs of the Body, through which the life, inherent in the total Body, expresses itself in particular functions of detail'.[27] Yet this did not mean that the rest of the body 'can dispense with the organs', nor did it mean that the body conferred on the organs their power of life. The organic conception of the Church did not mean that, 'the rest of the Body, even all put together – much less than any and every individual member of it – is already *de jure* a minister, or that the authority of the ministers to minister is derived from, or is conferred by, the mere will or act of the Body'.[28]

At this point the enduring appeal of the organic body image is co-opted in the service of the rationale for the ministry, its origin and relation to the body. For the crucial argument Moberly followed his father's Bampton lectures of 1868. Whilst the 'strength and health' (well-being) of the natural body was needed to enable each particular member to fulfil its function yet 'no one of these separate members or organs derives its own peculiar functions nor the power to exercise them in the first place from that strength and health'.[29] The parallel was drawn with the case of a priesthood, 'strictly representative in its own proper being, yet receiving personal designation and powers, not by original derivation from the body which it represents, or continual reference to it, but by perpetual succession from a divine source and spring of authorizing grace'.[30]

The argument was important and can be traced in different forms throughout the recent history of the discussion on ministry. It is a form of vitalism – 'spring of authorizing grace' – that emphasises infusion of capacity from outside a

25 Ibid., p. 65.
26 Ibid., p. 66.
27 Ibid., p. 68.
28 Ibid., p. 69.
29 Ibid., p. 70.
30 Ibid.

framework in contradistinction to possibilities from within.[31] The ministry belongs to the body, in the sense of being a part of the whole. It does not operate as an intermediary between the body and the life of the body. Thus we might say the ministry is *of* the body of Christ. Yet the body does not capacitate the ministry to fulfil its functions in and for the body to which it belongs. Capacity here refers to 'mode of authorization' and, as we shall see, this is effected from beyond the body – from above, by transmission of a divine commission. The theory offers a certain protection for the authority and the continuity of the ministry within the exigencies of time and space. However, when considered from 'the earthward side' this commission is mediated through those who hold office in the body. The agents of the authorisation are *of* the Church, not out of or above the Church. The circle is thus completed through the historical process. Such a procedure for authorisation raises many more questions concerning the relation between the authorising agents and the body than the theory can adequately explain. At this point Moberly retreats to a mechanistic account of the relation between Church and ministry.

At any rate in the late nineteenth century, Moberly found support for his view in Charles Gore and in a more general sense from the Free Church scholar, Dr Milligan.[32] Moberly wrote in the early days of modern biology and advances over the ensuing century suggest more complex biological analogies emphasising the interdependence and mutual animation of the parts and the whole of the body, for the very life and well-being of the parts (including 'the ministry). An evolutionary account of the life of the body cannot accommodate the more mechanistic strand in Moberly's account of ministry.

Ministry from 'Above' not 'Below'

Yet Moberly's intention was clear; he wishes to present a sharp distinction between (a) the ministry representing the whole body that 'wields, ministerially, authority and powers' which 'inherently belong to the collective life of the Body as a whole' and (b) the notion that 'every member of the Body is equally of right a minister, or that, if there be a distinctive right to minister, it is conferred by the voice of the Body simply, without authorizing or enabling empowerment of directly and distinctly Divine ordaining'.[33] This distinction between a ministry derived from above or from below was, in Moberly's view, 'of absolutely vital importance for the understanding of the rationale of ministry'. Ultimately the analogy with the biological body fades; the parts (that is, 'the ministry') of the whole do not have their strength and health 'in the first place' from the whole. The appeal to a supra-natural, transcendent bestowal of authority was critical.

---

[31] See Chapter 9.

[32] Moberly, *Ministerial Priesthood*, pp. 71–2.

[33] Ibid., pp. 72–3.

Moberly's either/or presumed certain ways of understanding the interaction of divine transcendence and immanence. A somewhat bifurcated divine action was implicit in his account. It reflects a two-nature Christology in which there is a strong delineation between Christ's divinity (from above) and humanity (from below). Ministry follows this pattern and hence in Moberly's view has its origins either from above or below. It is an issue that haunts the Moberly and associated Catholic traditions to which I have already drawn attention in Chapter 2 in its contemporary Roman Catholic guise[34] and to which I will return in Chapter 7. The domains of Christ's action are sharply differentiated and this has an associated ministerial form. The result is an approach to the relations between the ministry and the body of Christ that appears similarly closed. The resultant ministerial Nestorianism is in tension with more integrative accounts of the nature of the Church and its ministries. I shall address this matter specifically in Chapter 7.

The Ministry and the Laity: The Basis for Differentiation

In the chapter on the relations between the ministry and the laity Moberly was engaged in an argument about the representative nature of the Church's priesthood. Against Lightfoot, Moberly argued at length that the association of sacerdotal functions with a representative priesthood are not antithetical ideas but belong together, especially when the nature of sacerdotal ministry is interpreted in a reformed Catholic manner. Lightfoot's position had given particular emphasis to an original conception of Christian ministry that gave a certain priority to the sacerdotal and representative functions of the *whole Christian body*. Accordingly, he had argued that the 'priesthood of the ministry is regarded as springing from the priesthood of the whole body'.[35] We may be surprised to discover that Moberly considered such a view, whilst capable of misinterpretation, in line with his own position. Thus the 'representative' priesthood 'implied, in a real sense, the priestly character of the Church as whole'.[36] But it did not imply that members of the Church 'other than her ordained ministers are authorised to stand as the Church's representative *personae*'.[37] For Moberly it seemed there are two priesthoods within an 'inclusive priesthood of the Church Body': that is, the priesthood of the Christian layman [*sic*] and the priesthood of the Christian minister.[38] The latter 'is so representative of the community that what he does they do, and what they do

[34] See the discussion of Philip Rosato's approach to the relations between the ministries of the baptised and the ordained in Chapter 2.

[35] Moberly, *Ministerial Priesthood*, p. 76.

[36] Ibid., p. 78.

[37] Ibid.

[38] Ibid., p. 87.

they do through him', but this did not mean 'that what they corporately did through the act of their president they could equally do through any member whatever'.[39]

In Moberly's view there was a clear differentiation between the ministry and the laity and it is developed in relation to the nature of representation. This idea has become quite central in ecumenical discussion since Moberly's time. Part of the continuing dispute has centred round the origin of representative ministry. Here Moberly put the alternative options to his own quite bluntly: representation *via* either 'mere popular appointment' or 'distinction of ministers is mere matter of politic convenience'.[40] Yet Moberly knew that such a sharp delineation could not be absolute or at least was tempered by the recognition that the 'general Church body' was deeply involved 'in preparing for and concurring with the Divine act'.[41] 'Though ministerial appointment is certainly not human in place of being Divine, yet neither is it Divine quite apart from being human also'.[42] Evidently there was a place for authorising 'from below' but only as preparatory to and concurring with 'the Divine act'. Thus 'even what is most distinctively Divine in ordination is still conferred *through* the Church'.[43]

Ministerial authorisation *through* the Church, perhaps *by* but in no wise *from* the church. The prepositions become critical. Moberly's theological intuition will not surrender a substantive reference to God's solemn call and act in the authorising of regulated office that yet has to be 'uttered' through and in the body of Christ. He lamented the loss of a more emphatic 'lay voice' in the process and procedures of ordination as signalling that 'aspect of the priesthood as representative of the congregation'.[44] The identity of relation earlier posited between the ideal and real Church finds a faint echo in his recognition of the human element in ordination. In the interests of theological and logical consistency he could have been more open and innovative at this point. But he could not see any other option save for a dangerous naturalising of the ministry. To this extent his position almost invited a strong counter action. The conflict between clergy and laity continues.

A Question of Degree or of Kind?

What then was the correct way to identify the difference between ordained ministry and laity? Was it one of function, degree or kind? Moberly considered this under the category of 'character'. In ordination the 'character' 'conferred, and is indelible, is a status, inherently involving capacities, duties, responsibilities of

39 Ibid., p. 88.

40 Ibid., p. 89.

41 Ibid.

42 Ibid.

43 Ibid.

44 Ibid.

ministerial life'.[45] But, precisely because this 'character' did not imply a degree of personal and moral superiority to laity, the ministry was representative and not vicarious; a matter of consensus among Anglican theologians at the time. The reason for this distortion was to be found, in Moberly's view, in a lack of lay education. Moberly did not inquire into this and it may have been expecting too much of him to have seen clearly the roots of the problem in the long history of clerical domination of theology in the West. Moberly found support from Lightfoot, Gore and the Evangelical Liddon in affirming the difference between the ordained ministers and laity being one of 'degree' and/or 'function' not one of 'kind'. Both receive spiritual endowments; the laity's were 'personal' the other was 'corporate'.

Two things are worth noting. First, Moberly qualifies Liddon's reference to 'function': 'That is to say, of course, not in kind, apart from functional capacity; not in kind except just so far as distinctive authority to represent the Church by public performance of her corporate functions, of itself constitutes, *in a limited sense*, a difference of kind'.[46] This qualification, which holds to a difference in kind, 'in a limited sense', is precisely what has continued to weave its ambiguity through a century of ecumenical conversations with greater and lesser intensity as evidenced in the current ARCIC documents' appeal to a 'different realm of the gifts of the Spirit'. Exactly what ontological weight ought to be accorded this depiction of difference is contested.

Second, Moberly quotes approvingly and without qualification a further comment of Liddon's to the effect that: 'The priestly institute in the public Christian body was the natural extension of the priesthood which the lay Christian exercised within himself.'[47] In the modern discussion the notion of the particular priesthood as an 'extension' of the corporate priesthood has become a critical issue in clarifying the relation between lay and ordained ministries. For those in the Moberly tradition, 'extension' signals authorisation 'from below'. Yet I have already observed Moberly's willingness to countenance the idea of the priesthood of the ministry 'springing from the priesthood of the whole body'. I shall return to this issue later in this exposition.

Certainly Moberly had no wish to denigrate the laity as such and seemed entirely unconscious of the curious disjunction he imported into his scheme when he extolled the virtues and dignity of the laity. They were, after all 'the people of God', the *laos*.[48] It was evidently a category into which those in 'the ministry' no longer fitted.[49] This implicit closure of the boundary between ministry and laity

---

45 Ibid., p. 92.

46 Ibid., p. 96, my italics.

47 Ibid.

48 Ibid., p. 98.

49 This view had its roots in the early Church's development of the notion of the laity in response to clerical differentiation. See Alexandre Faivre, *The Emergence of the Laity in the Early Church*, trans. David Smith (New York: Paulist Press, 1990) for references to Tertullian (p. 46–7) and Clement of Alexandria (p. 55) – where laity even appears to include

was in tension with the more forward-looking aspects of Moberly's argument. But unfortunately it was entirely consistent with his defence of apostolic succession. The idea was clear: 'The work [of ministry] is God's work, and the authority to undertake it must be God's.'[50] The constitutive character for ministry is the charisma of the Spirit. This was the basis for the divine commission and the 'one warrant' for 'any form of *self sufficing or independent* Church ministry'.[51] It was a revealing comment. An organic conception of the body of Christ was antithetical to such an 'independent' tradition of ministry.

Such a commission 'from above' not 'from below' – that is, 'from God essentially and not man [*sic*]' – was the indispensable element. Thus, even in other methods of ecclesiastical appointment, wherein the 'congregation could constitute a minister' the undergirding belief must be 'that that which speaks through the choice of the congregation is God's voice'.[52] The difference for Moberly between this procedure and apostolic succession was that the latter offered a certainty and surety that transcended the dangers of any human devising. It achieved this by a particular 'ministerial' method or continuity, of transmission. Could it hold up at the bar of historical investigation? A good part of Moberly's energies were devoted to the defence of the theory on the basis of the evidence of the New Testament and early documents of the Church. His scholarship is now dated and susceptible to 'special pleading' (*pace* Hanson[53]). Furthermore, as we shall see later in this chapter, the discussion of apostolic succession has undergone some significant development. However, for our purposes a number of matters relating to Moberly's handling of the material remain relevant.

Some Critical Assessments

First, Moberly's treatment of the ministries in the early Church, particularly in the New Testament, seems to be seriously at odds with his earlier theology of the Church as an organic body. Now it seems there are emergent and strong lines of differentiation among the three orders – bishops, priests/presbyters and deacons – and between these orders and the other ministries. The fluidity of ministry in the early Church solidifies in Moberly's assessments and he tends to minimise

---

women – and Origen (p. 61). Faivre writes: 'At the beginning of the third century, the term 'lay' was used to describe men – and not, it would seem, women – who belonged to the church, but were not bishops, presbyters or deacons or who were not, in a more general way, members of the clergy' (p. 69). Thus the critical development over the course of time has been the expansion of the notion of laity such that in modern ecumenical discourse the *laos* refers to the whole people of God. See Chapter 7.

50 Moberly, *Ministerial Priesthood*, p. 100.

51 Ibid., p. 103, my italics.

52 Ibid., p. 105.

53 Hanson, Introduction to Moberly, *Ministerial Priesthood*, p. xx.

the significance of other ministries. For example, the role of evangelist was more a 'description of employment' rather than office.[54] The prophet could never have constituted another early order; in fact this function seemed inherently disruptive and was destined to fade out. It was essentially 'an individual inspiration' not a 'dignified order of ministry'. Beyond the enduring three orders hierarchically established, the other *charisms* of the Spirit belonged to the individual as such, bearing testimony to the 'infinite variety of personal spiritual endowment'.[55] Their corporate function and contribution to the life of ecclesia had been effectively screened out by Moberly. This serious ecclesiological error has haunted the Christian Church for many centuries. In modern times it has been challenged by the emergence of the charismatic movement in the second half of the twentieth century. Moberly's apostolic paradigm either assimilates all *charisms* into the three ministerial offices or simply ignores them. The 'organs' of ministry are highly restrictive and a certain ecclesial impotency is the result. It points to the fundamental incompatibility of Moberly's 'apostolic paradigm' with a more organic and relational understanding of the ecclesia of God.

Second, within the three orders – bishops, priests and deacons – a hierarchical pattern emerges in which an originally inchoate and unarticulated episcopally ordered Church is firmly in place by the mid second century. Fluidity and lack of clarity about the relations between the terms, presbyter, bishop and their relations to the apostles is simply a sign that the 'realities were in advance of the words'.[56] From early times the 'inner substance of episcopacy had an existence without a title'.[57] Moberly always has one eye to the threat of Presbyterianism.[58] He can countenance an emergent episcopacy, '*eo nomine*', but 'never to be "evolved" – for that would imply that it did not, in essential completeness, exist before.... That which was to come ... was the stereotyping, by titular contrast, of a difference inherently familiar, not the revolutionary creation of a novel distinction'.[59] The emphasis was clear: transmission by devolution from an 'outside agency', not appointment by evolution from within the ecclesia. It was a neat theory that offered confidence and certainty about the pedigree and credentials for episcopacy. But it could only be maintained by arguments from silence, a somewhat selective

54 Ibid., p. 162.
55 Ibid., pp. 161–2.
56 Ibid., p. 186.
57 Ibid. p. 186.
58 For example, ibid., pp. 186, 189.
59 Ibid., p. 219.

reading of history and a particular view of the historical process.[60] Its persistence in different guises in Anglicanism is remarkable.[61]

Moberly on Representative Priesthood

As Hanson notes, Moberly's defence of apostolic succession 'is not what we read him for today'. His real contribution was his exposition of the representative nature of Christian priesthood. This theme has already been touched on in relation to Moberly's discussion of the relation between the ministry and the laity. However, its fullest development occurs in the concluding chapter of the book on the nature of Christian priesthood. Moberly argued that the Anglican Reformers had recovered a more primitive and original understanding of priesthood as a pastoral office[62] and in this context were able to retain the language of sacrifice and priesthood. But the important theological issue was not so much a question of nomenclature but the nature of priesthood itself.

Moberly's inquiry was thus rooted in Christology. Here he noted that Christ's sacrifice includes Calvary – 'an indispensable preliminary' – 'yet it is not Calvary taken apart, not Calvary quite so directly as the eternal self-presentation in Heaven of the risen and ascended Lord, which is the true consummation of the sacrifice of Jesus Christ'.[63] His dying remained 'an ever present and perpetual attribute' of an eternal heavenly offering. Thus is Christ a priest forever, 'by the eternal presentation of a life which eternally is the "life that died"'.[64] Moberly followed Westcott and Milligan, 'Christ pleads what he *is*'. Yet this sacrifice belonged to the divine love and self-giving, not in the abstract but as it has occurred through 'consecration of death'. 'Such a definition of sacrifice carries with it … a corresponding definition of His priesthood' wherein Christ is priest 'in that he is the eternal offerer of this devotion of love, which, though human, is living because it died'.[65] 'The priesthood of Christ, then is Divine love under conditions of humanity' having both a 'manward [*sic*] and Godward aspect'.[66]

---

60 Moberly's recognition of the emergence of episcopacy has affinities with Newman's theory of homogenous evolution in which true developments will be found to have antecedents which embody the development in a less developed form. Continuity of substance is thus ensured. Yet Moberly does not develop his idea.

61 For further discussion see Chapter 10. The matter does raise some knotty questions for Anglicans. For example, does it operate de facto as a dogmatic principal or perhaps a principal of dogma? How has it been tempered or covertly retained through more recent reflection on the nature of apostolic succession of the whole church?

62 Moberly, *Ministerial Priesthood*, p. 226, cf. 299.

63 Ibid., p. 246.

64 Ibid.

65 Ibid., p. 249.

66 Ibid., p. 250.

Given Moberly's earlier organic conception of the Church as the body of Christ, the correspondence between the sacrificial priesthood of Christ and the Church was axiomatic: 'If Christ is priest, the Church is priestly'.[67] In the New Testament the 'priestliness of character is a correspondence which outflows upon the Church from the person of Christ' and as such 'Priesthood is not abolished, but consummated in Christ's Church'.[68] The rich imagery of the New Testament of the priestly character of the body of Christ did not in the first instance refer to apostles or presbyters 'but of the body as a whole, and of it just because it is the body of Christ; of it because of Him; and therefore of it, the whole, not of a part of it merely'.[69] This primary ecclesial reference for priesthood pointed to the danger of so deprecating the words priest and priestly that 'the priesthood of the layman must go to'. Moberly moved in another interesting direction: 'The priesthood of the ministry is to be established not through deprecation, but through exaltation, of the priesthood of the body as a whole'.[70] The Church's priesthood is 'really her identification with the priesthood and sacrifice of Christ', 'by outward enactment ceremonially, and by inwardness of spirit vitally', both informed with the 'Spirit of Love'. In relation to the world 'the Church is God's priest'; in relations between the baptised there too is the exercise of a 'real corporate priesthood'.[71] Both relations involve a 'for-other-ness'. Moberly's reflections on the nature of the corporate priestly life have an enduring value in their outer directed self-effacing quality.[72]

What then of the priesthood of Christ's ordained ministers? 'The priesthood of the ministry follows as corollary from the priesthood of the Church. What the one is, the other is'.[73] The reason being, 'that the priesthood of the ministry is nothing distinct in kind from the priesthood of the Church'.[74] Moberly insisted that it was no part of his argument 'to draw an essential contrast between the priesthood of the Church and of the ministry. The powers, and privileges, the capacities, are the powers and privileges and capacities of the body as a whole'.[75] Thus those who 'actually celebrate do but organically represent, and act for, the whole'. In exercising this duly authorised ministry the priest is called to both an outward and inward 'priestliness of spirit' in a representative manner as befits a leadership with

67 Ibid., p. 251.

68 Ibid.

69 Ibid., pp. 253–4.

70 Ibid., p. 254.

71 Ibid., p. 256.

72 Moberly's view of the priestly life is quoted approvingly by the former Principal of Ridley Hall and now Bishop of Sheffield, Christopher Cocksworth, in his recent co-authored book. See Christopher Cocksworth and Rosalind Brown, *Being a Priest Today* (Norwich: Canterbury Press, 2002), p. 15.

73 Moberly, *Ministerial Priesthood*, p. 257.

74 Ibid., p. 258.

75 Ibid.

an accent on pastoral oversight of Christian body.[76] Oversight finds its 'highest typical expression' in leadership in Eucharistic worship.

Moberly never tired of reiterating that 'the priesthood of ministry and of laity are not really antithetical or inconsistent, but rather correlative, complimentary, nay, mutually indispensable ideas'.[77] Though in a note he acknowledged that it was more accurate to speak of a priesthood of the whole body for there was no priesthood of the laity in which the collective priesthood of the ministry did not share. The note is interesting and revealing. The priesthood of the ministry shares in the priesthood of the body by baptism, but do they have another priesthood? The answer is yes, but it is evidently not different in kind, except in a limited sense, by virtue of a particular ministerial function. But the function is a representative one and thus integrally related to the corporate priesthood. As Moberly was quick to point out, it did not really matter from which angle one approached the issue: either from ministerial priesthood and thence to the 'dignity and power of the priesthood of the laity' or from the 'lay priesthood', 'and mount from thence to its *concentrated meaning* in those who are set apart personally to represent the collective priesthood'.[78]

It is difficult to avoid the sense of an unreconciled antinomy embedded in Moberly's exposition. There is, on the one hand, a sharp differentiation between the two priesthoods by virtue of the divine apostolic commission. On the other hand, there is a strong and robust representative account of priesthood derived from and shaped by Christ's priesthood. This latter conception is a more integrative and mutually sustaining notion of the priesthood of the Church and its ministry – the 'concentrated meaning' of the 'collective priesthood'. The two approaches do not sit easily together. The latter approach contains the kernel of promise in Moberly's account of ministry that has proven so fruitful in the Church. Behind this lies Moberly's inquiry into the doctrine of priesthood in the New Testament. Here he found priesthood rooted in the doctrine of the incarnation (springing from the self-giving of Jesus) and a corporate priesthood in Paul, Hebrews, John and Peter.[79] These matters were not developed by Moberly though it led Anthony Hanson, over seventy years later, to speak of Moberly's central insight, 'at least embryonically', of the idea of 'the extension of the corporate priesthood to the ordained priesthood of the Christian Church'.[80] In 1897 the implications of this for the wider ministries of the Church was not something at the front of Moberly's mind. His concern was directed to the nature and authority of the ordained ministry. In the ensuing years the increasing emphasis on the corporate nature of the Church's priesthood became the new ground upon which Moberly's project had to be re-thought.

---

76 Cf. ibid., p. 299.

77 Ibid., p. 262.

78 Ibid., my italics.

79 Ibid., pp. 263–78.

80 Ibid., p. xv.

Conclusion: Promise and Problems for Christian Ministry

Moberly's *Ministerial Priesthood* was a significant and influential systematic theology of ministry and set the benchmark for succeeding generations. The true value of the work only emerges through a patient exposition of the main lines of his inquiry. From the vantage point of a century on Moberly's work takes on a particular relevance if not urgency. Within a coherent theological account of ministry from the perspective of late nineteenth-century Anglo-Catholicism, *Ministerial Priesthood* identified issues that would be revisited and developed over the course of the century. Embedded in Moberly's exposition are future trends and tensions within the ministry of those Catholic and Protestant communions that share with Anglicanism a commitment to a differentiated and publically authorised representative ministry. I would point to the following issues in particular.

First, his endeavour to situate ministry within the life of the Christian community is critical. The appeal to the Pauline notion of the body of Christ enabled him to draw upon a rich imagery that emphasised connectedness and integration. It was by no means fully developed and indeed harboured within it some serious problems. Yet the interrelation between church and ministry for an exposition of ministry was a sign of things to come.

Second, his articulation of a representative priesthood derived from Christ, manifest in the 'collective priesthood' of the whole Church and given its 'concentrated meaning' in the priesthood of ministry was prescient of future developments in an ecclesiology of ministry. This representative priesthood received its shape and content from Moberly's fine exposition of the sacrificial love of God in Christ and the Spirit of Love. There are many things worthy of note here. In particular a self-giving 'for-other-ness' emerges as the dynamic informing pastoral priesthood. His defence of sacrificial language (nomenclature, for example, priest) – in relation to the eternal self-offering of the ascended Christ – and link to Eucharistic presidency have been insights pursued in Anglican ecumenical dialogue for decades and remain critical in contentious issues such as 'lay presidency' at the Eucharist.

Moberly's fundamental conception of representative priesthood provided the basis for his examination of the relations between the ministry and the laity. In the context of the body of Christ and the collective and ministerial priesthood, Moberly laid the foundation for a much more collaborative understanding of the ministries of the ecclesia. He may not have been an innovator in this but he did offer a rich and careful systematic account of the ministry of the Church.[81] This remains one of the most important issues in the Church as it considers its purpose, mission and calling in the twenty-first century. The above are signs of promise and identify trends in subsequent ecumenical thinking and practice in ministry.

---

81 Avis (*Anglicanism and the Christian Church*, p. 170) has drawn attention to the influences on Moberly. Stretching back behind Gore and Lightfoot, Avis points to the unacknowledged influence of F.D. Maurice on the notion of representative ministry.

Moberly mapped something of the emerging horizon of the Church's ministry and provided some theological clues to inform the journey.

However, Moberly's work also signalled some problems and tensions that have continued to accompany the Anglican Church and other communions. His defence of the Tractarian idea of apostolic succession was robust but has not stood the test of time. More recent developments in understanding the apostolicity of the Church and its faithful endurance have broadened the discussion considerably.[82] Yet the question of apostolic succession remains contentious even if more cautiously appealed to. Anglicans have continued to argue both internally and ecumenically about what is necessarily entailed in 'the historic episcopate'. Moberly's somewhat mechanistic account is of little use though his intuition concerning a necessary authority for ministry is indispensable.

A deeper problem is the fundamental incompatibility of Moberly's mechanism for transmission – operating independently of the ecclesia – with his conception of the body of Christ in which a representative priesthood is a correlative and complimentary priesthood to the collective priesthood. The disjunctions generated by these differing conceptions of the relationship of ministry to church continue to haunt Anglicanism.

The upshot was that Moberly's account of the relation between ministry and laity lacked sufficient integration. It was not clear how, in this *theories* of ministry – because there are at least two – there existed a genuine mutuality of relation between lay and ordained. There was certainly no hint in his exposition that the laity might enhance the ministry of the ordained let alone exercise ministries in their own right. It may be unreasonable to have expected much else in his time. Indeed, the manner in which he set the issue – ordained and laity – has now been superseded by recognition that the ministry involves a multiplicity of ministries of the whole Church. The Church is increasingly attuned to the tendency of the traditional ministry to assimilate and smooth out diversity and richness among the many ministries. Moberly belonged to the moderate Anglo-Catholic wing of the Anglican Church and his account of ministerial priesthood provided the most coherent though not uncontroversial doctrine of ministry in the Church of England in the first half of the twentieth century. Greenwood considered the Moberly tradition idiosyncratic and only serving to thwart the Church's attempt to articulate a theology that embraced the ministries of the whole people of God.[83] This may be premature though as we have already seen the theory of representative priesthood was skewed in a clerical direction by the 'foundational myth' of a rigid form of divine commission.

---

[82] See John Burkhard, *Apostolicity Then and Now: An Ecumenical Church in a Postmodern World* (Collegeville: Liturgical Press, 2004).

[83] Greenwood, *Transforming Priesthood*, p. 31. He says of Moberly that 'he represents for [*sic*] a significant strand within the Church of England's understanding and practice of ordained ministry that indeed is far from extinct today, though increasingly to be found in a defensive and idiosyncratic position' (p. 11).

Moberly's account embodied a tension between an integrative understanding of the relations between ordained and the whole Church driven by his representative theory of priesthood and a bifurcated two realm doctrine of ministry and Church. These two emphases coexist in his exposition. A more open and interconnected theory of representative priesthood operates in parallel with a tight 'stand alone' doctrine of 'the ministry' established via a mechanistic doctrine of ministerial transmission. This tension remains within the Anglican tradition. Ministry from 'above' or 'below' is an unfortunate way to depict the tension though it does contain a grain of truth. And it does draw attention to the emphasis on ministerial origins which as been such a major preoccupation of the Church in the twentieth century.

How the wider Church might develop a more appropriate understanding of the ministries and their authority remains on the agenda of the contemporary Church. The following two chapters will briefly trace some of the trends and tensions in the development of ministry as exemplified by Moberly. In doing so they highlight both the possibilities and problems associated with the development of collaborative ministry.

Chapter 5
The Question of Purpose: Ministerial Order and Pioneer Ministry

This chapter traces the fortunes of the Moberly ministerial paradigm in two key Anglican works, Michael Ramsey's *The Gospel and the Catholic Church* (1936) and Anthony Hanson's *The Pioneer Ministry* (1961). Both authors represent important engagements with the issues raised in the previous chapters and both rework and develop the Moberly tradition. Finally, both provide foundations for subsequent developments in ministry that have proved influential for the ministry and mission of the Anglican Church and the wider ecumenical scene. The chapter highlights the recovery of the purpose of ministry in the life of the Church.

Michael Ramsey: Episcopacy 'The Utterance of the Gospel'

When Michael Ramsey wrote *The Gospel and the Catholic Church*, he did not inquire into the nature and authority of ministerial priesthood. Rather, his attention was focused on the relation between the gospel and the Church, in particular its Catholic order and structure. As Hanson notes, 'Moberly and Gore would not have seen the point of doing this'.[1] But the context was decidedly different in the fourth decade of the twentieth century. In Ramsey's approach the philosophical idealism of Moberly has been displaced by an emerging biblical theology with its debt to Karl Barth. The doctrine of the incarnation is now deployed in a less abstractive sense,[2] as focused on the dynamic activity of God in the passion and resurrection of Christ. Ramsey writes in a more self-consciously ecumenical world. His apologia for an episcopally structured church is designed to commend the Anglican way in future Church reunion.

Within this framework Ramsey grounded the reality and life of the Church in the life, death and resurrection of Christ. Church and Christology were related in an essential manner. Moving beyond the familiar 'church as extension of the incarnation', Ramsey argued for a thoroughgoing organic conception;

---

[1] See Hanson, Introduction to *Ministerial Priesthood*, p. x.

[2] The contemporary German scholar, Dietrich Ritschl refers to the 'seduction of autonomous concepts' like 'incarnation' which easily become divorced from their larger frameworks of meaning and be invoked to justify all manner of theological statements (*The Logic of Theology* [London: SCM, 1986], pp. 185–6). His comments are particularly relevant for Anglicanism.

'not primarily in terms of an institution founded by Christ, but in terms of Christ's death and resurrection of which the one Body, with its life and its order, is the expression'.[3] It was a refreshing and theologically driven approach. 'For it seems not only that Christ creates the Church by dying and rising again, but that within Him and especially within His death and resurrection the Church is actually present.'[4] As a result, said Ramsey, 'we must search for the fact of the Church not beyond Calvary and Easter but within them'.[5] For Ramsey, the passion of Christ and the being of the Church are correlative realities: 'the fact of Christ includes the fact of the Church'.[6] Suggestively Ramsey states that 'Christ is defined not as the isolated figure of Galilee and Judaea but as one whose people, dead and risen with Him, are His own humanity'.[7] Theologically, Church and Christ are given in and with each other, a correspondence is posited between the being of the ecclesia and the humanity of Christ. This correspondence is corporate in nature. There is an echo here of Bonhoeffer's depiction of the Church as 'Christ in the form of community'. The Church as the body of Christ is nothing less than 'Christ Himself in His own being and life'.[8] Moberly's appeal to the Pauline conception of the Church as the body of Christ is here given deeper and richer theological bite. Although the air of an idealist ecclesiology still hangs over it – for example, the seeming unproblematic identity between Church and Christ – this is tempered with the strong emphasis upon the passion of Christ as the form of the Church's own life of continual dying and being raised.[9] The foundations are thus laid for what has been recently termed Ramsey's paschal ecclesiology.[10]

What part does the ministry have within such a conception? For Ramsey any suggestion that apostolic orders – bishops, priests and deacons – are separate or independent from the Church is quite inimical to his organic understanding of the Church. He sees this error deriving from the influence of Augustine on the Western Church's tendency to treat the validity of orders as something separate from the reality of the Church.[11] Ramsey commends the more theologically coherent position of Cyprian wherein 'the validity of orders depended upon their

---

[3] Michael Ramsey, *The Gospel and the Catholic Church* (London: SPCK, 1936), p. 7.

[4] Ibid., p. 19.

[5] Ibid., p. 7.

[6] Ibid., p. 34.

[7] Ibid., pp. 33–4.

[8] Ibid., p. 35.

[9] Though Ramsey warns of an 'mere immanentism' and recalls that to 'know the Church is not to know the inexhaustible truth of the Christ' (ibid., p. 35).

[10] See Ross Fishburn, 'Michael Ramsey's Pashcal Ecclesiology' (unpublished PhD thesis: Melbourne College of Divinity, Melbourne University, 2008).

[11] See Ramsey, *Gospel and Catholic Church*, pp. 151–4, 218–20. For an interesting an important reappraisal of Augustine and Cyprian's different approaches to orders and the Church see Colin Buchanan, 'Anglican Orders and Unity', in David R. Holeton (ed.),

derivation from and exercise within the one life of the whole Church'.[12] From this perspective the catholic structure of the Church is neither an addition to nor extension of the incarnation but rather the very 'utterance of the gospel'.[13] It is the logical outworking of his understanding of the relationship between Christ and the Church and recovery of a Cyprianic ecclesiology of orders. But in Ramsey's theology it is brought into correspondence with 'the utterance of God's redemptive love'.[14] It is axiomatic for Ramsey that the episcopate is of the *esse* of the Church, 'though baptism is the first mark of churchmanship'.[15]

Ramsey's argument for an episcopally ordered Church was influential and had the merit of providing a constructive theological argument for the Church and its ministry. This was associated with a more realistic approach to the historical development of the threefold order. Although he continued to affirm the importance of the apostolic succession he did so from consideration of its place within the whole body. Arguments about the devolution or evolution of episcopacy – for example, Lightfoot's argument about original parity of orders – so important to Moberly, lost their force when episcopacy was 'seen primarily as an organ closely related to the Gospel, and to the one Body' particularly where 'Grace is bestowed always by our Lord himself and through the action of His whole Church'.[16] Thus the 'succession of bishops is not an isolated channel of grace, since from the first Christ bestows grace through every sacramental act of His body'.[17]

It is useful to recall that it was during the same period that Karl Barth was arguing that the doctrine of the Trinity was not simply a synthetic theological statement but the Church's true analysis of the revelation of the Word made flesh.[18] The root and ground of the doctrine of the Trinity was the revelation of God in Christ. It was not isomorphic with but yet intrinsic to the reality of revelation. As such it was an analytic rather than synthetic statement. The analogy holds for Ramsey's own approach; the reality of an episcopally ordered Church constituted an analytic rather than synthetic judgement in relation to the gospel.

In the course of the twentieth century Ramsey's Christological focus has been further enriched with reference to the agency of the Spirit; Pneumatology has become a critical component in ecclesiology. Associated with this has come a greater appreciation of the eschatological dimension of the Christian faith. Both these developments modify the heavy institutional frame of Ramsey's

---

Anglican Orders and Ordinations, Liturgical Studies 39 (Cambridge: Grove Books, 1997), pp. 16–28, esp. 21–8.

12 Ramsey, *Gospel and Catholic Church*, p. 152.

13 Ibid., pp. 54, 208.

14 Ibid., p. 67.

15 Ibid., p. 84.

16 Ibid., p. 82.

17 Ibid., pp. 82–3.

18 Karl Barth, *Church Dogmatics*, trans. G.W. Bromiley and T.F. Torrance; vol. 1, pt. 1 (Edinburgh: T&T Clark, 2nd edn, 1975), pp. 348–83, esp. 377–83.

ecclesiology.[19] Furthermore, the traditional Anglican distinctions in relation to the episcopate; is it of the *esse*, *bene esse* or *pleni esse* of the Church may cease to have any relevance or make any sense, at least on a more fully integrated, organic and dynamic approach to church, ministry and the symbols of catholicity.[20] However, the important point in the present context is that Ramsey saw clearly the essential interconnectedness between gospel, Church and Catholic order.

But what of ministry more generally considered? This question was not on Ramsey's horizon though his more general exposition of the relation of the members of the body of Christ is suggestive. He speaks of the one priesthood of Christ being shared within the body.[21] His focus is an ethical one. What ought to be the mark of the mutual relations within the body of Christ? Here the key is the conforming of Christian lives to the pattern of Christ's own dying and living. In this way does the Christian participate in the 'marks of the Church'.[22] Overcoming individualism through death to self is the means whereby the members of the body of Christ know their dependence upon each other, 'wherein the relation of member to member and of function to function begets humility and love'.[23] In this context it is clear that the gifts of individuals 'belong to the Body and are useful only in the common life of the Body'.[24] The trouble at Corinth was that the Corinthians had 'taken the things of Christ in an individualistic way instead of *merging themselves and their gifts in the one Body* and so learning to die and live'.[25]

Ramsey's attention to the *charisms* of the Church remained largely undeveloped in this work. Its implications for an understanding of the relations between orders and the diversity of *charisms* of the Church is still being unravelled. He was more concerned how the inner coherence of the body of Christ and its many *charisms* was related to the passion of Christ. In this context he wanted to show that 'the backbone of the whole was and is the Episcopate, succeeding the Apostolate'.[26]

---

19 Avis, *Anglicanism and the Christian Church*, p. 307, is critical of Ramsey's 'special pleading' for apostolic succession' and his negative judgement on the 'orders of protestant bodies' (see Ramsey, *Gospel and Catholic Church*, p. 219).

20 This is the view of Stephen Sykes in his reflections on the importance of the 'symbols of catholicity' in Anglican–Lutheran conversations on episcope in 1987. Sykes' referred to the episcopate as a 'symbol of catholicity', 'an element in a system of communication'. From this viewpoint the above distinction collapses for in 'an integrated system no one abandons part of the "language" as simply inessential, if it expresses something which cannot be precisely said in any other way'. See Anglican–Lutheran Consultation, *Episcope in Relation to the Mission of the Church Today* (Geneva: Anglican Consultative Council and The Lutheran World Federation, 1988), pp. 19–20.

21 Ramsey, *Gospel and Catholic Church*, p. 84.

22 Ibid., p. 45.

23 Ibid., p. 44

24 Ibid.

25 Ibid., p. 51, my italics.

26 Ibid., p. 81.

In this context he wished to affirm that the Church's 'life in grace does depend upon the succession of Bishops, whose work, however, is not isolated but bound up with the whole Body'.[27] Exactly how this was the case within the life of the body – in relation to the functions and charisms of the ecclesia – was not particularly clear nor, it seems, of much interest to Ramsey. He was clear, for example, in the ordination of priests that Christ was acting 'through His whole Church whereof the parts derive their power from the whole'.[28] Thus it was that every act of grace 'is an act of the whole Church' and 'Bishop, presbyters and people exercise their share in the one priesthood of Christ'.[29] As such 'each order by its own function represents a part of the truth'. This was fine as far as it went. Ramsey was intent that each order 'learning its dependence, glorifies not itself but Christ whose Body is one'.[30] Dependence here was in relation to Christ. The mutual dependence of one in relation to the other was at best obliquely present.

Ramsey offered an updated and modified version of the Moberly paradigm.[31] Whilst Moberly's apostolic tradition operated *via* an external relation to the Church, Ramsey had developed a more integrative and organic account of the ministry in relation to the Church. A theological rationale for the embedding of the episcopate in the Church had been proposed. Whether it could stand up to further theological scrutiny was another matter.

However in *The Gospel and the Catholic Church*, Ramsey had little to say about the inner relations between Catholic ordering and the whole body of Christ, in particular how the people of God might enhance the episcopate. In this Ramsey's ministerial focus was narrow and clerical. Furthermore, he seems to have simply assumed Moberly's doctrine of representative priesthood and pursued his particular ecumenical concerns. However, on the positive side Ramsey had provided a stronger theological base for a future discussion of the relations of the ministries. For if it was the case that ecclesial order was so organically related to the Gospel of Christ, as Ramsey supposed, then what of the ministries and their associated *charisms*? There is nothing in Ramsey's account to suggest it was otherwise and much to suggest that a fully rounded doctrine of ministry might be very fruitfully developed along the Ramsey line. This would necessarily have to include an account of the relation between catholic orders and other ministries as well as a more general account of the interrelationships of the ministries. But that project was not yet on the horizon of the Church.

In the course of the twentieth century the Anglo-Catholic tradition of Moberly, filtered through theologians like Ramsey, was alive to the need for a more integrated account of the relation between Church and ministry. It was also engaged in an attempt to provide a more nuanced account of the derivation and nature of the apostolic office

[27] Ibid., p. 83.

[28] Ibid., pp. 83–4.

[29] Ibid., p. 84.

[30] Ibid.

[31] This is also the assessment of Avis, *Anglicanism and the Christian Church*, p. 172.

in the Church. The importance of these two issues was considerably heightened by the ecumenical movement and the impact of historical critical studies on the origins of Christianity. Yet the question of mode of authorization of ministry, in particular the apostolic office, and the quest for a more integrated account of the relations between church and ministry, were not always easy to reconcile. This difficulty was recognised by Austin Farrar and Anthony Hebert in the 1946 essays on *The Apostolic Ministry*.[32] From positions firmly within the Moberly tradition[33] they drew attention to the different emphases on the doctrine of ministry found in the New Testament. The organic conception of the body of Christ of the letters to the Corinthians and to the Romans pointed to 'members, all functioning in mutuality by divine appointment and grace, make up the one mystical Christ, animated by one divine Spirit.'[34] A Church structure emerged which 'is simply vocational and depends on a lively prearranged harmony between the vocations'. However, in contradistinction to this organic conception, in Ephesians notions of 'priority and derivation' are introduced with Christ as head and 'vital channels of the Body' named by which growth and health occurs. In this alternative conception the apostle is 'Christ's creative instrument as a Christian first created by Christ, through whom more are created.'[35] Thus, the apostolic mission of the first twelve 'creates the 'people' which was formerly no people'.[36] In this scenario the unity of the Church 'is the unity of the apostolate in equal and harmonious derivation from Christ'.[37] Of these 'two circles of ideas' Farrar was in no doubt that the emphasis in the New Testament was 'upon divine commission and creative apostleship'.[38]

Anthony Hebert, alert to the different patterns of ministry in the New Testament (that is, organic and hierarchical), identified the double conceptions of ministry;

---

32 Anthony Hebert, 'Ministerial Episcopacy', in Kenneth Kirk (ed.), *The Apostolic Ministry: Essays on the History and Doctrine of Episcopacy* (London: Hodder & Stoughton, 1946), pp. 493–534; Austin Farrar, 'The Ministry in the New Testament', in Kirk (ed.), *Apostolic Ministry*, pp. 113–82.

33 Indeed Hebert's 'Ministerial Episcopacy' seemed to be self-consciously developed in relation to Moberly with an emphasis on representative priesthood and an attempt to map out the relations between the 'special priesthood of the clergy' and the 'universal priesthood of all Christians'. In Hebert's unfortunate reference to the 'priesthood of the laity' he drew attention to its threefold expression; liturgically – 'in their share in the offering of the eucharistic sacrifice' (Hebert, 'Ministerial Episcopacy', p. 520); the offering of priestly lives in the world – symbolised in the offering of the bread and wine; and the priestly life of intercession and care for others in the world. By contrast the 'priesthood of the clergy' was located for the most part within the Church and congregation.

34 Farrar, 'Ministry in the New Testament', p. 175.

35 Ibid, p. 174.

36 Ibid. Farrar was the one largely responsible for the identification of the first apostles as the *shaliach* (Aramaic for Greek *apostelos*) after the manner of the Jewish messenger (*shaliach*).

37 Ibid.

38 Ibid, p. 179.

'as at once representative of the church as a whole and of Christ to the Church, at once within the Body and sent to it'.[39] The latter conception was guarded by St Paul's notion of the apostolate 'within the Church'.[40] Hebert acknowledged, as few had done before, that 'the correlation of the two is far from easy'. He went on to remark that 'this antithesis gathers up in itself the whole difficult problem of the Christian ministry, both on the practical and theoretical side'.[41] His insight was prophetic and later he made his own important contribution.[42] An important feature of the above two exponents of the tradition was their recognition that within the canon of Scripture multiple 'circles of ideas' coexisted and needed to be reflected in the ongoing life of the Church. A theory to account for their apparent antithesis was becoming increasingly urgent.

The Moberly tradition had thus bequeathed some problems for future generations. With the question of reunion on the agenda it was almost inevitable that energies within the Anglican camp would focus on advocacy for episcopacy as the appropriate form for the future Church's ordering. The emphasis on orders per se confirmed for many a prevailing clerical ethos. It was similarly difficult to avoid the sense of a continuing two-track theory for ministry operating more or less in parallel and unsynthesised. This was only confirmed by the lack of any positive rationale as to what the body of Christ might bring or offer to those in orders. The potentialities of the Moberly tradition on representative priesthood for the wider discussion of the Church's ministries for the most part lay dormant though perhaps not extinct.

Anthony Hanson: Pioneer Ministry as the Church *in nucleo*

When, in the early 1960s, the Anglican scholar and priest Anthony Hanson turned his attention to the matter of the Church and the ministry the context was quite different from Moberly's seven decades before. Hanson, with a background in Anglo-Catholicism, had spent twelve years in India and been involved in the formation of the church of South India. His reflections on Church and ministry were thus developed within a mission context where the *apostolicity* of the Church

---

[39] Ibid, p. 514.

[40] The reference is critical but it raises question about any tension between the two conceptions or indeed if they exist in fact. Thus John Robinson argued that the supposed tension between the ministry of the Church and the ministry of the apostles to the Church 'is an unreal one' in that both ministries 'are set by Christ in the Body and for the body' ('Kingdom, Church and Ministry' in K. Carey [ed.], *The Historic Episcopate* [Westminster: Dacre Press, 1954], p. 14).

[41] Hebert, 'Ministerial Episcopacy', p. 511.

[42] Anthony Hebert, *Apostle and Bishop: A Study of the Gospel, the Ministry and the Church Community* (London: Faber & Faber, 1963).

and its ministry was paramount. This provided him with a critical perspective on his inherited Anglicanism.

Weakness of the Catholic Doctrine of Ministry

In his book *The Pioneer Ministry*, Hanson offered a lucid and critical overview of the Pauline doctrine of ministry and its implications for the relation between church and ministry. There is no doubt that his approach significantly opened up the discussion of church and ministry and in doing so recognised a debt to Moberly and provided deeper foundations for more recent reflection on the relationship between the ministries. This will become apparent as we briefly follow Hanson's argument.

Hanson recognised that the problem with the 'Catholic' doctrine of ministry was its lack of integration with the Church. The 'Catholic' doctrine 'first separates the ministry from the Church, and then delivers the Church bound hand and foot into the hand of the ministry'.[43] The relation between church and ministry was 'external' and 'legal' rather than 'internal and organic'.[44] Authorization through a source independent of the body of Christ, yet representative of that body but not accountable to it, was problematical, to say the least.[45] What resulted was a kind of 'catholic gnosticism'.[46] In this context the ministry appeared as constitutive of the Church; an instrument of its unity and coherence. The being of the Church was in this way dependent upon the ministry, a matter that became explicit in the ecumenical arena.[47] Hanson identified this in scholars like Gore and Moberly.[48] The theory implied that the ministry could function apart from the Church. The laity became superfluous in the theory.[49] Hints of this could be discerned in Ignatius of Antioch's image of the relation of the ministry of the ordained and the laity where the bishop was the lyre, the presbytery the strings and the laity the choir.[50]

On the other hand scholars like Moberly were equally insistent on the organic conception of the Church within which the ministry functioned in a representative manner. However, this representative character was tenuous and unidirectional for it could offer no compelling account of the significance of the priesthood of the Church for the life and well-being of the representative priesthood. The antithesis, noted earlier by Herbert, between the organic and more hierarchical conceptions of ministry arose, in Hanson's view, from a poorly developed understanding of the

43 Hanson, *The Pioneer Ministry*, p. 139.

44 Ibid., pp. 139, 147.

45 Ibid., p. 145.

46 Ibid., p. 150.

47 Ibid., p. 164.

48 Ibid., p. 139.

49 Ibid., p. 88.

50 Ibid., p. 113.

relationship between the Church and its ministries. The nature of this relationship 'was a subject which has been strangely neglected by theologians'.[51]

Apostolic Ministry as Church in nucleo

Hanson argued that the 'role of the faithful remnant in the Old Testament was assumed by the apostles and disciples in the New Testament'.[52] This was borne out from his studies of the 'faithful remnant' of Israel and the doctrine of ministry in the Pauline letters. He referred to the Church's existence before Christ's coming as the commonwealth of Israel, 'kept from apostasy by the faithful Remnant'.[53] In Paul's teaching the first disciples 'were the faithful Remnant and … their apostolate sprang from this fact'.[54] In the Pauline context of the 'foundation of the apostles and prophets (1 Cor. 12:24–30; Eph. 2:20) Hanson argued that the apostles 'were the Remnant and therefore were the first Church'; the 'apostles are the ministry because they are the first Church'.[55] The ministry is 'the pioneer Church'.[56] This was a challenge to the familiar argument of *The Apostolic Ministry* that the Twelve had been appointed by divine commission to rule over the faithful remnant.[57]

Hanson concluded that the emergence and growth of Christianity followed the pattern of Christ, ministry, Church.[58] Whilst this might have led to the view that the ministry was prior to the Church, in fact Hanson argued that the pioneer ministry of the early apostles did not create the Church, rather 'the ministry is originally the Church *in nucleo*'.[59] 'The ministry shows in miniature what the Church should be'.[60] The ministry was thus 'the first church' or the 'rudimentary church'. Thus in 1 Corinthians 3:18–4:16 we learn that 'the task of the ministry is to serve the Church, but to serve it by itself living out the suffering, redeeming life of Christ in the world, in order that the Church as a whole may do likewise'.[61] The notion of the ministry as exemplar for imitation was strong for Hanson. Thus the first Christian ministers so identified with Christ's life that they became 'in a sense *alteri Christi*' not in an exclusive sense but only 'in order to induce the Church as a whole to do

---

51 Ibid., p. 58.

52 Ibid., p. 20.

53 Ibid., p. 43.

54 Ibid., p. 45.

55 Ibid., p. 63.

56 Ibid., pp. 87, 164.

57 Ibid., pp. 93–4, 98. Cf. Lionel Thornton, 'The Body of Christ in the New Testament' in Kirk (ed.), *Apostolic Ministry*, p. 104.

58 Hanson, *The Pioneer Ministry*, p. 65, cf. 75.

59 Ibid., p. 115, cf. 86, 94.

60 Ibid., p. 60.

61 Ibid., p. 62.

likewise'.[62] The nature of this ministry was gathered up in the Pauline idea of the 'ministry of reconciliation' which had been given to the whole church.[63]

The means by which this originative ministry devolved was fluid.[64] Hanson said it 'passes over into the hands of the Church, what we today would call the laity'.[65] This passing over pointed to the fact that in the Pauline churches 'the ministry does not really do anything that the rest of the Church cannot or must not do'.[66] The accent was on apostolic function rather than office as such.[67] The task of the pioneer ministry was thus to pass on the apostolic mandate of the Church for the people of God to fulfil. Thus, contrary to the RV and RSV translations of the period, Hanson argued that the removal of the comma after 'saints' in Ephesians 4:12 was more in keeping with the Pauline notion that *diakonia* is the work of the whole body of Christ.[68] The 'double relationship' of the ministry to both Christ and the Church did not entail the suggestion 'of the ministry doing anything which the Church as a whole cannot do'. Rather it was the case 'that the ministry is the pioneer in Christian living for the Church, as Christ was the pioneer for all of us'.[69] The pioneer ministry was thus a representative and exemplar ministry.[70]

Hanson's argument was innovative, particularly in his linking of the idea of the faithful remnant with the Pauline doctrine of ministry. His approach found sympathetic resonance with an earlier tradition developed by F.J.A. Hort in *The Christian Ecclesia* (1897). Hort had stated that 'the Apostles became themselves the first little Ecclesia, constituting a living rock upon which a far larger and ever enlarging Ecclesia should very shortly be built up slowly'.[71] This view of the apostles as constituting the 'first rudimentary Ecclesia' had been subsequently adopted by Bishop Headlam in 1920 when he referred to the apostles as the Church 'in embryo'.[72]

Ministry and Church in Relation

Hanson had provided a more solid and integrative theological account of the relation between ministry and church.[73] Though on occasions it did not appear entirely consistent. Thus the ministry did not constitute the Church nor did it have

[62] Ibid., p. 82.
[63] Ibid., p. 81.
[64] Ibid., p. 89.
[65] Ibid., p. 98, cf. 89.
[66] Ibid., pp. 76, 155.
[67] Ibid., pp. 97, 106.
[68] Ibid., p. 105. As noted in Chapter 2 this matter remains contested.
[69] Ibid., p. 62.
[70] Ibid., pp. 109, 155–6
[71] Cited in ibid., p. 137.
[72] Cited in ibid., p. 142.
[73] Ibid., pp. 87, 141.

an existence independent of the Church. Indeed the Church was not dependent upon the ministry for its being.[74] Yet the ministry 'is essential to the Church and yet not constitutive of the Church's existence'.[75] He was struggling to give voice to the fundamental reality of the ministry as the pioneer Church. In this conception church and ministry could not be thought apart from each other. Yet he was anxious to avoid any hint of the ministry reasserting itself over against the Church and thus did not press the inquiry at this point. For this reason he was not particularly clear in identifying the dynamic between ministry and Church. He spoke of one 'passing over into the other'. Certainly a more fluid and dynamic relation was posited. Yet this was not pursued and he finally reverted to the usual categories in asserting that the Church constituted the ministry.[76] The possibilities for a fuller relational understanding of church and ministry could not emerge. Hanson was still operating within an incarnational Christology but not a fully fledged Trinitarianism.

Pioneer Ministry in the Context of Mission

Hanson had offered a theological account for the continuing generation of new Christian community driven by apostolic witness which continually passed over into the new communities that were similarly called to fidelity in apostolic witness. Hanson's doctrine of ministry assumed a dynamic ecclesia under the impulse of its own apostolic mission. It was not a theory for maintenance of the presently constituted Church. Indeed 'in a situation where the Church is divided or static the task of the ministry cannot be adequately carried out'.[77] The missionary and ecumenical environment of the Church of South India was very different to the more settled and assured Church on English soil. Apostolic dynamism rather than stasis was the critical difference. Hanson recognised that his doctrine of ministry was undergirded by a stronger eschatology than traditional Anglican ecclesiology.[78] The Church was an ongoing creative activity of an apostolic gospel rooted in Christ and the *missio Dei*.

It was a challenge to the Catholic tradition, and significantly shifted the emphasis from questions of valid and regular orders, and historical pedigree to the demands of mission and the imperative of the gospel.[79] The apostolic ministry was set within an uncompromising horizon of the ever-expanding ecclesia of the apostolic God. How fared the tradition in relation to this approach? With the heavy institutionalisation of the Church and loss of the eschatological dimension of the kingdom the pioneer ministry had 'entirely disappeared' by the middle of the third

74 Ibid., pp. 139, 113.
75 Ibid., p. 109.
76 Ibid., pp. 123, 157.
77 Ibid., p. 155.
78 Ibid., p. 109.
79 Ibid., p. 87.

century.[80] Subsequent relations between church and ministry were 'hardened'. The 'standardising' of the catholic doctrine – in which ministry exercised a certain priority over church – was evidenced in Cyprian.[81] This particular catholic tradition was as entrenched in Protestantism as in Roman Catholicism.[82] More recent Anglicans had even managed to 'out-Romanize Rome'.[83] The bright light for Hanson was Luther who recovered an integration of ministry within the ecclesia through the doctrine of baptism.[84] Hanson drew attention to the tantalising but unexplored notion of Richard Hooker's that 'the true original subject of all power' was in the whole church visible.[85]

This baptismal basis for the church/ministry nexus and its association with the 'true and original power' of the Church provided the basis for a more adequate doctrine of ministry. It was precisely the direction in which Moberly's ministerial priesthood was heading. 'If Moberly had taken his admirable doctrine of representative priesthood seriously, he too would have arrived at this conclusion'.[86] The 'conclusion' was thus: 'The priesthood of the ministry is mediated through the priesthood of the Church; both are derived from Christ's priesthood'.[87] This was Hanson's development of the embryonic idea in Moberly of the idea of 'the extension of the corporate priesthood to the ordained priesthood of the Christian Church'.[88] However 'mediation through' and 'extension of' are not identical in meaning. The matter is complex and is the subject of the next chapter. The language presses the limits of an incarnational Christology without an accompanying Pneumatology. Hanson embedded traditional orders more firmly within the body of Christ and to this extent he made some progress in overcoming the disjunction between church and ministry.

Hanson also provided a richer framework for explaining the relations between all the ministries of the apostolic community of Christ. Hanson wrote in 1961 with a new wave of ecumenical dialogue on the horizon. His focus remained on the presently constituted ordained ministries. He did not have a great deal to say about the relations between the ministries. He was certain that the apostolic function was

---

80 Ibid., p. 118.

81 Though as we have seen in the discussion on Ramsey, the more serious problem was the Augustinian tradition that separated the question of the validity of orders from the Church.

82 Hanson, *The Pioneer Ministry*, pp. 124–5.

83 Ibid., p. 151.

84 Ibid., pp. 121–2.

85 Ibid., p. 131.

86 Ibid., p. 166. Hanson felt that Moberly's position entailed conferral of ministerial authority by Christ 'apart from the Church' rather than through it (ibid., p. 139). However this may not be entirely fair to Moberly, who also referred to ministry *through* the Church, from its 'earthward' perspective.

87 Ibid., p. 152.

88 Hanson, Introduction to Moberly, *Ministerial Priesthood*, p. xv.

indispensable[89] in the Church 'to be the pioneer in Christian living, in worship, in evangelism, in care for the flock'.[90] In this way the ministry 'leads the way in dying'.[91] This ministry 'is essential to the Church and yet not constitutive of the Church's existence'.[92] Furthermore, the Church was served by an apostolic ministry and the Church 'must join in that service'. The mutuality intended here is clear. It pointed to the fact that 'the ministry is not something given to the Church from outside to create it and hold it together: it is rather something given in the Church of Christ to be the Church, to be and do that which the Church, following it, must be and do'.[93] This seemed particularly the case in the missionary situation for there 'it is more obvious that the apostolate belongs to the whole Church and therefore must be exercised by every individual Christian *as well as by the ministry*'.[94] The implications of this are unclear though Hanson noted later that 'does not mean that the functions of the ministry gradually devolve upon laymen'.[95]

The Lure of Clericalism

This comment did beg the question of what to make of the wider community of disciples, their relation to this essential ministry and what lustre they might bring to the apostolic task of the Church. It was an area that Hanson had not really addressed. If he had he may have uncovered a problem embedded in his scheme. It became explicit when he asserted that there would always be 'a need for the ministry, for there is always a need for the nucleus *of the Church*, always perhaps a need for the faithful Remnant'.[96] It was a revealing comment. From the pioneer ministry co-terminus *with* the Church, Hanson had moved to the pioneer ministry *of* the Church. And this ministry – he meant ordained ministry – now apparently functioned as a remnant *within* the faithful flock. It is entirely contrary to the logic of his thesis. The result was that eventually in his argument the clerical frame re-emerges. Or perhaps it is a tacit recognition of the dialectic between the dynamic, generative activity of the ecclesia and the necessary moments of stasis, consolidation and forming of networks and functions for endurance. The apostolic ministry in all its variety cannot be entirely fluid, passing over from one community to the next without form, boundaries and symbols of endurance. How the pioneer ministry was a part of the wider apostolate of the *laos* remained unclear. Hanson had unconsciously merged the 'ordained ministry' with the ongoing apostolic ministries of the ecclesia. Following the example of the pioneers was excellent

---

89 Hanson, *The Pioneer Ministry*, p. 88.

90 Ibid., p. 109.

91 Ibid., p. 75.

92 Ibid., p. 109, cf. 104.

93 Ibid., p. 105, cf. 155.

94 Ibid., p. 146, my italics.

95 Ibid., p. 155.

96 Ibid., p. 109, my italics.

advice. Exactly what this meant for the relations between the ministries that emerged in this process remained unclear or confused. The possibility of new and richer *charisms* of the apostolic Spirit emerging; and their relation to the traditional orders remained an undeveloped area. In 1961 it was not in his field of vision.

Yet Hanson had highlighted a critical dimension of the relation between church and ministry and to this extent he was a forerunner of more recent developments that have opened up the question of ministries both within as well as between the churches. He was a pioneer but it is not clear how his insights have been taken up. On the one hand he claimed to have rejected a 'catholic gnosticism' on ministry and church.[97] On the other hand it is arguable that his identification of the 'pioneer ministry' with 'the pioneer church' offered clues as to the direction a renewed catholicity in ministry might develop. In this respect he showed that the Moberly tradition, when shorn of its ideological distortions, had fruitful possibilities for the reconciliation of the ministries within a new focus on apostolic mission. How this has unravelled itself in the second half of the twentieth century is the subject of the next chapter.

---

[97] Ibid., p. 147.

Chapter 6
The Question of Reach: Representative Priesthood and the Ministries of the *laos*

The Pioneer Ministry was reissued in 1975, and Hanson opined that there had been little Anglican material directly devoted to the topic of ministry in the intervening 14 years and that his own work had attracted little attention. The next two decades were marked by new ecumenical dialogues throughout the churches informed by a growing interest in a communion ecclesiology with an associated renewal in Trinitarian thinking. This was the period in the wake of Vatican II when conciliar documents on the people of God, ministry and ecumenism had given fresh impetus to open and expectant dialogue among the churches.[1] It was only in the last decade of the twentieth century that the fruits of this ecumenical and ecclesiological reflection brought forth more substantive contributions from Anglicans on the nature of ministry. In the intervening period the lines of development are less clear.

The foregoing discussion on the interpretation of the Moberly tradition has highlighted some trends and tensions that can be tracked in the more recent decades. It will be no surprise to find the not unfamiliar problems of the Catholic tradition reappearing in new forms and contexts. There are also signs of promise of a greater emphasis on collaboration between the ministries emerging out of a richer ecclesiology of ministry. The present chapter explores some of these developments in terms of the emerging consensus on representative ministry and the remarkable expansion in the ministry of the people of God. It highlights the expanding reach of the ministries of the people of God in the service of mission. The significance of such developments for a theology of collaborative ministry is developed in Part III.

---

[1] The key document is *Lumen Gentium*, Decree on Ecumenism and Decree on Ministry and Life of Priests, in Austin O'Flannery (gen. ed.), *Vatican Council 2: The Conciliar and Post Conciliar Documents* (New York: Costello Publishing Company, 1981).

Representative Ministry: Consensus and Confusion

Ecumenical Dialogue

Perhaps the most important, though not the most obvious feature of contemporary discussion on ministry, has been in the area of the nature of representative ministry. Moberly's 'ministerial priesthood' has strong and powerful echoes in the ministry statement of *Baptism, Eucharist and Ministry*. While the heavy emphasis on ordained ministry has been lamented by many critics it remains true that the reality of the priesthood of the whole Church (Moberly's 'collective priesthood') and the priesthood of the ordained (Moberly's 'ministerial priesthood', a far more satisfactory term theologically) has received strong endorsement ecumenically. The priesthood of the Church, like the priesthood of those ordained, is derived from Christ. *Baptism, Eucharist and Ministry* is not particularly clear as to the nature of the interrelationship between the two priesthoods though the general priesthood is recognised as generative of a variety of ministries following the royal, prophetic and priestly ministry of Christ.

Recognition of the significance of the priesthood of Christ as the source and energy for ministry has also been an important element in the Anglican–Roman Catholic dialogue (Anglican–Roman Catholic International Commission: ARCIC) from 1973.[2] However in this dialogue, as observed in Chapter 2, a tension re-emerges. A 'common Christian priesthood' ('the priesthood of the people') entered through baptism is identified.[3] 'Christian ministers' share in this 'common priesthood' and are 'representative of the whole Church' particularly in presiding at the Eucharist. 'Nevertheless their ministry is not an extension of the common Christian priesthood but belongs to another realm of the gifts of the Spirit'.[4] Subsequent clarifications by ARCIC only serve to confirm the problem. The priesthood of 'the people of God' and 'the ordained ministry' 'are two distinct realities which relate, each in its own way, to the high priesthood of Christ … which is their source and model'.[5] This somewhat gnostic differentiation between 'different realms of the Spirit' and reference to 'distinct realities' represents a regression from Moberly's depiction of ministerial priesthood as 'the concentrated meaning' of the collective priesthood. In the *Final Report*, both priesthoods come from Christ, the 'great high priest', but their inner relation remains obscure. The resultant 'unsynthesised antinomy' points to a continuing unresolved tension in the tradition.[6] The double procession theory of priesthood suggests an ecclesiology in

2 Anglican–Roman Catholic International Commission, *Final Report*.

3 Ibid., par. 13, p. 36.

4 Ibid.

5 Ibid., par. 2, p. 41.

6 See Brent, *Cultural Episcopacy*, p. 61. See Chapter 2 for further discussion.

which ministry and church are somewhat separate. It is at odds with the avowed commitment to an ecclesiology of *koinonia*.[7]

Anglican bilateral and multilateral dialogues over the past two decades reveal significant preoccupation with questions concerning the commensurability of Anglican orders with other Protestant communions. Within an ecumenical setting where the intention is to address sticking points to further unity such a focus is entirely understandable and Meissen and Porvoo Common Statements indicate some remarkable advances. A number of features of such dialogues are relevant for our present purposes. First, it is almost axiomatic that the doctrine of the Church is developed as the foundation for reflection on ministry. Here the concepts of *koinonia*, baptism and mission recur. Thus the Anglican–Lutheran Helsinki dialogue states that the churches 'have rediscovered the communal character of the Church at a time of loneliness and estrangement. The Church lives in *koinonia* and is a community in which all members, lay or ordained, contribute their gifts to the life of the whole.'[8] From a slightly different perspective the Anglican–Reformed dialogue states the matter: 'The church is sent by God to witness in the world to his unlimited grace. Only in this double perspective of mission and of new life in Christ as experienced as the free gift of grace can ministry in the church and ministry of the church be adequately understood.'[9] The missionary and eschatological context is the new reality within which and from which the question of the church's ministries are considered. Hanson's critique in *The Pioneer Ministry* of the separation of church and ministry and its divorce from the imperative of mission is here being intentionally redressed. A consensus, echoing Michael Ramsey's thesis many decades before, seems to have been reached that church, gospel and ministry are necessarily related to each other. The *Porvoo Common Statement* draws particular attention to this.[10]

Second, associated with this is recognition that the gifts of the Spirit are bestowed on the body of Christ through individuals for the sake of the whole Church. Representative ministries of word and sacrament belong within this wider domain of the *charism*s of the Spirit. Third, this ecclesial context for representative ministries has been associated with a renewed understanding of the apostolicity of the whole Church.[11] Whatever is thus said of ordained ministries is only said in relation to the ministry of the whole people of God as they together serve the *missio Dei*.[12]

---

7 Anglican–Roman Catholic International Commission, *Final Report*, par. 3, p. 30.

8 *Anglican–Lutheran Dialogue*. Report of the Anglican–Lutheran European Regional Commission, Helsinki (London: SPCK, 1982), par. 48, p. 21.

9 *God's Reign and Our Unity*. Anglican–Reformed Dialogue (London: SPCK,1984), par. 73.

10 *The Porvoo Common Statement*, par. 11, p. 11.

11 Ibid., pars. 36–40, pp. 22–4.

12 For an excellent Anglican contribution see, *Apostolicity and Succession*. House of Bishops Occasional paper (London: Church House, 1994).

These features of contemporary ecumenical dialogue constitute powerful trends in the way in which ministry is treated in Anglicanism and across the ecclesial spectrum. Tensions remain for Anglicans because the methodological starting point – that is, the Church and its ministries – unravels itself into scenarios that are challenging for traditional positions on Church order. For example, questions and tensions remain *among Anglicans* over the extent to which Protestant Churches signatory to the Meissen Common Statement have a *fully* representative episcope and how that matter might be overcome.[13] Ecumenism, as so often happens, is the field upon which unresolved internal Anglican conflicts are manifest. The form and prerequisites for a representative ministry remain contested. Certainly the relations between such a ministry and the wider ministries is not a matter that has been seriously addressed in the ecumenical dialogues. Evidently such an inquiry is not perceived as having anything to contribute to discussion about the nature of representative ministry.

Church Reports on Ordination and Priesthood

The theme of representative priesthood has been the subject of a number of reports in the Church of England. A report of the mid 1970s on *The Theology of Ordination* referred to 'a distinctive ministry' within the general ministries.[14] The priesthood of this distinctive ministry was 'not to be equated' with the 'unique priesthood of Christ' nor the 'corporate priesthood of the whole Church' even though 'the ministers of word and sacrament are not excluded from the corporate priesthood'.[15] It is a remarkable statement though the tradition we have been examining may have been partly responsible for the need to deny any such exclusion. The report noted that even though the corporate priesthood derived from Christ, 'this is not to be confused with the distinctive charismata associated with the ministry which, as was seen above, are bestowed upon individuals'.[16] For the most part this report offers a somewhat traditional approach. Thus within the apostolic succession of Christ's Church there is an apostolic ministry 'to *guarantee* the transcendence of the apostolic message, and to ensure the fulfilment of the Church's mission'.[17]

---

13 See *The Report of the Meissen Commission, 1991–1996*. General Synod, GS Misc 490 (London: Church House, 1996). This report indicates that under Canon B12 'episcopally ordained' would have meant, 'in the context of its time', 'ordained by a bishop in the historic succession'. Thus Protestant ministers of the Evangelical Church in Germany would have to be re-ordained in order to officiate as priests or deacons in the Church of England (see pp. 75–6). Whether, 'in the context of its time' would have to necessarily bind the present Church of England is *the* contested matter within Anglicanism.

14 *The Theology of Ordination*. Report by the Faith and Order Advisory Group of the Board for Mission and Unity, GS 281, ND, p. 5.

15 Ibid., p. 8.

16 Ibid., p. 7.

17 Ibid., p. 9, my italics.

The distinctive ministries 'coexist alongside'[18] – in an unexplained relation – the charismatic community where gifts are given liberally.[19] Such general ministries are 'the context for ministry'. When the report considered 'Other Forms of Ministry', it recognised the impact of the Charismatic and Renewal movements producing a multiplicity of ministries 'not unlike that which we see in the New Testament'.[20] In relation to the many ministries the ordained ministry 'acts as an articulating focus for the total life of the priestly body of the Church'.[21] A representative ministry emerges to which the people of God evidently do not contribute and moreover pose some difficulties in relation to the rationale for ordination and eucharistic presidency.

Some different emphases are evident in *The Priesthood of the Ordained Ministry*, a 1986 report for the General Synod.[22] This report offers a much fuller and integrated account of the nature of ministerial priesthood. Anxiety about the identity and function of the representative priesthood drives the exposition. The emergence of a 'distinctive ministry' has its roots in Hanson's notion of the apostles as 'the nucleus of the new messianic community'.[23] The main emphasis in the report is on the development of the 'distinctive priesthood' in history. Although there is little that is new in this report nevertheless its text is revealing. In commenting upon the ARCIC reference to the priesthood of the ordained belonging to a different realm of the gifts of the Spirit compared to the corporate priesthood the report notes that this indicates that the former 'is not simply a delegation "from below"'. It is the Moberly tradition, though in fact its immediate point of reference is the Lutheran–Roman Catholic Dialogue reference to delegation 'from below'. The background to this is Vatican II's *Dogmatic Constitution of the Church*, wherein it is stated that 'the church's ministry cannot be derived from the congregation, but it is also not an enhancement of the common priesthood, and the minister as such is not a Christian to a greater degree'.[24]

The implication of this particular discussion is that the priesthood of the people is 'from below' though it too is derived from Christ. The tension is explicit but apparently unacknowledged. The *different* realm of the gifts of the Spirit is clearly not a realm 'from below'. It must be 'from above' where Christ is. The Christological bifurcation implicit in the Moberly tradition is here exposed. The common priesthood from below and the representative priesthood from above correspond to the double reality of the humanity and divinity of Christ. The analogy is compelling. The argument – as already observed in Chapter 2 –

---

18 Ibid., p. 16.

19 Ibid., pp. 4–5.

20 Ibid., p. 16.

21 Ibid., p. 17.

22 *The Priesthood of the Ordained Ministry*. Report of the Board for Mission and Unity of the General Synod of the Church of England (London: Church House, 1986).

23 Ibid., p. 18. Hanson was on the committee.

24 Cited in ibid., p. 83.

has been developed with some sophistication by the Jesuit theologian, Philip Rosato. He refers to the ordained representing Christ's 'transcendent headship of, and the baptised his immanent presence to the Church, and through it, his headship of and presence to humanity'.[25] Whilst these two separate modalities of Christian priesthood are said to be 'orientated to each other' nevertheless, in Rosato's account, they seem to move in two different directions – that is, from above (ordained; 'transcendent headship') and below (baptised; 'immanent presence'). These categories, whilst not synonymous with the divinity and humanity of Christ, perform the same function in the scheme of mediation of divine grace. It is hard to resist the conclusion that the two-natures problem in Christology has been transferred into the two priesthoods of the Church, the ordained and baptised. Given the long and contested history of attempts to develop an adequate account of the two-nature doctrine, it is no surprise that a doctrine of ministry indebted to this Christology will produce such unsynthesised antinomies. The problem of the relations between the body of Christ and its representative ministry; between the ministry and the ministries, cannot be unravelled on the basis of a defective or incoherent two-nature doctrine of Christ. *The Priesthood of the Ordained Ministry* bears testimony to the fact that when an almost exclusive Christological focus drives the doctrine of ministry there will be continual conflict between the different realms from which ministry is derived Christologically. The logical response will be strong closure and sharp boundaries for the ordained ministry. Representative priesthood cannot then be properly representative and certainly the priesthood 'from below' cannot add anything to the priesthood from above.

In this report the representative ministry has become a 'special ministry' that 'is not simply derived from the priestliness of the whole community'.[26] We are on familiar territory here but it is remarkably uninformative. What if such a 'special ministry' was not 'simply derived' but complexly derived, perhaps through some idea of 'mediation through' as Hanson earlier suggested. The report states that the special ministry is 'not a magnified form of the common priesthood'.[27] Presumably this is intended to rule out notions of 'concentration' and 'extension' though they are all very different. Concentration is quite different from magnification.

The doctrine of representative ministry receives its most mature and dynamic articulation in the 1987 *Education for the Church's Ministry*, ACCM paper. The theology of ministry articulated in this report has provided the basis for ongoing critical reflection on the nature of the ministries and their inner relations. Robin Greenwood's relational theology of ministry is clearly in debt to it. The report is an example, albeit in report form, of how a doctrine of ministry might be developed beyond the exclusively Christological paradigm. To be more accurate the report endeavours to think through a Trinitarian approach to the ministries of the Church. The emphasis is on a dynamic understanding of the relationship

---

25 Rosato, 'Priesthood of the Baptised', p. 260.

26 *The Priesthood of the Ordained Ministry*, p. 99.

27 Ibid.

between church and ministry whereby the latter 'is the ministry of Christ in the Church and expectations for this ministry should arise from the task and nature of the Church'.[28] The Church's task is to serve the *missio Dei* in the world. This is the horizon for the ministry of the whole people of God and 'within that' an ordained ministry. Both ministries, corporate and ordained, 'are bound to each other' and the ordained minister 'recognises the activity of God in and for this corporate ministry, represents it to the members of the Church, focuses and collects it in a co-ordinated pattern and distributes it in service of God's work in the world'.[29] The report goes on to speak of the 'interanimative quality' that exists between the ordained ministry and the 'community of the Church'. I will develop this further in relation to the wider ministries of the Church.

Theologians on Ministry

The issue of representative ministry was addressed in 1979 by Richard Hanson in *Christian Priesthood Examined.* Hanson was critical of the cultic and sacerdotal influence on Christian understandings of priesthood and called for such notions to be 'discarded altogether or drastically modified'.[30] It was an issue to which Moberly, in argument with Lightfoot, had given considerable attention. A sacrificial dimension to ministerial priesthood was justified on the basis of a reformed Catholic understanding of the ascended Christ's eternal offering. It was a finely nuanced argument that still remains theologically serviceable. When Hanson turned to the topic of 'true priesthood' he discarded the older doctrine of apostolic succession and argued that the priesthood of the 'official ministry' was 'inevitably in a certain measure a channelling and concentration of this priesthood [of all Christians], which was the church's priesthood and an expression and realization of Christ's priesthood'.[31] Thus Hanson proposed the idea of a representative priesthood, which 'rests upon the priesthood of all baptised Christians', a 'concentration of the priesthood of Christ's people'.[32]

A decade later the two Hanson brothers brought the embryonic dimension of the Moberly tradition to its term in proposing that 'the priest only posses his [*sic*] priesthood because the church posses a priesthood, the derived priesthood of Christ. Christ our great high priest exercises his priesthood through the church, and the church in virtue of this corporate priesthood authorizes certain people to act on its behalf'.[33] The position is not uncontroversial but it is the logic of an integral relationship between church and ministry. It is invoked by Robin

[28] Ibid. p. 27.

[29] Ibid., pp. 28–9.

[30] Richard Hanson, *Christian Priesthood Examined* (London: Lutterworth Press, 1979), p. 99.

[31] Ibid., p. 100.

[32] Ibid., pp. 102–3.

[33] Hanson and Hanson, *The Identity of the Church*, p. 153.

Greenwood in *Transforming Priesthood*.[34] Resistance arises because the scheme retains a linear feel: Christ, Church, ministry. Perhaps this is where the language of 'extension' fails in a way that 'concentration' might not. Certainly the Anglo-Catholic Moberly invoked the latter word.

Anthony Hanson's non-lineal identification of the 'pioneer ministry' with 'the Church' provides the basis for a notion of concentration of the priesthood of the ordained. However, as we saw in Chapter 2, contemporary Anglicans of a more Catholic persuasion, as progressive as they are in many areas, resist the language of concentration.[35] This is, in part, quite understandable given their tenacious hold to a two-track theory of priesthood. On this basis the language of 'extension' and even 'concentration' undermines the distinctions they believe necessary to sustain a Catholic doctrine of priesthood and ministry. Anthony Hanson's 'solution' may require further exploration but it seems to me he has at least offered the Moberly Catholic tradition a way forward. Minimally it will involve a reappraisal of the underlying Christology of their doctrine of ministry in relation to an accompanying Pneumatology.

Recent reflections on ministry and priesthood by Anglican theologians show the influence of ecumenical dialogue, church reflections and wider developments in ecclesiology. The contributions of Robin Greenwood (*Transforming Priesthood*) and William Countryman (*Living on the Border of the Holy*) will be considered in more detail in the following chapter. However, both these theologians offer creative attempts to renew and transform understandings of ministry and orders within the framework of a relational ecclesiology embedded in creation (Countryman) and the *koinonia* of the apostolic Church (Greenwood). Countryman, writing out of the liberal Catholic tradition of Anglicanism, develops an account of a 'fundamental priesthood' rooted in creation and the human being in the image of Christ. His notion of a 'sacramental priesthood' offering an iconic representation of the 'fundamental priesthood' is a creative development of Moberly's ministerial priesthood. It is an important and suggestive work which points a way forward for a renewed theology of orders within the catholic tradition. Whether Countryman's approach overcomes the divide between the two priesthoods is a matter that will be taken up in the next chapter.

Robin Greenwood, from a broad-Church tradition, has developed a relational theology of mission and ministry. He draws heavily upon recent Trinitarian theology and its offspring *koinonia* ecclesiology. These conceptual coordinates provide the framework for a fresh understanding of the ministry of the whole body of Christ and the place and significance of those in orders within this community. The Church as a complex and dynamic network of persons in relation to each other, God and the world seems to underlie Greenwood's ecclesiology. In this scheme 'there are no positions of permanent subordination', and none are ever

---

34 Greenwood, *Transforming Priesthood*, pp. 152–4.

35 Carnley, *Reflections*, p. 175.

'to be interpreted as being set apart from the community'.[36] Whether he has given a sufficiently full and integrated account of the nature of relationality as it unravels itself in the life and mission of the Church is a matter that will also be addressed in the following chapter. The appeal to relational language is tricky and may unintentionally embed unresolved problems in a more contemporary discourse.

Both theologians point to the continuing relevance and importance of the tradition of ministerial priesthood. No doubt they would be highly critical of Moberly's approach. Yet Greenwood's development of the relation between ordained and the corporate priesthood appears to be significantly in debt to Moberly's theory of representation, especially in his appeal to ordained priesthood as concentration of the priesthood of the Church.

Ecclesiology for Ministry: Koinonia *and Baptism*

The general theological background to the discussion of representative priesthood has been dominated over recent decades by the theme of *koinonia*.[37] Communion ecclesiology has been a driver of the ecumenical scene for a number of years and it has drawn heavily from developments in Trinitarian theology as exemplified in the writings of scholars from across the ecclesial spectrum.[38] When the accent is on the communitarian nature of the ecclesia energised and directed in a Trinitarian manner conditions are established for a more open and explorative inquiry into the nature of Christian ministry. Communion ecclesiology requires a ministry that nourishes community and mission. The ministries of the whole people of God can be rethought within such a frame. A representative ministry will necessarily be crafted in relation to an ecclesiology of *communio*. However, the appeal to *koinonia* is not unproblematic and it can just as easily provide a new housing in which many unresolved tensions in ministry and church continue. Differences over the language of priesthood and the appeal to an incarnational Christology as the foundation for ministry may continue to operate in an unsynthesised way alongside a Trinitarian ecclesiology of *koinonia*.

More specifically the immediate background to discussion of priesthood and ministry has been the consensus reached in the ecumenical world on the nature and purpose of baptism. *Baptism, Eucharist and Ministry* set the benchmark for

---

36 Greenwood, *Transforming Priesthood*, pp. 166–7.

37 See, for example, the World Council of Churches Canberra Statement, 'The Church as Koinonia: Gift and Calling', in Michael Kinnamon (ed.), *Signs of the Spirit: Official Report of the Seventh Assembly of the World Council of Churches* (Geneva: WCC; Grand Rapids: Eerdmans, 1991), pp. 172–4 and The Fifth World Conference on Faith and Order, 'On the Way to Fuller Koinonia', in *On the Way to Fuller Koinonia: Official Report of the Fifth World Conference on Faith and Order*, ed. Thomas Best and Gunther Gassmann; Faith and Order Paper no. 166 (Geneva: WCC, 1994), pp. 223–7.

38 For example, John Zizioulas (Orthodox); Colin Gunton (Reformed); Miroslav Volf (Free Church); Jean Tillard (Catholic).

this and the importance of baptism as the sacrament of initiation into the Christian community cannot be over-emphasised. It has become a feature of ecumenical dialogues, particularly between Anglicans and other Protestant churches. Baptism is the foundational sacrament of incorporation into the community of the triune God. Both the Meissen and Porvoo Common Statements proceed from a strong doctrine of the Church as the community of those baptised into the triune God. This leads to recognition of the ecclesial integrity of each others' communion through a renewed appreciation of the theological significance of baptism as the sacrament of fundamental *communio* in Christ and the Spirit.[39] This has provided the basis for the development of an ecclesiology of ministry in which notions of representative ministry have a natural relatedness to the body of Christ. Questions of validity of orders are framed first within the ministry of all the baptised and more deeply undergirded by what might be termed a baptismal ecclesiology. This ecumenical sacrament of communion can provide a foundation for honour and dignity being accorded the ministries of the different churches. The significance of this was highlighted in a discussion paper for the 1993 World Council of Churches Conference on Faith and Order wherein it was stated: 'There is an important ecumenical convergence concerning the fact that ecclesial ministry should be approached in terms of our shared baptism which enables the whole people of God to share in Christ's ministry'.[40] Anglican theologians have recognised the importance of a baptismal ecclesiology as a basis for ecumenical understandings of church and ministry.[41] Such an approach also has the potential to inform conversations within particular churches like Anglicanism as to the relations between its many ministries, the way authority is shared and decisions made, and appropriate structures for accountability. However, exactly how an emphasis on baptismal ecclesiology alters the emphasis on an ecclesiology of *communio* is a work still in progress.

A baptismal ecclesiology embeds the representative ministry within Christ's community. But it does not immediately clarify how to give an account of such a representative ministry nor the nature of the relations between the ministries. Indeed, conflict in Anglicanism over the question of Eucharistic presidency indicates how contentious is the issue of representative ministry in relation to the people of God.[42] Hence, in spite of the remarkable ecumenical progress over the past few decades on ordained ministry issues to do with the nature and identity of

---

39 *The Porvoo Common Statement*, par. 17, p. 11, par. 32 g, p. 19; *On the Way to Visible Unity*.

40 *Towards Koinonia in Faith, Life and Witness*. Discussion paper, Fifth World Conference on Faith and Order, Santiago de Compostela. Faith and Order Paper no. 161 (Geneva: WCC, 1993), par. 70, p. 31.

41 For example, Avis, *Anglicanism and the Christian Church*, appeals to a 'baptismal paradigm' as a foundation for understanding the Church, pp. 300–311.

42 *Eucharistic Presidency*. A Theological Statement by the House of Bishops of the General Synod, GS 1248 (London: Church House, 1997).

ordained ministers and their relations with the wider body of Christ, both within and between churches, remains firmly on the theological agenda. The Moberly tradition of representative priesthood has a great deal to offer this theological conversation. A critical issue it will have to address concerns the reciprocity envisaged between the representative ministry and wider ministries. The weak point so far has been the inability of the tradition to give anywhere near an adequate, let alone compelling, account of how the *laos* adds dignity, lustre and power to the ministries which represent it. This is even more problematic in a period of the Church which has witnessed a veritable abundance of ministries exercised by the people of God. The relationship between the ministry and the many ministries has to take stock of the priesthood of the whole Church. This leads to the second main trend in the contemporary discussion of ministry.

The Priesthood of the People: An Abundance of Ministries

An Invisible Priesthood?

Whether it is between churches or within churches there is an increasing pressure to give an account of those ministries that fall outside the traditional threefold pattern of ordained ministry. In 1897 Moberly wrote a chapter in *Ministerial Priesthood* on 'The Relation between Ministry and Laity'. It probably fairly described the current state of the issue. In Moberly's categories ministry was co-terminus with the ministry of bishops, priests and perhaps deacons: basically those in Holy Orders. Besides this there existed the laity. If he had been pressed on the calling of the laity he would no doubt have referred to their life of worship, witness and service in the world. In an important sense for Moberly there was nothing particularly different between clergy and laity. He was insistent that both shared the same powers, privileges and responsibilities relevant to being Christian. Indeed this was the great strength of his theology of representative priesthood. It was genuinely a representative doctrine of ministry notwithstanding some of its theological baggage. The danger was that those acting in a representative capacity simply assimilated every aspect of ministerial life to themselves. However, in principle at least the laity, by virtue of their share in the priesthood of Christ as people of the Church, were called to share the life of Christ in the world. Insofar as Moberly's sights were trained on articulating a theology of ministerial priesthood he did not consider the kind of questions that have arisen later about the wider ecclesial ministries. It is quite remarkable that he actually wrote a chapter on the relations between ministry and laity. If he finally saw them set over against one another he was probably not that out of step with his day. But he had provided a theory for a much richer account of their relations. Yet his theory also incorporated into it features concerning authorization of ministry that effectively undermined a truly representative ministry. The laity added nothing to the character of the ministry and appeared the passive recipients of the ministrations of the clergy.

Ramsey's focus on church order and the gospel did not seem to offer much joy on the topic of the wider ministries. Again his sight was fixed on other matters. However again, like Moberly, Ramsey laid some foundations for the contemporary discussion of the ministries that we do well to consider. Principally his organic conception of 'order as an utterance of the gospel' assumed the status of an analytic judgement. Order was a necessary implicate of the gospel. If that could be sustained then much more was theoretically at stake than simply the claim that episcopacy was of the *esse* of the Church. That the Church orders its life in response to the gospel is hardly an add-on or secondary matter. Ramsey's argument was in relation to Catholic order, the threefold pattern of the tradition. But in a new context, when ordering of the ministries in relation to the death and resurrection of Jesus Christ now has to take stock of the multiplicity of the *charism*s for ministry manifest in the Church, Ramsey's analytical judgment justifies a radical reappraisal of the ministries and their relations. The notion of 'Catholic order' can no longer be contained within a clearly defined and differentiated set. A new opening has occurred, the boundaries are more osmotic than previously imagined, and new realignments amongst the Spirit's *charism*s are taking place. Order is not being jettisoned, simply being re-ordered. The present chaos of ministries is the creative edge of new order. If ministerial order in this wider, more dynamic sense is an analytic of the gospel; a necessary implicate of what it means to be sharers in the priesthood of Christ then all ministries of the Spirit are to be welcomed and honoured. All such ministries belong to each other and enhance the other. New differentiations and orderings will necessarily arise precisely because the Spirit's *charism*s are not vague and undifferentiated but because they are the very opposite. Ramsey's argument for episcopacy may deliver far more than he imagined for the present time. The critical issue is how a renewed catholic ordering might be justified within this wider horizon.

The same might well be said for Anthony Hanson, though from a different perspective. The pioneer ministry was the Church in 'miniature', *in nucleo*. The key for Hanson was that the pioneer ministry did not and could not do anything other than what the whole Church was called to be and do. The apostolate was co-terminus with the ecclesia. The pioneer ministry was the Church: the pioneer Church was the ministry. Church and ministry were one and the same. This reading of the Pauline doctrine of ministry was a natural consequence of a missionary Church. It pointed to an ongoing generative mission in which the apostolic ministry of reconciliation was self-perpetuating. This was Hanson's base and it clearly has major implications for the abundance of ministries of the Church today. Such ministries belong to the apostolic dynamic of the gospel. Differentiations of ministries, following the Pauline missionary pattern, are a necessary part of the total ministry. Fluidity, dynamism and emphasis upon function rather than office were the leading ideas of Hanson's conception of the pioneer ministry. Such things are highly relevant to our present contexts, particularly in those parts of the Church where there is a vision for the renewed apostolic mission of the gospel. The pioneer ministry generates an abundance of ministries.

However, as Hanson observed, in the course of time the eschatological vision undergirding the Church's apostolic task faded and a more settled institutional form of ecclesia emerged. The pioneer ministry disappeared. It is for this reason that Hanson imports into his scheme the idea of a 'pioneer ministry' *within* the ecclesia as a more or less enduring element of its life. The purpose is that such a ministry will constantly recall the Church to its true apostolic mission. A representative ministry necessarily appears but its purpose is to enable the whole Church to fulfil its calling to be apostolic. But what of the relations between the 'pioneer ministry', or the ordained, as it became for Hanson and the wider apostolate? As we have see he was not clear on this. He wrote out of and for a missionary-orientated church. The trajectory of this approach is clear but how it would operate in more static ecclesial environments is problematic. Indeed, Hanson acknowledged that the pioneer ministry was difficult to undertake in such contexts.

The three theologians I have been looking at, in different ways attempted to develop a theology of ministry related to the Church and the gospel. Whilst the question of the rationale of the representative ministry preoccupied their minds, the implications of their work has proven fruitful for consideration of understanding wider ecclesial ministries and clues are given about the relations between the ministries. This is an important conclusion for the Anglican Church that has a poor track record of reflection upon the role and significance of the 'laity'. Moberly's 'collective priesthood' has, for the most part, seemed invisible.

Certainly there is little evidence of sustained theological attention on the question of the laity. In 1963 John Robinson turned his attention to the subject. He did so having first differentiated the representative nature of the ordained ministry from a conception very different – that is, a 'vicarious ministry'. Where the latter conception dominated 'every concession made to the laity will inevitably be and appear to be at the expense of the clergy'.[43] A representative ministry focused on being a 'servant of the servants of God' generated 'a tremendous increase and release' of ministry. When this occurred then one ministry 'expands automatically with the expansion of the other'.[44] Robinson was on the borderlands of a genuine collaborative approach to ministry. He was ahead of his time in the Church of England.

Robinson referred to the recovery of the 'priesthood of the laity' though he was just as insistent on promoting the 'laity of the priesthood' whereby 'the whole church, ordained and unordained alike, is called to be a lay body'.[45] He meant by this that the Church 'is essentially and always a body which is immersed in the world'. Robinson was influenced by the Roman Catholic, Yves Congar's

---

43 John Robinson et al. (eds.), *Layman's Church* (London: Lutterworth Press, 1963), p. 16.

44 Ibid., p. 17.

45 Ibid., p. 18.

Theology of the Laity and the appeal for a 'genuine laicity'.[46] He also appealed to Bonhoeffer's call for 'authentic Christian worldliness'.[47] For Robinson it was a question of right orientation in regard to the calling of the whole Church, beyond self and for the world. He recognised two kinds of laity: Church-centred and world-centred. The latter needed most help and the notion of 'the genuine laity of the priesthood' provided a theological base for renewal of action of behalf of the kingdom in the world. As usual with Robinson his brief reflections were insightful, prescient and discomforting. The ministry of God for the coming kingdom was an inclusive ministry; both Christians and non-Christians might be found working for the kingdom through the structures of the world. The *laos* was at root an eschatological idea and so was the ministry to which God called the Church.

In 1985 a little over two decades after Robinson's essay, a working party of the General Synod Board of Education produced the first Church of England report for 80 years on the laity entitled, *All Are Called: Towards a Theology of the Laity*. In the course of the Common Statement the report noted:

> There remains an unresolved theological division in the Church of England, which seriously affects our understanding of the Church and the position of the laity in it. This concerns the differentiation between the priesthood of all believers, into which all Christians enter through baptism, and the sacramental priesthood which is the special calling of some particular members of the Church.[48]

The statement noted that whilst some Anglicans believed that priests were 'sacramentally distinct' from other members of the Church other Anglicans believed that those ordained differed from laity in function only, that is, to equip the members of the Church for its ministry in the world. The report further pointed to the tension between those who believed that priests depend for their call and authority 'solely from God' and others who maintained that such authority came not only from God 'but derives also from the members of the Church'. Others took an intermediate position; the authority for the 'special priesthood' 'rests partly on a call from God' but also upon a 'clear recognition' of this call by the Church who acknowledged the representative authority in particular people from among the body. The report was not designed to settle this 'long-standing controversy' but it recognised the serious problems such differences had created for the Church and the abuse of power. Each of the above positions had given rise to a belief that laity were 'second-class citizens'. One essayist considered that this problem had

---

46 Yves Congar, *Lay People in the Church: A Study for a Theology of Laity* (Westminster: Newman, 1957).

47 Robinson et al. (eds.), *Layman's Church*.

48 *All Are Called: Towards a Theology of the Laity*. General Synod, Board of Education (London: Church House, 1985), p. 5.

been perpetuated by the tendency in the ARCIC statement on ministry to set apart clergy from laity and link the former to Christ in a unique way.[49]

The report was critical of a 'persistent clericalism' – 'undue influence of clergy' – that involved both clergy and laity. It noted the heavy emphasis in ecumenical discussions on the ordained ministry; one result of which was that this ministry became 'a kind of fly-paper that attracted all sorts of questions about the fate of Christianity in the modern world'.[50] Within an increasing secular society Christian lay identity had become overly focused on the 'domestic activities of the institutional Church'. The report adopted a similar approach to John Robinson 20 years earlier in pointing the laity to the world beyond the visible institutional Church. This was also in line with recent ecumenical statements such as *Baptism, Eucharist and Ministry*. The Bishop Chair of the report recalled that all bishops and clergy 'have been laymen at one time'.[51] It was an unfortunate comment reflecting a primitive conception of 'laity' and only served to highlight how deeply ingrained and unconscious the problem of the separation between clergy and laity was. The need for reconciliation on this internal issue of the Church remains on the agenda. When the vocations and ministries of the people of God are sublimated by incompetence or out of anxiety to preserve clerical identity the result is an invisible priesthood and a ground swell of frustration. The Spirit's work ought never to be so grieved.

A Priesthood of the Ministering Spirit

Both on the ecumenical scene and for the Anglican Church one of the decisive features of the recent period in ministry is the growth of the ministries of the whole church. Today it is not so much a question of the ministry in relation to the laity but rather in relation to the wider ministries. The significance of this was noted in *Baptism, Eucharist and Ministry*, where the new accent on the work of the Holy Spirit as the liberating and renewing power of the Church was clearly recognised.[52] In this context it was noted that: 'The Holy Spirit bestows on the community diverse and complimentary gifts.'[53] These gifts were given 'for the common good' and were manifested in 'acts of service' both within the community and 'to the world'. Drawing on the New Testament, the variety of gifts included 'communicating the Gospel in word and deed, gifts of healing, gifts of praying, gifts of teaching and learning, gifts of serving, gifts of guiding and following, gifts of inspiration and vision'.[54] The ministries of the Spirit were for the whole people of God and individuals had a responsibility with the assistance of the community

---

49 Ibid., p. 14.

50 Ibid., p. 13.

51 Ibid., p. 35.

52 *Baptism, Eucharist and Ministry*, 'Ministry', par. 2, p. 20.

53 Ibid., par. 5, p. 20.

54 Ibid.

to 'discover' their gifts and 'to use them for the building up of the Church and for the service of the world to which the Church is sent'.[55] It was an important paragraph significantly placed before the lengthier discussion on the ordained ministry. Such gifts were the *charisms* of the Spirit. Their focus and purpose was not confined to the region of personal piety (as Moberly had suggested) but was directed outward for the strength and well-being of the community and world. They were ecclesial gifts signifying the calling of the whole people of God to be a ministering community of Christ.

Baptism, Eucharist and Ministry had drawn attention to the remarkable changes that had been taking place in the churches through the Pentecostal and charismatic movement in the course of the century. Ecclesial life now breathed a pneumatological air and this was reflected in Anglican Dialogues with other churches. Two years after *Baptism, Eucharist and Ministry*, the Anglican–Reformed dialogue surveyed the differences and challenges for the two communions noting that the scene was now 'further complicated by the rise of the "charismatic" movement within both our communions'.[56] This complication had been around since the late 1960s in the Anglican Church in the West and much more a feature of general church life in wider parts of the Anglican communion for a great deal longer. The dialogue referred to the new emphasis 'on recognizable tokens of the Spirit's presence as the proper mark of full membership' and attempted an even-handed, if cautious approach. Thus whilst 'we must welcome and cherish all the signs in our time of a new quickening by the Spirit in the lives of our members' it was also necessary to maintain the eschatological perspective which understood all such manifestations of the Spirit as pointing the Church towards 'a goal that lies beyond our sight'.[57]

A discussion paper for the Fifth World Conference on Faith and Order at Santiago de Compostela in 1993 prepared under the direction of the Anglican theologian, Mary Tanner, picked up the theme of *Baptism, Eucharist and Ministry*. 'All have received the gifts of the Holy Spirit and, therefore, all are ministers. It is in this context that both the ordained ministry and the ministry of the laity must be envisaged'.[58] Exactly how to envisage the ordained in relation to the wider ministries was not clear though the context was inescapable.

The *Porvoo Common Statement* represents a new level of integration in Anglican ecumenical conversations on the related themes of *koinonia* and the work of the Spirit. Drawing upon the work of *Baptism, Eucharist and Ministry*, Porvoo referred to the Holy Spirit as bestowing on the community 'diverse and complementary gifts'.[59] The constituting power of the Church was the triune God 'through God's saving action in word and sacraments'. Baptism 'confers the gracious gift of the Spirit'. As such all members were called to participate

55 Ibid.

56 *God's Reign*, par. 58.

57 Ibid.

58 *Towards Koinonia in Faith*, par. 70, p. 31.

59 *Porvoo Common Statement*, par. 18, p. 11.

in the 'apostolic mission' and for this purpose all the baptised received 'various gifts and ministries by the Holy Spirit'.[60] This was the corporate priesthood of the whole people of God and it was a priesthood related to ministry and service. This corporate priesthood was essentially an apostolic community participating in the mission of the triune God and within this there was an 'apostolic succession of the ministry'. However here the *Porvoo Common Statement* takes a new twist directly related to the recognition of the gifts and ministries of the Spirit of the corporate priesthood. Now the accent on the ordained ministry is the 'co-ordination' of the diversity of God's gifts: 'this diversity and multiplicity of tasks involved it [the Church's unity] in calls for a ministry of co-ordination'.[61]

Anglican reflection upon ministry through ecumenical dialogue bears witness to the significant developments that have been taking place in the area of the gifts and ministries of the whole people of God. However such reflection has been undertaken in the service of the question of the recognition of ministries between the churches. The focus has been the issue of the commensurability of ordained ministry among the churches. To that end the dialogues have lacked any extended reflection on the nature of the wider ministries per se. And there remains a certain fuzziness on the relationships between *charism*, gift and ministry. It does appear that where ministry is specifically under view it relates to the ordained ministry. The Spirit's *charism*s are for service. The relation between the ministry and the ministries in terms of gifts is not explored, nor is it anywhere addressed exactly how the diversity and multiplicity of *charism*s of the corporate priesthood contribute to the well-being, release and expansion of the traditional threefold pattern of ministry.

The sense that all is not exactly clear and that extended focus on the representative ministry may require further consideration of such matters is reflected in the various Meissen consultations. Thus as a result of the Fourth Meissen Theological Conference in 2001 it was agreed to work towards: 'deeper theological agreement in our understanding of the ministry and ministries (for example, the ministry in its relation to the royal priesthood of the baptised, the nature of the diaconate and the issue of the "threefold ministry")'.[62] However the pressure seems to be coming from the European Protestant Evangelical churches.[63] Anglicans have not been unmindful of the issue as evidenced in the 1986 report on the *Priesthood of the Ordained Ministry*. Here it was noted that:

> [The Church was understood] by the first Christians to be ministerial in the sense that it was constituted by a wide but interconnected series of these gifts, given by the Holy Spirit for the building up of the one Body.... Paul asserts that all

---

[60] Ibid, par. 32 (i), p. 20.

[61] Ibid., par. 42, p. 24.

[62] *Making Unity More Visible*, The report of the Meissen Commission, 1997–2001 (London: Church House, 2002), p. 50.

[63] *Report of the Meissen Commission, 1991–1996*, p. 58, wherein this issue and others were raised by the Evangelical churches 'again and again'.

> Christian ministries contribute to one corporate ministry and mission.... The key concept of the earliest New Testament evidence is thus the idea of a ministry of the whole 'priestly' people of God in which particular ministries must find their place as part of a coherent whole.[64]

This approach is sharpened and expanded in the 1987 ACCM paper, *Education for the Church's Ministry*. Here the accent is on a genuine 'corporate ministry' of the whole people of God. The ordained ministry subsists within this larger ministry 'recognizing, coordinating and distributing the ministry of others'.[65] As such the ordained and other ministries are 'interdependent' and 'interanimative' and each 'brings the other to be'.[66] The idea that the ministries 'bring each other to be' is a radical and innovative approach to the ministries of the Church. It points to a profound mutuality in ministry wherein each ministry bestows life and energy on other ministries. Yet the idea does not seem to appear in the modern literature and thinking on priesthood and ministry in the Anglican Church. However, there is more than a hint that in an earlier time something different was at least envisaged as an Anglican ideal. It is contained in the second collect for Good Friday and appears in the 1549 *Book of Common Prayer* and in subsequent English prayer books.[67] The collect is worth quoting in full:

> Almighty and everlasting God, by whose Spirit the whole body of the Church is governed and sanctified; Receive our supplications and prayers, which we offer before thee for all estates of men [sic] in thy holy Church, that every member of the same, in his [sic] vocation and ministry, may truly serve thee; through our Lord and Saviour Jesus Christ, who liveth and reigneth with thee, and in the unity of the same Spirit, ever one God, world without end. Amen.

This collect, freely translated by Cranmer from the earlier Roman rite, presumes that all members of the Church have a vocation and ministry.[68] The reference to 'vocation and ministry' was added in the 1549 *Prayer Book* and points to Lutheran influence. In this collect ministry is clearly an inclusive term. How such ministries might be coordinated and collaborate in the service of the gospel remains an important and urgent issue in a period which has witnessed such an explosion of ministries among the people of God.

---

[64] *Priesthood of the Ordained Ministry*, par. 34, pp. 17–18.

[65] *Education of the Church's Ministry*, par. 30, p. 29.

[66] Ibid., par. 29.

[67] For a comparison of texts from earlier Roman rite through to 1662, see F.E. Brightman, *The English Rite: Being a Synopsis of Sources and Revisions of the Book of Common Prayer*, 2 vols. (London: Rivingtons, 1915), 1:372–3.

[68] For discussion of changes from the Roman rite to 1549, see George Harford and Morley Stevenson (eds.), *The Prayer Book Dictionary* (London: Isaac Pitman and Sons, 1913), p. 214.

It is not surprising that, in the light of the expansion of ministries over the last few decades, the diaconate has remerged as a significant order within the Church. In particular the permanent diaconate has become a growing trend in Anglican ministry throughout the communion.[69] This order straddles both liturgical life and orientation to the world. It functions as a truly representative ministry for the people of God precisely because the priesthood of the people is much more conscious of its own ministerial calling and vocation. The ministries of the people are now properly represented within the threefold pattern of ordained ministry. Thus the renewed diaconate is not a problem for the corporate priesthood but it is a challenge for the other orders in so far as the permanent diaconate is no longer simply a stepping-stone to priesthood. The order has an integrity in its own right and compels the Church to rethink its understanding of interdependent ministries.

The Church of England report on the diaconate noted the ecumenical consensus that all Christians have received a gift or *charism* through baptism and that all are called to minister 'in one way or another'. The report went on to argue that ministry was more than Christian discipleship. 'The latter embraces all we think, say or do' though 'it is not necessarily public, representative or formally accountable'.[70] Ministry 'is a form of service that is representative of Christ and the Church in a way that is publicly acknowledged and publicly accountable, either explicitly or tacitly'.[71] The distinction may be overplayed given what is generally said about the whole Church as a ministering community. Thus, later in the report it is stated that the deacon's task is, 'like that of all of the ordained', 'to promote, release and clarify the nature of the Church' and 'encourage and coordinate the diaconal ministry of the people of God'.[72] In this way the diaconate does not detract from the wider ministries but rather, 'as an ecclesial sign of the *diakonia* of Jesus Christ, can enhance the sense of commissioned service among all the Church's ministers, lay and ordained'.[73]

The above brief reflections point to a renewal of the priesthood of the people through rediscovery of the *charisms* of the ministering Spirit. The emergence of lay ministry has thus become one of if not the central feature of the life of the Church. As Stephen Croft notes:

> Many parts of the Church, including the Church of England, have begun to ordain women; charismatic experience and spirituality has played an increasingly important role in church life; there has been growth in a more creative use of liturgy. Alongside all of this has come a recovery of the theology of the whole

---

69 See *For such a time as this*: *A Renewed Diaconate in the Church of England*. Report to the General Synod of the Church of England of a Working Party of the House of Bishops, GS1407 (London: Church House, 2001).

70 Ibid., p. 27.

71 Ibid.

72 Ibid., p. 36.

73 Ibid., p. 46.

> Church as the people of God and of the ministry of the laity alongside that of the clergy. Baptism and not ordination is seen as the foundation for the ministry of the whole people of God.[74]

What this points to is a new way of being the Church. In this new way the corporate priesthood has emerged out of the shadows and become a visible testimony to the abundance of ministries given by Christ through the Spirit.

Conclusion: Continuing Trends and Tensions in Ministry

The present and the preceding two chapters have traced some of the key developments in ministry over the past century. This has been undertaken through a series of case studies on the Anglican tradition as it has interacted with other churches and engaged in its own critical reflection. I have identified trends and tensions in ministry in the two domains of representative ministry and the ministries of the corporate priesthood. We have tracked these developments through selected ecumenical dialogues, internal reports of the Church, and in the work of a number of theologians who have written substantial pieces written on ministry.

The trends indicate a continuing preoccupation with questions of ordained ministry particularly in relation to the wider ecumenical movement. Recognition of ministries across ecclesial boundaries is the pressing issue. Within that frame we have noticed significant developments on the nature of the Church as an apostolic and missionary Church in which all are called to serve through ministries and gifts of the Spirit of Christ. At the heart of this ecclesiology is the idea of the Church as a communion. Anglicans have linked this to a baptismal ecclesiology and thus provided a foundation for consideration of ordained ministry. This has meant that the representative ministries of the Church have to be rethought in relation to the doctrine of the Church and the wider ministries. However, we have also seen that this rethinking has not progressed very far on the issue of the relations between the ministries. With a notable exception the idea that the wider ministries may contribute to and capacitate the ordained ministries has not really emerged on the Anglican agenda. Debates over lay presidency and anxiety over the role and identity of the ordained point to unresolved issues of the ministry within the body of Christ. The recent period has witnessed fresh attempts to develop an integrated and dynamic understanding of ministry. The keynote here has been the character of a church that is focussed on the mission of God.

At the same time we have also observed the renewal of ministries of the people as the gifts of the Spirit enable all to participate in the apostolic mission of God in the world. The Charismatic movement and general conscientisation of the laity

[74] Stephen Croft, *Ministry in Three Dimensions: Ordination and Leadership in the Local Church* (London: Darton Longman and Todd, 1999), p. 10.

at a time of significant challenge to the Church in the West has been a feature of Anglicanism. The recovery of the reality, power and integrity of the corporate priesthood has been a noticeable trend. This is signalled in the renewal of the diaconate of the Church.

The trends also carry tensions or rather matters requiring further reflection and resolution. I have already noted the issue of the relations between the ministries. This has deeper roots observed in the Moberly tradition identified in an earlier chapter. The issue here was the tendency to give priority to ministry over church or at least separate the two. Lack of integration at this fundamental point affected subsequent reflection on questions to do with validity of orders, place of the clergy, and passivity of the laity. We observed this problem as it wound its way through the Anglican tradition in the modern period. Emphasis was necessarily placed on separation rather than a more collaborative approach to ministry. This only engendered conflict between clergy and laity and an anxiety to shore up respective positions.

I also noted in the Moberly tradition – as developed through Ramsey and Hanson – a shift in emphasis such that the ministry and its ordering was brought more intentionally and theologically within the orbit of the gospel and the Church. This more integrative tradition has always been present, particularly in Moberly, though this organic relation between church and ministry was subject to a distortive theory of apostolic transmission, operating externally to the life of the Church. This element in the tradition has been subject to continual critique and refinement. Apostolicity has been broadened to embrace the whole of the Church. However, the appeal to the 'historic episcopate' continues to exert a significant influence in the Anglican Church. The interpretation of this phrase is contested within Anglicanism. For as long as this remains a tension within Anglican ecclesiology Anglicans will find ecumenical dialogue both a sign of hope and highly problematic, especially in dealing with other Protestant churches.

Part of the unresolved tension in Anglican ministry was also brought to light in the 1986 report on the priesthood of the ordained. Here the problem of a two-nature Christology underlying the distinction between the two priesthoods – ordained and corporate – was exposed. The Moberly distinction between the divine commission for apostolic orders 'from above' compared with authorizations 'from below' has been endemic in the Anglican tradition. Given the heavy emphasis upon Christology as the driver for a doctrine of ministerial priesthood it is almost axiomatic that the rationale for ministries will end up assimilating problems associated with the two-nature Christology. The most obvious expression of that problem in the doctrine of ministry is in the failure to properly integrate the two priesthoods. As observed in Chapter 2 this problem is not the preserve of the Catholic tradition and includes Protestantism as well. The two-nature Christology invariably struggled to explain the nature of the union and either assimilated one nature to the other or ended up with a bifurcated Christ. This helps to explain much of the difficulty faced by the churches over the vexed question of the ministries. When the decisive focus and basis for differentiated ministries is Christological the effect is to close off ministry to the laity by assimilating all ministerial functions to the ordained. A counter reaction occurs when the functions of ministry are democratised and representation is undermined. This is a feature of much of current practice in Anglican ministry. Its roots however can be located in a Pneumatology 'from below'.

Many of the present unresolved issues relating to the identity and role of the ministry and relations between the many ministries find their roots in the theological drivers operating from either Christological or Pneumatological domains. The foregoing reflection on trends and tensions in Anglican ministry over the course of the last century indicates that ministry, unsurprisingly, is a field upon which important issues are processed in relation to the doctrine of God. The mix of church, ministry and the gospel of Jesus Christ is an inescapable feature of reflection on the theology and practise of ministry. In Part III, I will consider how some of the tensions noted above might be rethought in the interests of a more collaborative and ecumenical theory of ministry.

PART III
Towards a Collaborative Theory of Ministry

Chapter 7
Ministries in Relation: The Quest for Integration

Introduction and Overview

This chapter inquires into the relations between the ministries of the Church. It is particularly concerned to inquire into the relation between those ministries for which the Church has traditionally ordained certain persons and the wider ecclesial ministries. The disjunction between these two domains has a long history and, as we have observed in Parts I and II, the issue of the relations between the ministries remains unresolved. Moreover the rapid development of the diversity of ministries of the whole people of God has only increased the pressure to clarify the basic relation between what has been traditionally termed 'the ministry' and the wider ministries of the laity.

It is odd that in the field of Christian ministry – one that has generated a plethora of literature – there is such a paucity of reflection on the inner relations of the ministries in the modern period. As we saw in Chapter 2 the contemporary understanding of Christian ministry is exceedingly complex and somewhat tangled. Difficulties in nomenclature, relation to baptism, uncertainty and conflicts over the relation between ordained and lay ministry, and ecumenical challenges regarding the mutual recognition of ministries all contribute to a fairly confused and anxious climate in which the topic of ministry is discussed and practised. Such matters are hardly insignificant for the Christian churches as they consider how they might coordinate their common mission in the world. Lack of clarity and internal confusion about the nature of the ministry is a serious inhibitor of the Church's witness to the gospel. Failure to properly coordinate the ministries of the people of God (both within a church and between the churches) dissipates energy and thwarts the development of responsible engagement with the world.

Our preliminary discussion (Chapter 3) highlighted the importance of the relationship between church and ministry as an indicator of likely problems in the way ministry was understood and operated. For example when the focus was on ministry – undergirded by a strong Christology – sharp boundaries between ordained and lay ministry could emerge. In this scenario the ordained ministry operated over against and somewhat unrelated to the life of the Church. Where the focus was on Church, and ministry was seen as a Spirit-led activity, the result was a plethora of ministries. The danger in this pneumatological emphasis was that ministry might easily collapse into a list of tasks distributed within the social world of the ecclesia. This occurred for essentially pragmatic reasons related to perceived needs but without clear focus or purpose in relation to the mission of the Church. It was unclear how the Church's continuity and form over time was sustained.

Notwithstanding the emergence of Trinitarian and relational discourse in contemporary ecclesiology it seems that a fully Trinitarian account of the ministries still awaits us. A litmus test for both the lack of such an account and a focus for its application was around the question of the relation of the ministries. Indeed, a continuing difficulty observed throughout our earlier explorations was the lack of a coherent and theologically grounded rationale for a truly collaborative relation between 'the ministry' and the ministries.

The above issues re-emerged in Part II, in the examination of the recent tradition on ministry in the Anglican tradition. Anglicans have given significant attention to the identity and rationale for the threefold ministry of bishops, priests and deacons, particularly within the ecumenical environment of the twentieth century. But as we have seen the tensions as well as the promise of the Moberly tradition has meant both a strong focus on a representative priesthood and little attention to the relations between the ministries of the people of God. Tensions between doctrines of ministry derived from Christology and Pneumatology are evident and remain unresolved in contemporary Anglican practice. This can be observed in the variety of issues on the Anglican agenda regarding ministry: lay presidency, women in orders, the impact of the Charismatic movement/Pentecostal churches, increasing participation of the whole people of God in ministries of a diverse sort, church planting and the development of new ministries, as well as a general lack of understanding of the identity and purpose of ordained ministry within the current mix of church activity. The abundance of ministries that have emerged in the twentieth century exists alongside the traditional threefold ministerial orders. How they work together without diminishing the other; indeed how they might enhance and expand the ministries of the other remains an issue that bears importantly on how the Church fulfils its apostolic calling in the world.

Certainly the heavy investment by Anglicans in the ecumenical scene and the consequent focus on the question of the recognition of ministries across the denominational divides has been clearly in evidence. The importance and necessity of a properly constituted representative ministry has been a preoccupation of such dialogues. Yet this has proved and still continues to be one of the most intractable issues the churches face with regard to their ecumenical life. A lot of ink has been spilt on the issues involved. Yet this *inter-church* issue on ministry is closely related to the *intra-church* issue of the inner relations between the ministries. They are almost mirror images of each other. The ecumenical conversation has thus two aspects: both within a particular communion and across communions. The fact of an emerging abundance of ministries impacts upon a church's self-understanding of its formal and public ministry – realignments are taking place *within* communions which are far from complete and still conflictual. Yet at the same time the dialogues *across* the communions of the Church often presuppose more stable identities for ordained ministries than is the case. Both conversations circle around each other. Neither conversations are particularly clear about how the ministries actually work together and for what purpose.

The resolution of these matters is beyond the scope of this chapter. However a more modest proposal for our present inquiry can be stated in the following question. Is there a way of understanding the inner relations between the ministries of the Church that justifies genuine collaboration and confers enriched ministerial capacities upon all ministries? This is the nub of the issue that will be of particular concern in the present and succeeding chapter. A theory to undergird and make sense of such a view of the ministries may be hopefully of value for the Church's ecumenical and missional calling.

From another perspective this chapter represents a preliminary exploration of how the ministries of the Church are 'interanimative' of each other in such a way that they 'bring each other to be'. This suggestive phrase from *Education for the Church's Ministry* invites further consideration.

The following three chapters (7, 8 and 9) are an experiment to see what arguments might commend themselves for a deeper integration of the ministries of the Church. The present chapter will develop a preliminary analysis of the trends and tensions already observed in the relations between the ministries. Three forms of relation are discussed: disjunctive, implosive and integrative. The integrative ideal is persistent in the modern period and points to a more collaborative ministerial practice. Yet what is lacking is an adequate theory to justify a sustained collaborative ministry. This issue is addressed in chapters 8 and 9.

Ordained and Lay Ministry: Forms of Relation

Disjunctive Relation

From our inquiry so far what might be inferred about the inner relations of the ministries? Within Anglicanism a dominant tradition from Moberly to the current period evidences a disjunctive relation between the ministries; the ministry is construed as separate and\or over against the life of the Church. In Moberly's day it was discussed in terms of 'the ministry' and the 'laity' and these basic terms remain current. Yet, as we have seen, the sharp delineation between ordained and lay – arising from the mode of authorization of the former ('from above') – was in tension with a more integrative account of the relation between the ministry and the 'collective priesthood' (the priesthood 'from below'). At root the tension reflected the different ways in which ministry and church were related. With Michael Ramsey the basic disjunction remains though again we noted the potential embedded in his approach for a more integrative account of the ministries of the church.

In ecumenical dialogue the ARCIC deliberations on ministry, as observed in Chapter 2, also evidence a disjunctive relation between the ministries, albeit in a contemporary and more nuanced form. Where the 'common Christian priesthood' and 'priestly ministry' are 'two distinct realities' there is no intrinsic relation between the two. It remains fundamentally an external relation. At best the relation is indirect through a Christological source. The priesthood of Christ funds two different priesthoods; a common priesthood and a distinct priestly ministry. It is entirely unclear how the ordained ministry 'shares' in the common priesthood yet is a 'distinct' priesthood from a different realm of the gifts of the Spirit. As noted in Chapter 2 a 'parallel track' theory of ministry results.

However, if the priesthood of Christ is generative of ordained and common ministries, as argued in ARCIC, then minimally some account has to be given of the relationship between these two domains of ministry. The discussion at this point is remarkable for its failure to take up such a challenge. A fully relational account of the ministries would require the joining of the three nodes – Christ, ordained and baptised – wherein a dynamic relational quality operates. It is the manner of the union between the differentiated ministries which subsist in Christ that is critical.

Excursus: Ministerial Nestorianism

Yet to talk of the nature of the union between ministries in the one Christ has echoes of the Nestorian controversy from an earlier age. Nestorian Christology struggled to give an adequate account of the union between the humanity and divinity of Christ.[1] The 'Nestorian heresy' has a ministerial form in an unreconciled relationship between a 'special priesthood' – 'from above' – and the 'common priesthood' – 'from below' – both of which derive from Christ.

Nestorius presumed the unity of Christ – the unity of the *prosopon* – and attempted to give an account of the manner of the union between the two concrete realities in Christ – that is, the Godhead which subsists in the Logos and 'manhood [*sic*] in Christ'. He spoke of the 'conjunction' (*conjunctio*) of the two natures and less frequently of the 'union'.[2] However, his emphasis was always upon the differentiation of the two natures even in their union. Not quite 'division at any price' but perilously close it might seem. Where the doctrine of ministry is filtered through Christology the overlaps with Nestorianism are revealing. At a primary level the unity of the ministries is assumed by reference to the one priesthood of Christ. Where the emphasis then falls on the concrete ministries of the ordained and the baptised we note the following features: (a) the over-riding focus is on the ordained and (b) the ontological difference between ordained and common priesthood lurks close at hand. By analogy with Nestorius the unity of the priesthood is established at a different level from the level at which the differentiation in the ministries is articulated. At the secondary level (concrete ministries) the 'co-joining' of the

---

[1] See Aloys Grillmeier, *Christ in the Christian Tradition*, vol. 1, *From the Apostolic Age to Chalcedon (451)*, trans. John Bowden (Atlanta: John Knox Press, 2nd revd edn, 1975), pp. 443–87, esp. 457–63.

[2] Ibid., p. 459.

ministries is poorly handled; the 'special priesthood' and the 'common priesthood' remain essentially disconnected. Furthermore, in the same way that patristic Christology had difficulty giving an adequate account of the humanity of Christ in the incarnation of the Logos, so too the contemporary Church has struggled to give an adequate account of the contribution of the common priesthood to the priesthood of Christ. The merit of Nestorius is that he at least saw there was a problem and attempted to tackle it directly, if ultimately unsuccessfully. The analogy with Nestorianism, notwithstanding the different categories in which the two problems are discussed, may nonetheless prove illuminating for our own struggles regarding the reconciliation of the ministries within and between the churches and why they are so intractable.

At the least here we have an interesting example of how an ancient Christological controversy has been relocated into the practical field of ministry. It is not surprising that difficulties in the field of ministry, given their roots in a long-standing Christological problem over the two-nature theory, have persisted and do not admit of an easy solution. The Christological framework is seriously flawed.

The argument here is that the disjunction between the priesthood of the ordained and the common priesthood presses back to problems in the application of a two-nature Christology. But this problem is difficult to identify for two reasons: (a) because of the sophisticated way in which the Christological argument can be developed according to the double modality of Christ's relation to the Church – transcendent and immanent – and (b) because the basic problem is obscured by the invocation of the Spirit as the context and conferer of ministerial gifts. In this latter case the lurking Christological difficulty is masked by reference to the work of the Spirit.

The disjunction between the two priesthoods points to a failure to transpose into ministry the Trinitarian dynamics founding and energising the priesthood of Christ in the Church. The end result is a parallel-track theory of Christian ministry: one for the ordained and the other for the rest. In this conception there is nothing that the latter can offer to enhance the ministry of the former, save obediential following. The logic of the disjunctive relation between ordained and lay is that discussions of ministry rarely, if ever, inquire about the ways in which lay ministry might contribute to priestly ministry. It cannot get onto the agenda because it is not relevant to the identity and purpose of those in orders.[3]

One result of this basic conception is that the ministries remain permanently in conflict with each other. The conflict moves in two directions. In one the ordained ministries dominate and/or assimilate the ministries of the people. This has been a long-standing problem for the Church. It generates clericalism that can be fostered by both clerical and lay people. In the other direction the purpose and function of the ordained is negated or undermined by an emergent and self-possessed laity who may view the ordained as inimical to the mission of the Church in the

---

[3] Peter Carnley's recent discussion of lay and ordained ministry is a case in point (*Reflections*, pp. 156–80).

world. A covert lay leadership can emerge. The conflict moves in either or both directions and arises out of fundamental disjunctions in the self-understanding of the priesthood of Christ in the Church.

An Implosive Relationship

The disjunctive relation between ordained and lay ministry was characteristically a feature of a doctrine of ministry developed Christologically. Where the emphasis was more discernibly Pneumatological the relationship between the ministries was always in danger of imploding or dissolving altogether. As we have observed in Chapter 2 and 3, where ministry is related primarily to the *charisms* of the Spirit, this generates significant challenges for the traditional ministerial offices. The orderings of the ministering Spirit continually generate novel and new forms of ministry that move freely across traditional boundaries. The Spirit effects new alignments and challenges stable forms. *Charism* as the primal expression of gifts can lead to ministerial office and order being displaced or ceasing to have any intrinsic purpose. The Spirit 'blows where it wills' and the shape and forms of ministry give expression to this constant reshaping and renewing. The ossification of stable ministerial forms is a constant danger; they can be 'left behind' as irrelevant. The primacy of *charism* dissolves existing relations and reconfigures the ministries in new and surprising ways.

This, of course, is not uncommon in the modern era of Pentecostalism and the Charismatic movement of the last half of the twentieth century. Its challenge to the traditional orders of ministry was identified in Chapter 3 following the lead of the New Testament scholar, James Dunn. The charismatic movement has and continues to have a significant impact within the churches including the Anglican Church. The Church of England Doctrine Commission's report, *We Believe in the Holy Spirit*, represents an important response to current developments and a recognition of the challenge that such an emphasis has in the Church and its ministries.[4]

However, the pneumatological emphasis has a long lineage and has deep roots in the Judaeo-Christian tradition. The prophetic tradition of Israel and the Church is but one manifestation. Tertullian's sharp critique of the Church of his day and his subsequent move to Montanism is an early and well-known example of a renewed emphasis in the Church on the Spirit as the active agent in all forms of ministry. Whilst it seems that Tertullian, in his Montanist period, never abandoned notions of the special priesthood of the clergy[5] nevertheless his emphasis on the Spirit as the agent for ministries of the Church gave a certain priority to the general priesthood and represented a challenge to the status quo in respect to ecclesial

---

[4] The Doctrine Commission of the Church of England, *We Believe in the Holy Spirit* (London: Church House, 1991), especially chs. 3 and 5. The current discourse on 'emerging Church' and 'fresh expressions' also raises questions about traditional orders of ministry.

[5] Bulley, *The Priesthood of Some Believers*, p. 170.

orders. What looked like chaotic behaviour from one perspective was also, from another perspective, precisely the way in which the Church could recover its faithfulness and holiness through the exercise of the *charisms* of the Holy Spirit. It is interesting that of all the early church theologians Tertullian was particularly alive to the relationship between the ministry and the ministries. He gave particular attention in his 'Catholic' as well as his Montanist period to the proper balance between the 'special' and 'general' priesthood. His emphasis upon the latter – for example, the Levitical model for priesthood is applied to the faithful[6] – and his stress on the continuity between the two priesthoods – same disciplinary regulations for both[7] – made for 'a theologically rich understanding of the general priesthood, richer than any before him'.[8] It also points to early tensions emerging between ordained and laity and the need to keep the two integrally related.[9] In Tertullian's case the ordained ministry was a subset and ecclesiastical expression of the priesthood of the faithful.[10]

We also noted in Chapter 2 that precisely because of the tendency to dissolve settled ministerial forms, a Spirit-generated ministry had a degree of occasionalism about it. There was a danger of losing those stabilities necessary for ecclesial endurance through time and space. Ordinarily they are expressed – at least in part – through particular public and formally authorised ministries that function as important symbols of continuity and visible signs of the presence of the community of Christ. The radical diversification of the ministries of the Spirit requires counterbalancing and reciprocal stable forms of endurance and witness. And where such have been marginalised, the unlimited open space can become an empty void. The dissolution of all concrete and continuing relations between the ministries, formal and informal, authorised and free-acting, creates conditions for new orders of public ministry out of a chaotic and fluid system. This is not unusual and can be creative but unchecked it can simply mean that new forms of domination emerge. The problem within Pentecostalism of the unchecked authority of the charismatic leader is well known. The emergence of the 'apostle' in contemporary Pentecostalism is relevant here.[11]

However, our exploration of the Anglican tradition in Part II, indicated that one of the great benefits of the work of the Spirit in the contemporary Church was the uncovering of the ministry of the whole people of God. That which had been invisible had in recent decades become more visible. We recognised an abundance of ministries funded by the *charisms* of God. New alignments are occurring, relationships between the ministries are being re-established in new, surprising and challenging ways both within and between the churches. Ecumenical dialogues

[6] Ibid., p. 166.
[7] Ibid., p. 318.
[8] Ibid., p. 174.
[9] Ibid., p. 173.
[10] Ibid., p. 318.
[11] Cannistraci, *Apostles*.

are increasingly conducted with reference to the work of the Spirit who bestows gifts upon the whole Church for the glory of God. Established boundaries between churches and within the different and divided communions are being dissolved; new forms of ministry are emerging. Perhaps the implosion of relations between the ministries is a necessary moment in ecclesial reformation and renewal.

Yet the Church is at a critical stage in its life where it urgently requires collaborative and mutually enriching ministries. This will require ministries that embody an interweaving of spontaneity and stability, open to new expressions and resilient through creative adaptation. But at this stage 'it is not yet clear what we shall be' (1 John 3:2). Certainly the pneumatological emphasis in the churches has had an unsettling influence. This is happening directly through challenging existing ministries and their purpose. It is also happening covertly or indirectly through the inner reconfiguring of ministries in relation to the work of the Spirit's *charism*s. Yet where the work of the Spirit is dislocated from the agency of the living Christ the resultant plethora of ministries may struggle to find proper reference to Christ. An emergent, immanentist, *charism*-led Church can very quickly lose reference to the Christ of the gospels; ministries can simply become expressions of personal whims and fancies. Under such conditions the philosophy of the individual gains religious legitimation. The gnosticism of the ancient world reappears in new and enticing forms. One response to this is to recover the enduring symbols of faith expressed through word, sacrament and an authorised public ministry. This was very much the approach of the great early church apologist Irenaeus. However, as we have observed in the foregoing chapters the search for more integrative approaches to the ministries is clearly on the agenda.

Towards the Integrative Ideal

Beyond the more traditional disjunctive relations and more recent tendency to dissolve the relations between the ministries there is a discernible trend towards more integrative approaches. The companion language for such a development is Trinitarian. We have already noted the importance of this for some contemporary Roman Catholic scholars. In this respect Edward Hahnenberg's, *Ministries: A Relational Approach* provides the most coherent and creative attempt so far to develop an integrative approach to the ministries of the Church. Although his focus is decidedly Roman Catholic nevertheless his insights are relevant across the ecclesial spectrum. His uncovering of the problems of a Christological or pneumatological undergirding for ministry is particularly illuminating. His relational approach is indebted to a richer Trinitarian dynamic.

Within the Anglican communion there is an emerging literature on Trinitarian relationality and its link to the dynamics of ministry. Robin Greenwood's *Transforming Priesthood* is a good example here. Perhaps more importantly the tenor of modern ecumenical dialogues certainly appeals to a renewal in Trinitarian ecclesiology as the backdrop for reflections upon the ministries of the divided churches. However, our inquiries into ministry have also identified a rich vein within Anglicanism of a more integrative kind. We identified this stream within Moberly's *Ministerial Priesthood* with his appeal to the organic conception of the Church and its ministry in relation to Christ. From his Anglo-Catholic perspective Moberly expressed it thus: the 'priesthood of the ministry follows as a corollary from the priesthood of the Church.... The powers, and privileges, the capacities, are the powers and privileges and capacities of the body as a whole ... [and those who celebrate] do but organically represent, and act for, the whole.'[12] Its importance has not been lost on Anglicanism, even from within the evangelical stream. Thus the former Archbishop of Canterbury, George Carey has drawn attention to Moberly's doctrine of representative priesthood as 'central to the concept of ministry in the Anglican Church'.[13] It was this thread in Moberly's argument that Anthony Hanson developed – with the aid of F.J. Hort and Arthur Headlam – in the *Pioneer Ministry*. Central to this was a reconfiguring of the relationship between ministry and the Church. As we have seen Hanson's integrative account of the ministries was premised on the argument that the originative ministry was nothing less than 'the church *in nucleo*': 'the first church' or 'the rudimentary church'.[14]

The closer relationship between ministry and church has continued to be an important theme in Anglican reflection upon ministry. This is reflected in Richard Hanson's *Christian Priesthood Examined* in which the representative priesthood 'rests upon the priesthood of all baptised Christians' and is a 'concentration' of the Church's priesthood.[15] Central here was an organic conception of ministry based upon a common baptism. *Baptism, Eucharist and Ministry* and subsequent ecumenical dialogues have, as we observed in Chapter 6, been clearly indebted to this fundamental insight. This fresher integrative approach underlies *Education for the Church's Ministry* and Hanson and Hanson's *The Identity of the Church*.

Over the last decade there have been a number of attempts to develop a fuller explication of what this more integrative account of the ministries might entail. Robin Greenwood's *Transforming Priesthood* and more recently *Transforming Church* are clearly indebted to the emergence of Trinitarian thinking in relation to the doctrine of the Church and ministry. Greenwood argues that a Trinitarian basis for ecclesiology, when applied to a doctrine of ministry, points to a relational understanding of ministries where the relation is not established through 'a process of causality of any kind' (for example, 'chain of individuals' or 'historically "guaranteed" line of apostolic communities'). Rather, the accent is upon 'interdependence'[16] wherein 'the entire church rather than the priest alone is said to represent Christ'.[17] In this context the priesthood of the ordained represents

---

12 Moberly, *Ministerial Priesthood*, p. 258.

13 Carey, 'Reflections upon the Nature of Ministry', p. 27.

14 Hanson, *Pioneer Ministry*, pp. 86, 94, 155.

15 Hanson, *Christian Priesthood*, pp. 100, 102.

16 Greenwood, *Transforming Priesthood*, p. 164.

17 Ibid., p. 145.

a 'focusing' of the priesthood of Christ's body.[18] The link of such a function to notions of 'intensification' or 'concentration' is not difficult to see, though the language has a longer pedigree than most imagine and can be traced back, through various interpreters of the recent Anglican tradition, to Moberly. Greenwood's claim that 'there is nothing that could be said of bishop, priest or deacon that is not in some way true of the Church as a whole'[19] has strong echoes in Moberly's earlier conceptions of the relation of the ordained to the 'collective priesthood'. This might well come as shock to both Greenwood and his critic, Carnley.[20] The latter rejects notions of the priesthood of the ordained focussing or intensifying the priesthood of the Church.[21] Rather he aligns himself with the ARCIC position that the priesthood of the ordained is different from the common priesthood not simply in 'degree' but in 'kind'.[22] The Anglo-Catholic Moberly was particularly careful at this point: the difference was one of 'degree' and/or 'function, not one of 'kind' except in a 'limited sense' related to 'functional capacities'.[23]

Yet as different as Greenwood and Carnley are on the matter of the derivation and function of the ministries both wish to highlight the interdependent and relational aspects of their conceptions of ministry and priesthood.[24] The theological intuitions point in this direction though problems persist in both approaches. Greenwood's rationale for the 'uniquely distinguishing role of the priest' may not be convincing and evidence too much debt to traditional notions of setting apart[25] which may be at odds with his notion that the ministries 'co-create' each other.[26] Carnley's proposal, that ordination involves not merely 'a setting apart of a person from the world, *but a pastoral distancing of an individual from the rest of the Church*' bristles with difficulties and offers no basis for genuine collaborative ministry wherein the ministries animate and enliven one another.[27]

William Countryman sets out on a different tact in developing 'the fundamental priesthood of Christians' grounded in 'the true life of humanity in the presence of God, illuminated by the priesthood of Christ'.[28] The basis for this is life in relation

---

18 Ibid., p. 142.

19 Ibid., p. 142. Compare Robin Greenwood, *Transforming Church: Liberating Structures for Ministry* (London: SPCK, 2002), p. 75.

20 Greenwood is deeply critical of Moberly for the latter's adherence to a sharp divide between the clergy and laity (*Transforming Priesthood*, pp. 7–11).

21 Carnley, *Reflections*, pp. 175, 179.

22 Ibid, pp. 172, 175.

23 Moberly, *Ministerial Priesthood*, p. 96.

24 Carnley, *Reflections*, p. 178.

25 See Carnley's criticism, ibid, p. 171; and Greenwood, *Transforming Priesthood*, pp. 143, 169, for references to ideas of the priest being 'set apart'.

26 *Transforming Priesthood*, p. 75.

27 Ibid., p. 175.

28 L. William Countryman, *Living on the Border of the Holy: Renewing the Priesthood of All* (Harrisburg: Morehouse, 1999); cf. Kenneth Mason, *Priesthood and Society*

to the Holy, a life of encounter at the borderlands between God and the world. A bond is thus established at the heart of creation between God, creation and a kind of natural priesthood arising from such encounter. It is an approach with strong affinities to the tradition of F.D. Maurice in Anglicanism. For Countryman the difference between this 'fundamental priesthood' of humanity and Christian priesthood is epistemological: 'If our Christian priesthood is unique, it is so only in that we have been graced, for no merit of our own, with the integrating clarity of that vision.'[29] Countryman refers here to the understanding that the truth that anyone encounters is at one with the 'Word incarnate in Jesus'. In this conception creation has ontological priority over the Church in relation to a ministering priesthood. An interdependence between creation and church is thus posited. On this view a ministering priesthood is clearly orientated towards the world.

What is not so clear in this approach is the logic of an ordained ministry. Humanity's 'need for religion with it sacramental priests' seems to be the key for Countryman.[30] The purpose of the sacramental priesthood is to model a form of life that allows the fundamental priesthood to 'more readily do its work'. The chief characteristic of the Church's sacramental priesthood 'is not its own power or authority or even its sacredness, but the way in which it emerges within and points towards the priesthood that is dispersed throughout the Christian people and the whole human race'.[31] Countryman has brought into focus the significance of the idea of the Holy as that to which and about which priestly life revolves for the sake of the priestly community and the wider humane race. This has the great merit of placing the discussion of ministry and orders within a richer context of creation and human society. Sacramental categories become critical and the ancient tradition of salvation through illumination is given a contemporary ring. Yet Countryman is unable to say how the fundamental priesthood contributes to the sacramental priesthood in any way notwithstanding his espousal of contemporary patterns of mutual ministry.[32] It is ultimately a one-way relation, the latter (sacramental priesthood) facilitating the work of the former (fundamental priesthood).

A recent book by Christopher Cocksworth and Rosalind Brown, *Being a Priest Today*, provides an excellent introduction to the ordained ministry today. For practical wisdom interwoven with the fabric of the ministry tradition in theology and Scripture this book is remarkable. It offers a fresh, humane and powerful vision for ministerial priesthood today. Here there is an aliveness to the relation between presbyter and people: 'Presbyters are not a caste outside the *laos*, they

---

(Norwich: Canterbury Press, 1992), ch. 2 (esp. p. 36) on the 'priesthood of humanity'.

29 Countryman, *Living on the Border of the Holy*, p. 137.

30 Countryman, *Living on the Border of the Holy*. The anthropological and sociological factors that underpin structures and symbols for meditation of the sacred are well known and ought not be dismissed. How they might be related to theological domains of sacral leadership requires careful thought.

31 Ibid, p. 138.

32 Ibid, p. 167.

are a category within the *laos*. They are members of the *laos* who are placed in a particular pastoral relation to other members of the *laos*.'[33] This emphasis upon the presbyter's particular placement within the people leads the authors to state that 'presbyters are defined by their relationship to other members of the *laos*'.[34] Following the lead of Moberly a century earlier the authors refer to this relationship in terms of an 'intense "for-other-ness"'.[35] And underlying this is the fact that 'Christian identity is fundamentally relational'. But what is the nature of this relationality? Drawing from early Church sources (for example, the *Apostolic Tradition of Hippolytus* and John Chrysostom) the authors point to the fundamental interdependence between presbyter and people observed in the New Testament: 'The presbyter needs the people to be a presbyter. The people need a presbyter to be the people of God'.[36] The one 'interanimates the other'. The instincts here are surely right. The book is an exploration of the inner life of the ordained who are called to serve the 'health and beauty' of the Church. Yet it is unclear in this relational approach exactly how, in the words of *Education for the Church's Ministry*, the ministry of the people 'brings the other [ministry of the ordained] to be'. The significance of the book is that it offers an engaging vision of what ministry that raises a people to holiness and truth might look like. The nature and dynamic of the reciprocity that might obtain here is unchartered. The integration is half complete.

Conclusion: Integration of Ministries an Elusive Ideal?

The search for more integrative relations between the ministries, and particularly between the ordained and wider ministries of the people of God, remains a continuing challenge and a somewhat elusive ideal. We note a number of aspects of this search by way of summary.

First, it is axiomatic that integrative and interdependent categories are the fundamental referents in ecclesial reflection on ministry. The appeal to the discourse appears uncontested. In the light of the recovery of Trinitarian theology and its application to the doctrine of the Church more or less across the ecclesiastical spectrum it is not surprising that the stock-in-trade language for reconceiving doctrines of ministry is deeply indebted to relational language.

Second, this development fits well with a renewed emphasis upon the ministry of the whole people of God and offers possibilities for new conceptualities to emerge and improved and reformed practises. In this way the newer discourses fund understandings of ministry more closely aligned with the missional nature of the ecclesia.

---

33 Cocksworth and Brown, *Being a Priest Today*, p. 15.

34 Ibid.

35 Ibid, pp. 8, 20.

36 Ibid, p. 19.

Third, the actual deployment of the language of relationality is quite varied and, as observed above, generates quite different conceptualities concerning the ministry of the Church. Indeed, the search for a more integrative approach to the ministries within the purposes of the Church is an unsettled and contested area of contemporary church life.

Fourth, this points to the difficulty inherent in any attempt to press Trinitarian language into the service of an ecclesiality of ministry. Traditional problems in the ministries and their inner relations – that is, disjunctive and implosive dynamics – can simply remerge within a new conceptuality. The strategies adopted by various apologists for ministry may indicate an intuitive grasp of the difficulty of the exercise. The priority of interdependent and relational categories is generally accepted and named. However, the search for more satisfying integrative understandings of ministry usually proceeds through attention to one particular ministry. Lines of connection and implications from reflection on one ministry are then made across the ministries. In short a Trinitarian rhetoric masks habitual defaults into either Christological or Pneumatological emphases with their accompanying difficulties and unresolved issues for the nature of Christian ministry.

Fifth, whilst such a methodology is wholly defensible what seems to fall out of view is the nature of the relation between the ministries per se. Moreover, the standard approach is to focus on the nature of representative ministry – ordained ministry – and then show how its embeddedness in the ministry of the whole people of God is generative of more respectful and interdependent relations between the ministries. The focus is thus on one node in the complex of ministries – ordained – and the wider ministries fall out of view. Inevitably this approach betrays a failure to press the Trinitarian dynamic of the ministries as far as it should be. Wholly commendable proposals emerge for reconceiving the priestly ministry of the ordained in relation to the people of God. But there is a distinct absence of reflection on the reciprocal nature of the relationship between the ministry of the ordained and other ministries. The result is an enhanced and healthier conception of the ordained ministry but it remains fundamentally unclear why and how, to use the words of J.A.T. Robinson nearly five decades earlier, the ministries of the people of God generate an ongoing mutual expansion of each other, let alone 'bring each other to be'. How this might be reconceived in the interests of an approach to ministry that is both collaborative and ecumenically serviceable is the subject of the two following chapters.

Chapter 8
Collaborative Ministry: A Dialogue between Theology and Science[1]

Introduction: Methodological Issues

The previous chapter offered a preliminary analysis of the different ways in which the ministries of the Church are related, particularly the ordained and wider ministries. This analysis highlighted the need for a method of inquiry that could uncover some of the deeper dynamics involved in creating, sustaining and renewing the ministry of the Church. I have already uncovered some clues for such an inquiry. For example, in the previous chapter, I noted that the relations between the ministries varies depending upon whether the underlying theological foundation is Christological or Pneumatological. A strong Christological focus for ministry was more often associated with a disjunctive relation between ordained and more general ministries. This approach usually generates a strong focus on boundary differentiations, that is, between the ordained and the ministries of the laity. Where Pneumatology dominates, the relations between the ministries tends to break down. The reason is that an emphasis upon the work of the Holy Spirit is associated with a multiplication of ministries. However in this case the relations between the ministries become increasingly blurred and/or diffuse.

The search for a more integrated approach to the ministries of the body of Christ was associated with a more consistent application of Trinitarian categories. But, as argued in the previous chapter, this latter strategy remained elusive and underdeveloped. Furthermore, it could also harbour within it distortions arising from over-emphasising Christology (disjunctive ministries) and/or Pneumatology (dissipative ministries) in the relations between the ministries.

Exactly how to develop a more integrative approach to the ministries of the Church is a key concern of this chapter. Specifically, we want to know how a richer theological understanding of the ministries would enable us to answer the question posed in the previous chapter: is there a way of understanding the inner relations between the ministries of the church that justifies genuine collaboration and confers enriched ministerial capacities upon all ministries? From an Anglican

---

[1] Chapters 8 and 9 had their origin in an article, 'Healing the Wound: Collaborative Ministry for Mission', *St Mark's Review: A Journal of Christian Thought and Opinion* 199 (2005): 3–11. A revised version subsequently appeared in *Ecclesiology* 3.1 (2006): 81–101.

point of view we want to know what justifications can be offered for Cranmer's Good Friday Collect, which stresses the vocation and ministry of all the faithful.[2]

As we have observed in earlier chapters, in recent years it has been common to begin an inquiry into Christian ministry with an appeal to Trinitarian doctrine. This doctrine has been used as a springboard for reflections on the Church as a communion in which relational categories become the norm for ministry. The appeal of Trinitarian categories is the possibility of a richer integrative approach to the ministries. However, this has not proven as fruitful as might be expected for resolving the question of the relations between the ministries. The transposition of Trinitarian doctrine into understandings of ministry remains underdeveloped. We might say that the Trinitarian field has been tilled extensively in recent years however its yield has not been great. This is the case notwithstanding the significant investment in Trinitarian and relational categories in discussions of ministry.

Is it possible to develop a general theory of ministerial order that justifies collaborative practice? And how might a general theory be conceived? On any account, this is a major undertaking and some might consider it foolish in the extreme. On the other hand it is precisely a general theory that seems required if the churches are to have a future together in mission.[3] A general understanding of ministry derived from first principles can provide conceptual apparatus that opens up new possibilities for understanding and practice. For example, a number of practical questions arise. How might Pentecostal, Protestant and Catholic traditions recognise a common future ministry embodied in their own life and between each other? How might the communions divided internally find a renewed vitality and coherence in ministries for the glory of God? A general theory provides a mediation between existing expressions of the ordering of the Church's varied ministries (formal and informal) and a future consensus that has so far proven elusive.

In current theologies of ministry there seems to be a distinct absence of intermediate categories, that is, general purpose concepts that facilitate the move from established discourses of meaning to new understandings.[4] It is not unusual to invoke Trinitarian language and weave this somewhat effortlessly into general accounts of ministries. Thus the doctrine of the Trinity may be proposed as foundational for ministry and as such provide the justification for all kinds of cooperative forms of ministry. But is this sufficient? Such accounts usually do not

---

[2] See Chapter 6.

[3] For a discussion of the value of general theories see Hardy, *God's Ways with the World*, p. 127.

[4] For discussion of intermediate categories see Hardy, 'Created and Redeemed Sociality'. Such categories 'serve as a two-way street' between the domain of the practical (empirical realities) and what Hardy refers to as the 'transcendental' or the higher level 'generic semi-interpreted theories'. The key for the present purposes is the notion of conceptual apparatus that operate as a 'two-way street' between a familiar discourse and set of meanings and richer and more dynamic understandings of divine and human interaction in the world.

go far enough and not surprisingly thwart the development of new approaches to perennial problems. Old problems remain trapped in patterns of meaning that tend to shore up pre-established positions. Little real progress in understanding can be made. This is evident in the knotty little problem of the relationship between those ministries for which people are ordained in the Church and those ministries exercised by the wider body of the baptised. I have never heard or read a single sentence that explains how the ministries of the baptised contribute and establish the ministries of deacons, priests or bishops. There is a disconnect here despite extensive explorations of the Trinitarian basis for all ministry.

The quest for a more integrative approach to the ministries of the Church is an attempt to uncover the inner order of the ministries. The concept of order is familiar in the field of the sciences and to this end a theology of ministry may benefit from a more indirect inquiry via a dialogue between theology and the sciences. This is not an arbitrary matter. The reason is that if the ministries are the way the household of God orders its life in the gospel then inquiry into the concept of order may yield wisdom for our understanding of ministerial order and those who inhabit 'holy order'. To this end the present chapter attempts a reconceiving of the problem of the ministries by recourse to the concept of order in science.

Accordingly, this chapter takes its cue from some of the insights of modern evolutionary thinking as it has been applied to social systems. In particular, the concept of order and associated themes of emergence, novelty and causation (whole–part influence) will be tested for their usefulness in understanding the dynamics of ministry within the ecclesial system. A primary concern will be to consider how insights from outside the discipline of theology might feed into the distinctly theological discussion of the ministry of the Church. The supposition is that theology can benefit from interaction with other disciplines for it to undertake its own work. Such an engagement offers the prospect of finding fresh conceptualities to uncover and explain the dynamics of ecclesial life and the practice of a truly collaborative ministry.

Orders and Order: An Emerging Ecclesial Pattern

Ministerial Order in the Early Church

The concept of order is central to an understanding of ministry and the dynamics of the ecclesial community. When it comes to ministry the concept can be understood in the broader sense of the regulation of ecclesial ministries or more narrowly in terms of a particularly defined official ministry. In this latter respect we note that the appeal to 'Holy Orders' is rooted in the early development of the threefold ministry (offices) of the Church in contradistinction from other orders of the *laos*. The term 'lay' is foreign to the scriptures and *klerikos* does not appear in the Septuagint and

New Testament.[5] The religious deployment of the idea of laity (*laikos*) appears initially in Clement of Rome writing to the Corinthian Church at the end of first century. In the context of division and discord, Clement's overriding concern seems to have been to re-establish proper order within the Corinthian Church.[6] To this end he appeals to an ideal ordering under God in which each has a particular 'rank'. Whilst the analogy with the idea of rank in the military is not difficult to discern, Clement also draws upon analogies with the Levitical cult of the Old Testament. He locates the ministries of the Christian community in terms of the orders of high priest, priest and Levite. Those designated as 'layman' (*anthropos laikos*) are assigned their own place and are bound by 'lay precepts'. However in trying to carve out a place for the baptised, Clement managed to cement a division between priesthood and laity.

Clement of Rome's use of the term *laikos* did not reappear until a century later in the writings of Clement of Alexandria and Tertullian. Tertullian, writing in the early years of the third century, was the first Western theologian to distinguish the *ordo* of the clergy from the *plebs* – what we call laity or *laos*.[7] Tertullian was alive to the increasing divide between clergy and the baptised and even in his pre-Montanist days he held a strong doctrine of the laity. Certainly by the time of Cyprian in the fourth century the lines had been established between clerical and lay life. From this early period tensions between the two would become a feature of the Church. The appeal to laity today reflects both the early tradition which distinguished laity from clergy and a more recent tendency to include all the baptised under the term laity or more usually *laos*. The conflation of these two usages can create confusion.

The threefold order of ministry (offices of bishop, priest and deacon) that had become relatively fixed and stable, at least from the sub-apostolic period, were now clearly distinguished from a general priesthood. Such an ordering of ministries, associated with Cyprian in the fourth century with a strong correlation of the

---

[5] *Kleros* has its roots in the Old Testament notion of 'casting lots' (receiving one's 'portion' or 'inheritance') and in the New Testament this idea continues, though in, for example, Col. 1:12 the 'lot' or 'inheritance' is with the 'saints in light' and clearly applies to the company of believers. Only later is the *kleros* associated with a particular group or 'lot', that is, the *klerikos*. Thus whilst the *kleros* is for the whole flock of Christ, the *klerikos* become a particular portion of the flock. See Faivre, *Emergence of the Laity*, p. 6.

[6] Ibid., pp. 18–19.

[7] Alan Hayes, 'Christian Ministry in Three Cities of the Western Empire', in Richard Longenecker (ed.), *Community Formation in the Early Church and in the Church Today* (Massachusetts: Hendrickson, 2002), p. 140. Only a few years earlier in 177 at Lyons, in a letter transcribed by Eusebius, there is no such distinction between clergy and laity. Rather, the *kleros*, 'allotted portion', here taking the meaning 'class' or 'order', refers to the martyrs (ibid., p. 133).

threefold offices with the priesthood of the Old Testament,[8] came to overshadow the fluid and dynamic aspects of ministry of an earlier formative period. Yet the actual history of the Church bears witness to a richly differentiated *ordo* of the Church that has included a wide variety of ministries with pre-eminence in the early Church being accorded the order of martyrs.[9] This variety was reflected in the distinction between 'major' and 'minor' orders of the medieval Church and the internal variety associated with the composition of the minor orders. Moreover the boundaries between these two fundamental orders were not entirely fixed.[10]

Underlying the notion of orders is a more fundamental recognition that the ordering of ministries belonged to the logic of an ecclesial world that was growing in complexity as it expanded throughout the Roman Empire. In this respect the internal ordering of the Church and its ministries was a dynamic feature of the social evolution of the Christian movement. There is nothing particularly unusual about such a development. Indeed it is to be expected. Hence the emergence of more sophisticated and layered orderings of ecclesial life over time was a concomitant feature of increasing levels of organizational complexity. This development was a natural feature of an expanding Church under the impulse of its own inner life in God. Yet as modern research into the formation of early Christian communities indicates, the emergence of an ordered life and ministry was neither a simple

[8] Ibid, pp. 148–53; Faivre, *Emergence of the Laity*, ch. 6. Faivre shows how for Cyprian the clergy do not belong to the laity.

[9] For the importance of the order of the martyrs see Hayes, 'Christian Ministry', p. 133. Hayes refers to confessors, prophets and teachers at Carthage (p. 138). For more on confessors, see Bulley, *Priesthood of Some Believers*, p. 256. The *Apostolic Constitutions* list a variety of officials with ministries, besides the threefold ministry: readers, singers, porters, deaconesses, widows, virgins, orphans (see, Frances Young, 'Ministerial Forms and Functions in the Church Communities of the Greek Fathers', in Longenecker [ed.], *Community Formation*, p. 162). For the variety of ministries in the New Testament see Patzia, *Emergence of the Church*, pp. 152–82, esp. 180. Patzia discusses apostles, prophets, teachers, evangelists, deacons, bishops, elders, pastors, plus 'anonymous leaders and spiritual gifts' (p. 179) and identifies 'charismatic ministries' (p. 182). Faivre, *Emergence of the Laity* (p. 215–16) refers to the 'functions exercised by the assembled people' – participation in the selection of clergy, especially bishops, discipline regarding penitents, consultation by the theologically able in matters requiring theological discernment, and the wider apostolate of the laity in the world (among the poor, slaves, craftsmen; among the intellectual and well-off parts of society; private or domestic spheres; political apostolate). Faivre makes special mention of the apostolate of the godparent through pre-baptismal catechesis. For a discussion of contemporary expressions of the charismata and associated ministries in Roman Catholicism, see Hahnenberg, *Ministries*; Fox, *New Ecclesial Ministries*. The emphasis in this material is on the explosion of lay ministries as a complement to traditional orders.

[10] See Chapter 2, p. 22, footnote 42. Compare Bulley, *Priesthood of Some Believers*, p. 295.

affair nor even throughout the early church. The emergent order was historically contingent; a matter that has generated significant conflict in Anglicanism.[11]

Order as Routinisation

How might the development of more structured forms of ministerial order be understood? Weber's theory of routinisation of an originative charismatic leadership into more stable institutional forms has proven useful and influential and been the catalyst for ongoing sociological studies on leadership, charisma and organization.[12] However, behind Weber lies the earlier work of the Protestant Rudolph Sohm. Sohm, an academic lawyer rather than theologian, argued in *Kirchenrecht* (1892) that primitive Christianity degenerated into the legal and ecclesiastical structure of early Catholicism.[13] This development was evidenced in the transposition from a divinely given charismatic order – with a focus on teaching – to a legal order with duly appointed officers. In this framework charismatic ordering gives way, under pressure of increasing organizational needs, to more complex levels of institutional ordering. This can be observed in the ancient Church's development from an 'early charismatic style of ministry to a more regulated and ordered one'.[14] The beginnings of this process have been discerned in the 'early catholicism' of the later epistles. The process meant that over time the charismata could be assimilated into particular offices, e.g., bishop.[15] Sohm and his heirs have exercised considerable influence on the history of interpretation of the development of ministry in the early Church among both Protestant and Catholic scholars.[16]

---

[11] The development of the historical critical approach to Christian texts and origins has highlighted the complex and fluid context of the New Testament and sub-Apostolic period. The late nineteenth century debate on ministry between Lightfoot and Moberly revolved around this. For further see the discussion in Chapter 4.

[12] See Max Weber, *The Theory of Social and Economic Organization*, trans. A.R. Henderson and T. Parsons, rev. and ed. Talcott Parsons (London: William Hodge and Co., 1947), pp. 334–53. For a more recent study see Thomas Csordas, *Language, Charisma and Creativity: The Ritual Life of a Religious Movement* (Berkley: University of California Press, 1997).

[13] For an excellent discussion of Sohm and subsequent discussion of his thesis see Campbell, *The Elders*, ch. 1. Sohm's book has never been translated into English.

[14] Patzia, *Emergence of the Church*, p. 181.

[15] Bulley, *Priesthood of Some Believers*, pp. 297–306. Bulley notes that with Cyprian the clergy 'and especially the bishop, monopolise the power and ministries of the church' (p. 301). Bulley also notes that evidence from Origen suggests that 'the major source of the laity's ministry was diminishing in people's experience and being increasingly dominated by the clergy' (p. 289).

[16] See Campbell, *The Elders*, pp. 11–19. Compare Nichols, *Holy Order*, pp. 24–5, 181; Martin, *The Feminist Question*, p. 109.

The obvious danger in the process of routinisation is over-regulation and control of the expression of the charismata and a general solidification and stratification of the ministries. This is exemplified in the sevenfold form of the 'sacrament of order' associated with the medieval Church. What emerges is a stable and somewhat elaborate, even artificial framework for differentiation and function of ecclesial ministries.[17] Whilst Calvin could highlight some of the absurdities and confusions of the medieval 'sacrament of order', and the sixteenth-century reforms produced a simplified version, nevertheless the fundamental commitment to a regularised institutional ministry remained intact.[18] Whether in Catholic or Protestant form the emphasis upon regulation of ministerial authority carries with it a tendency to obscure or render impotent the dynamic operating between the ministries. Yet the counter to this is not necessarily reversion to the primacy of charisma as the principle of order (the Sohm tradition). This may mean exchanging a highly regularised and delimited form of order for a dissipative and chaotic form, neither of which achieves a proper dynamic ordering of the ministries. The either/or dualism associated with the institutional versus charismata approach to order is an essentially conflictual model for ordering that lacks a rich and energetic dynamic.

This points to a deeper problem – that is, the social ordering of institutional life has for the most part been undergirded by a concept of order that is fundamentally static. This may be perceived as its very strength. In this context the measure of an institution's capacity to remain in harmony is correlated to its ability to return to a pre-existing stability following a disturbance. Where an ontology of order prevails that prizes harmony and balance above all else, ministerial orders remain sharply differentiated from other orderings of the vocations, discipleship and ministries of the people of God. The problem might not be the operation of hierarchical notions of order per se but rather the impact of an essentially static ontology of order. The inner drive to maintain stability propels the institution into a trajectory driven by deep-rooted conflict between established orders and forces of destabilization. Such a reading of the social evolution of the Church and its ministries is certainly possible and to some extent justified. Certainly the history of the prophetic tradition and the uneasy relationship between the institution and mystical traditions in Christianity bear testimony to the ways in which steady-state theories of order generate patterns of institutional dominance as a means to maintain stability of order in the wake of potential destabilizing threats. A static ontology of order actually generates institutional conflict as exemplified in, for

---

17 Nichols, *Holy Order*, ch. 3. Nichols also highlights the ongoing disputed nature of orders, for example, the particular ministries within the sacrament of order (was it really seven or was there only one basic order, episcopal, from which all flowed) and the ranking of the orders, especially the relation between episcopal and priestly orders.

18 Calvin pointed to the inability of the scholastic theologians to agree about the number of holy orders and the relations between them as evidence of lack of attendance to the Word of God. See Nichols, *Holy Order*, pp. 92–3 (referring to Calvin, *Institutes*, bk. 4, ch. 19, pars. 22–33).

example, constant friction in the history of the Church between clerical and lay ministries. Furthermore, in this context, conflict is essentially a response to human failure and improper use of power. But such ontologies also obscure some of the deeper dynamics of ecclesial life and thwart attempts to uncover the vitality of the ordering of the ministries of the people of God.

Ideas of Order and the New Sciences: From Static to Dynamic Categories

The Enduring Significance of Order

The above discussion points to the fact that any inquiry into the relations between the ministries might benefit from a more careful consideration of order as a feature of the social evolution of the Church. Such a line of inquiry benefits from interaction with a variety of disciplines where the concept of order is both central and problematic. The problematic aspect of the concept of order is immediately obvious in the modern antipathy towards order per se. It is difficult to make a case for order in a disordered age.[19] Order is under threat where human autonomy is prized above all else, and authority, as a consequence, operates internally rather than as an external referent. The revolt against conceptions of order as pre-given and imposed, as it were, from without has been a critical feature of the modern age. The supposition of the ancient tradition with respect to order was that the patterns of the cosmic and sacral realm offered templates for embodiment within social, cultural and religious domains of life. 'Order is heaven's first law' uttered Alexander Pope.[20] Within an Enlightenment framework order was considered inimical to human freedom rather than its natural compliment, associated more with compulsion and estrangement. 'The love of order turns to hate of order, and the "sacred order".'[21] Order has been removed from its transcendental throne. This can be linked to the displacement of the once powerful unitary Parmenidean tradition in philosophy and culture by an equally ancient tradition of Heraclitus. In this latter tradition process, flux and change are the dominant categories for thought and life.[22] In this context disorder rather than order becomes paramount.

Yet the problem of order remains even in the ascendency of its opposite: disorder. Even the root meaning for order from the Greek, *taxis* – meaning 'to place' or 'to set up', primarily of an army for battle, embodies an ambiguity since '"ordered" means either "possessing a pattern" or "having been forced into

[19] Helmut Kuhn, 'The Case for Order in a Disordered Age', in Paul G. Kuntz (ed.), *The Concept of Order* (London: University of Washington Press, 1968), pp. 442–59.

[20] Ibid., p. 446.

[21] Ibid., p. 444.

[22] See Colin Gunton, *The One, the Three and the Many: God, Creation and the Culture of Modernity*, Bampton Lectures, 1992 (Cambridge: Cambridge University Press, 1993), ch. 1.

a pattern"'.[23] Order belongs evidently to the 'sphere of human activity' and as such it can become an expression of the human 'will to power'. The history of civilizations bears witness to such an abuse of order. But the revolt from order only ensures that its potent dangers will re-emerge unchecked. Grappling with order seems to be a feature of human existence. How then might it be understood?

Order as a 'Mode of Togetherness'

Order might be best understood as a relational concept. More formally it can be described as a 'mode of togetherness'. 'Things are brought together by order. Now just as the basic mode of "togetherness" consists of the relationship of the whole to its parts, so also is order a relation in virtue of which many things function together as if they were but one'.[24]

From this perspective disorder and chaos 'bear traces of order'. The nature of order as a 'mode of togetherness' is further specified by reference to the degree or quality of togetherness. This can be discerned through attention to the intensity (or essentiality) and potentiality (or richness) of ordered relations.[25] This gives rise to notions of layered orders and hierarchy. The nomenclature is, in itself benign, but the history of abuse of order – dysfunctional and destructive 'modes of togetherness' which have denied or sundered intrinsic relations within order – has generated negative reactions to all ideas of hierarchy.[26] But in fact, as evolutionary biology and social evolution make abundantly clear, the emergence of ordered relations from simple to highly complex forms is intrinsic to the way the world actually works. The graduated ordering of the world is multi-layered, complex and elaborate in its hierarchical structuring. Layered and interrelated ordering is intrinsic to the differentiated richness of the world.

Any consideration of the concept of order will finally have to attend to the dynamics and process of growth and decay. A dynamic layered concept of order

---

23 Kuhn, 'The Case for Order', p. 445.

24 Ibid., p. 447.

25 Kuhn distinguishes between 'accidental' and 'essential' relations generated by order (ibid., p. 447). These correspond to two types of order: *ordo extrinsicus* (external order) and *ordo intrinsicus* (internal order) that are not sharply differentiated but representative of 'a scale between two extreme possibilities'. An example of the former is a pile of rubbish, of the latter, a living organism. In the former the objects in the pile might still belong together essentially when considered as 'spacial objects'. Whilst in a living organism a degree of 'independence' might still obtain for the components in the order. Again for the pile of rubbish there may be an internal order for the objects but they would not have any relation to the totality (weak interconnections). With the essentially ordered organism the internal order of the components is related to the comprehensive order. Thus we can have an 'order of orders' and successively more comprehensive orders.

26 This suggests that the task of finding new language to express the process and dynamics of order is critical in the rehabilitation of order and significance.

suggests that growth means the generation of 'higher order' whilst decay means that a higher order is replaced by a 'lower one'.[27] Recent developments in the understanding of chaos and order have provided deeper insights into the way even apparent decay can become the trigger for new emergent order. This will be followed up below.

Perhaps the most significant shift in the understanding of order in the modern period has been from an ontology of order that emphasised fixity and stability to a dynamic ontology of order that involves change, adaptation and capacity for novelty. Pre-modern notions of order funded the ancient conception of the world as an ordered domain reflecting a mythic/sacral divine realm. The Platonic realm of forms provided the metaphysical scaffolding and template for the patterning and ordering of the social world of human beings. Social forms and organizational life were the location for a mediation of deeper sacral patterns. Hierarchies below mirrored the eternal order. In such a context order was not so much discovered within the contingencies of historical existence as woven into them. The ontology of the social realm was thus stable and fixed.

In the Western tradition the breakdown of the medieval synthesis and the de-sacralisation of the prevailing metaphysical order led – at least from the seventeenth century – to a naturalising of order. The question about the transcendental source and ground of order was obscured. Order was not derived from an external preordained form but rather came to be seen as a distinctly human project,[28] something to be constructed within the social fabric of late seventeenth-century Europe. For John Locke, order was to be discerned from empirical observation, testing and measurement; for others, such as Descartes, it was more a matter of rational deduction. Immanuel Kant sought a mediation between the radical empiricism of Hume and the rationalism of Descartes, though Kant could still speak of the 'order of nature' and 'the order of things' 'in the grand traditional sense'.[29] These constructivist and naturalising approaches to order were the forebears of nineteenth-century developments. This period was full of ambiguity. On the one hand the revolt against a traditional metaphysics of order receives its sharpest form in Nietzsche's assertion of human will to power. Here the transcendental status of order has been entirely transposed into human categories. Yet, on the other hand, it is precisely in this period that seeds are sown for the remarkable developments

[27] Kuhn gives as an example of decay the situation where a population has become a coherent nation of people but then becomes a mass – a lower form of order, more manipulable and vulnerable to the imposition of an imposed order ('The Case for Order', p. 448).

[28] Insofar as the concept of order includes the human being as a creator of order this development was the natural outcome of a gradual loss of the sacred canopy and the consequent de-sacralising of the world. The emphasis shifts from the human being bounded by order to one who creates order. In the confrontation between the '*ordo ordinans* ("order ordering" – order as an active force in creating patterns)' and the '*ordo ordinates* ("order ordered" – order as already existing patterns)' the accent shifts to the former.

[29] Kuhn, 'The Case for Order', p. 443.

in biological evolution. The human being is both creator and discoverer of the implicate order of living organisms.

With the rise of an historical consciousness and Darwinian evolutionary thought in the nineteenth century, conditions obtained in which order came to be understood as an emergent property of nature, society and human endeavour. The static ontology of order associated with an earlier classical metaphysic had given way to a naturalised, de-sacralised, historically contingent and fundamentally emergent concept of order. Traditional conceptions of order had been destabilised to the point of being overturned. The earlier stable ontology of order had, on the face of it, been replaced by a more dynamic ontology of order. Yet this revolution did not necessarily dispense with hierarchies, though the direction was quite different: no longer top-down but rather from the bottom up. Order as an intrinsic relational feature of life re-emerges from below.

Order and the Science of Emergence

The problem of order, its origins, identification and continuing significance has remained on the agenda in the twentieth century through advances in the sciences.[30] In particular the modern period of the sciences has been the principal means for uncovering the richly dynamic implicate order of the world and human life. A particularly good example of this is in the area of evolutionary biology. Here the concept of order is linked to the emergence of successively higher levels of complexity in living organisms. More complex orders emerge which evidence and rely upon continuities with less complex forms. Yet these higher levels also evidence properties that cannot be explained by what has preceded them. New order evidencing novelty and discontinuity emerges through continuities. Higher levels of complex self-organization have what is described as 'emergent' properties. Scientist and theologian, Arthur Peacocke, describes the process thus:

> For the processes of the world exhibit an intelligible continuity in which the potentialities of its constituents are unfolded in forms of ever-increasing complexity and organization. These forms are properly described as 'emergent' in that they manifest new features which are irreducible to the sciences which describe that out of which they have developed. That qualitatively new kinds of existence come into being is one of the striking aspects of natural becoming. We witness the seeming paradox of discontinuity generated by continuity.

[30] In the biological sciences see Ilya Prigogine and Isabelle Stengers, *Order Out of Chaos: Man's New Dialogue with Nature* (New York and London: Bantam Books, 1984); Stuart Kauffman, *The Origins of Order* (Oxford: Oxford University Press, 1993); for social institutions, see, for example, Dennis Wrong, *The Problem of Order* (London: Harvard University Press, 1994).

> For nature adopts new forms of being that appear to be discontinuous, *at least in some respects*, with those from which they originate (my italics).[31]

Peacocke develops the theological trajectory of this insight from evolutionary biology:

> Hence belief in God as creator involves the recognition that this is the character of the processes whereby God actually creates new forms, new entities, structures and processes that emerge with new capabilities, requiring distinctive language on our part to distinguish them. God is present in and to this whole process whose discontinuities are grounded in its very continuities.[32]

The identification of 'emergent properties' in higher levels of complex organization implies a move beyond 'naïve reductionism' for 'the physiochemical investigator of living systems is again and again baffled by the lack of conceptual resources in received physics and chemistry to deal with such complexity [of living organisms] and with the demanding intellectual need for new ones'.[33]

As a complement to the process of emergence is the notion of 'top-down causality' or 'whole–part influence'. This has been posited to explain the way in which the parts of an evolving system – 'dissipative systems' that manifest 'order

---

[31] Arthur Peacocke, *Theology for a Scientific Age* (London: SCM Press, 1993), pp. 300–301.

[32] Ibid, p. 301.

[33] Arthur Peacocke, *God and the New Biology* (London: J.M. Dent & Sons, 1986), p. 27. For a careful and insightful discussion of different kinds of reductionism (methodological and epistemological) see chs. 1 and 2. In particular Peacocke describes three types of reduction. (a) 'Plain reductionism … when higher-level theories are reducible and higher-level processes are not autonomous'. This strong form of epistemological reductionism is indistinguishable from 'ontological reductionism' – all is reduced to physiochemical levels. (b) 'Non-reduction whereby not only are the higher-level theories non-reducible to lower-level ones but the higher-level processes are autonomous with respect to lower-level process'. This strong form of non-reduction ('strong organism') is open to the charge of 'vitalism' whereby a non-material cause has to be postulated in the higher-level system. (c) A 'weak' form of non-reduction 'when the higher-level processes are not autonomous (that is, the regularities of the higher-level processes are fully consistent with the laws of the lower-level processes) but the higher-level theories themselves are not reducible' (see pp. 18–19). Peacocke seeks a non-reductivist and non-vitalist account of living organisms. This means that he subscribes to the general position of scientists that nothing is 'added' to atoms and molecules when they 'adopt the complex organization which is characterised by living' (p. 11). On the other hand this does not imply for him that biological organisms are 'nothing but' the sum of the parts of atoms and molecules. In other words such complexes have 'emergent properties' not reducible to the constituent parts.

through fluctuations'[34] – are constrained to develop in certain patterns or order due to the influence of the whole upon the parts. Peacocke describes it thus:

> The notion of causality, when applied to systems, has usually been assumed to describe 'bottom-up' causation – that is, the effect on the properties and behaviour of the system of the properties and behaviour of its constituent parts. However, an influence of the state of the system as a whole on the behaviour of its component units – a constraint exercised by the whole on its parts – has to be recognised.[35]

Such influence has been variously described – 'downward' or 'top-down' causation – though Peacocke refers to it as 'whole–part constraint'. He cites the example of the Bernard phenomenon where individual molecules in a hexagonal cell, 'beyond a critical point'

> move with a common component of velocity in a coordinated way, having previously manifested only entirely random motions with respect to each other. In such instances, the changes at the micro-level, that of the constituent units, are what they are because of their incorporation into the system as a whole, which is exerting specific constraints on its units, making them behave otherwise than they would in isolation.[36]

The relationships between the constituent parts considered as a whole complex are new. The nature of their interactions is influenced by virtue of their incorporation into a complex whole which itself remains relatively open to more comprehensive determination from, for example, the wider environment. Peacocke argues for a complementarity between bottom-up and top-down causation. The exploration of the dynamics of such complementarity remains a work in progress. However we might briefly summarise the situation in the following terms: the whole is more than the sum of the parts; the parts are generative of higher level orders that involve novelty; the operation of the parts are constrained by their constitution as parts of a whole; the whole is only what it is because the parts are constituted as

---

[34] Peacocke, *Theology for a Scientific Age*, pp. 52–3. The notion of 'dissipative systems' (from the work of Ilya Prigogine) describes how in 'far-from-equilibrium, non-linear, open systems, matter displays its potential to be self-organizing and thereby bring into existence new forms' entirely through the dynamics of such systems under the constraint of the whole as it responds to slight fluctuations generative of significant transformations of the system at higher levels (pp. 52–3).

[35] Arthur Peacocke, 'God's Interaction with the World: The Implications of Deterministic "Chaos" and of Interconnected and Interdependent Complexity', in R. Russell, N. Murphy and A. Peacocke (eds.), *Chaos and Complexity: Scientific Perspectives on Divine Action* (Indiana: University of Notre Dame Press, 2nd edn, 1997), p. 272.

[36] Ibid, p. 273.

they are. This points minimally to a notion of living organisms as a dynamically ordered set of relations in which parts and whole contribute to the constituting of the entity and its functioning.

The unresolved nature of the direction and dynamic of order, and the significance of the complementarity of the bottom-up and top-down causality is particularly evident in the contemporary inquiry into brain/mind/consciousness. The psychologist, Malcolm Jeeves argues for an 'irreducible intrinsic interdependence': 'irreducible (in the sense that to get rid of either [mental and physical] is to tell less than the whole story) intrinsic (in the sense that it is part of the way the world is) interdependence (the mental and physical are correlated and complementary)'.[37] Interestingly the one uncontested result of the above developments is the fundamentally integrative nature of all orders of life. What is equally remarkable is the capacity for novelty that erupts from within deeply integrative sequences of complex biological development.

Developments in contemporary physics reveal a quantum world that is both resistant to ordering and expressive of an implicate order amidst chaos. Chaos and order appear to be reciprocally related: order has its 'seeds in the realm of chaos' and 'just as a smoothly operating machine can become chaotic when pushed too hard (chaos out of order), it also turns out that chaotic systems can give birth to regular, ordered behaviour (order out of chaos)'.[38] Instability appears to be the pre-condition for the emergence of new order. Thus not only is novelty integrally related to continuity; dynamic order is predicated upon the operation of chaotic systems and indeterminacy. It is relevant from natural biological systems to complex social systems and their organizational life.[39]

Conclusion: The Dynamic Ontology of Order

The dynamic ontologies of order revealed by the modern sciences raise questions for theological reflection about the nature of the world and divine agency. The dynamic and integrative world of the sciences is not inimical to deep ordering and patterns. On the contrary the latter seem to feed off such dynamism. The insights of the sciences have also had an impact upon the social sciences and the understanding of the social evolution of human communities and organizations.[40]

---

[37] Malcolm Jeeves, 'Toward a Composite Portrait of Human Nature', in Malcolm Jeeves, (ed.), *From Cells to Souls – and Beyond* (Grand Rapids: Eerdmans, 2004), p. 240.

[38] David Peat, *From Certainty to Uncertainty: The Story of Science and Ideas in the Twentieth Century* (Washington: Joseph Henry Press, 2002), p. 124, see also p. 136 for reference to 'seeds'.

[39] Ibid, pp. 143–5.

[40] See the excellent discussion of the application of the insights of modern science to institutional life by Margaret J. Wheatley, *Leadership and the New Science: Discovering Order in a Chaotic World* (San Francisco: Berret-Koehler, 1999).

Resilience, as the capacity to adapt and transform whilst maintaining a measure of *homeostasis* within rapidly changing environments, is a central feature of dynamically ordered systems.[41] Identity and continuity of institutional life is achieved through the complex interplay of the parts and whole of a system and fluctuations (perturbations) generative of new relations of order.[42] This can be challenging for 'Newtonian organizations in a quantum age' where sharp boundaries, poor information flow and inability to adapt, seriously impede the ability of an institution to fulfil its purpose. Dynamically ordered systems with richly interrelated rather than disjunctive and/or implosive structures require and are constituted by similar interrelated and dynamic forms of leadership.[43]

Minimally the above reflections on the concept of order in the contemporary sciences suggests that the question of the ordering of ecclesial life and its ministries may have much to gain from a creative interaction with the best insights of the other disciplines. This matter is the subject of the following chapter.

---

[41] Richard Newbold Adams, *The Eighth Day: Social Evolution as the Self-Organization of Energy* (Austin: University of Texas Press, 1988), p. 25.

[42] Ibid, p. 65, drawing on the work of Ilya Prigogine.

[43] Wheatley, *Leadership and the New Science*, ch. 2.

Chapter 9
One of Another: Dynamics of Collaborative Ministry

Ecclesial Ministries: A Set of Dynamically Ordered Relations

Forms of Ministerial Reductionism

The insights of Chapter 8 provide a rich framework for consideration of the relations between the ministries of the Church. How are they instances of a 'mode of togetherness' and what is the character of this togetherness? The disjunctive and dissipative forms of ministry outlined in Chapter 7 arise from a fundamental failure in the dynamic ordering of the ministries. The disjunctive relation – that is, ministries of ordained and lay function on parallel tracks – is undergirded by a static ontology that is unable to conceive how the emergence of novel ordering might be integrally related to the ministries that called it forth. Two things result. First, new ministries tend to be rejected or diminished because they cannot easily be integrated into the existing pattern of ordered ministry. Second a form of 'ministerial vitalism' is created based on the need to inject new order (novelty) into a system from 'outside'. An ordered ministry appears from outside the system seemingly by divine fiat. It arises from a rather wooden and mechanical form of revelation. The true naturalness of ministry in the body of Christ is obscured.

The problem of a disjunctive relation between the ministries was a problem associated in Chapter 4 with the Anglican R.C. Moberly's theory of apostolic succession. At first sight Moberly's theory of ministry appears to be a case of 'top-down' causality. However it betrays a failure to recognise and integrate the possibility of new order as an emergent property of the system. This is the problem of vitalism: an injection of external input is required to generate dynamism and life. It is fundamentally dualistic and cannot give an adequate account of the inner relations between the parts of the ministerial system. It is thus an overly simple explanation of complex ordering. This is characteristic of a disjunctive approach to the ministries driven by Christology without an accompanying Pneumatology. Such an approach inevitably fails to show how a rich complementarity obtains between emergent 'bottom-up', and 'top-down' processes for the ordering the ministries. It cannot show how the relations between the ministries are necessarily irreducible, intrinsic, and interdependent. The clerical/lay divide remains entrenched. As argued in Chapter 7 whilst the one Christ establishes the ordained ministries and is also the foundation for the common ministries these two domains of ministries operate in parallel. As we saw in Chapter 7 this is analogous to the age-old problem of the relations between the humanity and divinity of Christ.

The disjunctive relation between the ministries is fuelled by a fear of reductionism in which the higher orders of ministry are explained solely by reference to 'lower orders' – less complex forms of ordering within the whole. This is combated by an over-emphasis on a top-down derivation of the traditional orders. Yet this is not genuine top-down causality for it provides no basis for an integrative understanding of the ministries at different levels of ordering. As observed in the previous chapter genuine whole–part influence operates on the premise that the higher level can only be what it is because the less complex forms upon which it ('the order that orders') acts are already what they are. The dynamic is mutually sustaining. But this dynamic cannot be incorporated into a disjunctive understanding of ministry. Instead what occurs is a form of 'episcopal vitalism' – something added from outside the system. The vitalistic account of the ministry 'from above' can still appeal to concepts of emergence but it does not generate genuine novelty but a determinism from below.[1]

Where the relations between the ministries are constantly in danger of imploding (such as in Pentecostalism) the real problem is the inability of the ordering to maintain itself; it collapses back into more inchoate and diffuse forms. The dynamism is truncated and not fully realised for it is unable to reach higher levels of determinacy. Fluctuations in the system generate significant instability and drive the system into chaotic behaviour. Whilst this might conceivably become the occasion for new ordering to arise, the system dynamic is thwarted in its full operation. Possibilities for newer more complex and higher level ordering

---

[1] See Chapter 8, n. 33 regarding the concept of vitalism and Chapter 4 for the Anglican debate in the late nineteenth century. For a contemporary Roman Catholic argument along these lines see Martin, *The Feminist Question*, p. 109. Martin, appeals to an analogy from evolutionary biology for the development of the episcopal office. Martin invokes 'the model of a living organism that in its origins contains in an undifferentiated mode all that it needs to achieve its identity'. Office belongs 'to the intrinsic genetic code of the church'; the actual development of the office belongs to non-genetic (epigenetic) factors, for example, cultural factors in time and space. Martin sees similarities with another analogy from music wherein the score represents the 'basic genetic network' that needs to be performed by a company of musicians (epigenetic factors). The strength of this account of the emergence of ordered ministries is that it is able to recognise fluidity and diversity. What it cannot give an account of is the eruption of genuine novelty. The problem is not simply that Martin has ignored sociological analysis in favour of a biological model (See Stephen Sykes, 'To the Intent that these Orders may be Continued', p. 55) but rather that his use of the model is too simple yet delivers too much (women are necessarily excluded from office). The possibility of genuine novelty appearing through 'bottom-up' emergence – of discontinuity generated by continuity – and 'top-down causality' undermines the homogenous evolutionary model implied by Martin. Both Martin and the Anglican Moberly appeal to notions of emergence as a defence of traditional catholic orders. But their approaches do not provide a rationale for collaborative and mutually enriching relations among the ministries.

cannot arise where the whole operates as a flat hierarchy and there is a systemic refusal for higher levels of differentiation. What appears at first sight as a strongly dynamic system in fact turns out to be highly reductionist in its operation. Multiple orders of ministries continually emerge and return to their originative source. It is a unidirectional dynamic.

When, as in forms of Pentecostalism, there is fear of a controlling top-down ministry of the ministries (for example, mono-episcopacy) this acts to sublimate the potential energies of the ministries. They remain locked in underdeveloped systems susceptible to any perturbation, lacking the quality of resilience, easily assimilated into and transformed by the impacting environment. In short the dynamic is truncated, the ordering is immature and the relations between the ministries are neither perdurable nor sustainable but continually metamorphose into new forms lacking discernible continuities with their former constituents. Such a system also relies upon a form of 'Spirit vitalism' from *outside* to remain a living ecclesial form of life. The implosion of the ministries and lack of sustainable differentiations can only be overcome by a dualism between Spirit and matter. It is thus not surprising that, in order to compensate for this default in the system, contemporary Pentecostalism places renewed emphasis upon the higher order ministry of 'apostle' and the appointment of such ministries through the outside agency of the Spirit.[2]

Dynamically Ordered Ministries

A more richly ordered system would allow for the emergence of orders for the ordering of ministries. Such higher-level ministries would (a) have oversight of the ministries, (b) influence the pattern and expression of ministries, (c) be constituted in part by the diversity of the charismata, but (d) not be fully explained by reference to them. What would a 'more richly ordered system' look like? This is a critical issue for the churches today. In Part IV of this book I develop a relational ontology of orders (Chapter 10) and in that context articulate a 'grounded episcopate' (Chapters 11 and 12) as an example of how a more integrative and personal ordering of the ministries might work. In this conception a renewed catholicity from below necessarily connects different ecclesial traditions of order at more local levels where ecumenical work has a priority.

Ecclesial ministries that are dynamic ordered relations exhibit similar features to the ordering of complex entities observed in the discussion of the concept of order in the sciences in Chapter 8. The fundamentally integrative nature of their relations is not inimical to the emergence of more complex forms of ministry. Indeed, the broader ministries give birth to more complex levels of ministerial forms

---

[2] It is interesting that even here a quasi mechanical apostolic succession can be invoked to give confidence of the Spirit's anointing. For example the Houston blood line (from father to son) has a special place in the emergence and growth of Hillsong Pentecostal Church in Australia.

that are in continuity with the diverse charismata. The latter provide the building blocks for the emergence of the former. In the social evolution of complex entities such as an ecclesial system the emergence of ministerial office does represent genuine novelty in the system. Episcopacy is one important example.[3] But the precondition is the operation of ministries that contributed to the expansion and increasing complexity of the system. Ministerial offices cannot be reduced to their constituent parts –that is, those ministries that funded their creation, but nor can they be what they are without the presence and existence of the ministries.

Ministries at all levels are co-related, integrally and dynamically linked and in this way truly establish each other. They exhibit a genuine complementarity between an emergent ministerial order and a 'top-down' influence. Thus those higher level ministries act in such a way that the energy of the various ministries is released and directed for the purposes of the whole ecclesial system. The higher order ministries are thus confirmed in their purpose and significance as the 'lower ordered' ministries fulfil themselves in accord with the purpose of the whole. In this way the orders of ministry establish each other and foster each others' work and purpose. Thus can it be truly said that the ministry of the higher orders and the orders that brought them forth bring each other to be.

The above discussion suggests that ministries ought not be driven by fear of reductionism (that is, the Catholic fear of loss of essential order) and overcompensate by strong top-down bossing. Nor ought they be driven by fear of 'top-down' control (Pentecostal fear of sublimation by a dominant order) and thus reject the emergence of higher order oversight. Rather the ministries are irreducible, intrinsic and interdependent. All forms of vitalism are eschewed. The vitalities of the ministries are embedded *within* the system.[4] Theologically we might say that the transcendent agency of the Spirit is immanent within the natural ecclesial system generating a cruciform pattern of order. It is after all the Spirit of the crucified and ascended Christ that is present to and within the ecclesia. This points to an immanent Trinitarianism as the ultimate basis for ecclesial ministries. It also suggests that Christian ministry requires a doctrine of creation as much as a doctrine of redemption. But more of this below.

The inner relation between the ministries sketched above is what one ought to expect for an evolving social system that follows the general pattern exhibited in the world seen through evolutionary biology, physics and the social sciences. The central feature in these different but related domains is the operation of a dynamic ontology of order in which new orderings and novelty are woven into deep continuities. A further consequence is that the orderings of ministry are open

---

[3] For a discussion of the novelty of the episcopate in the ancient world see Robin Lane Fox, *Pagan and Christians* (London: Penguin Books, 1988), ch. 10, 'Bishops and Authority'.

[4] Though here we are clearly talking about a system that is open rather than closed, capable of regeneration and expansion through interaction with its environment and life-giving agency as the transcendental ground of system and environment.

to new development as in any adaptive system. The adaptation is successful if new forms emerge that both resonate with pre-existing forms yet engender new capacity for the system to expand. Ministries as a set of dynamically ordered relations is not a code for capacity to maintain a steady-state but rather points to a basic resilience in the system to respond creatively to new disturbances and information.

The Task of a Theology of Ministry

From this perspective the task of a theology of ministry is twofold. First, to uncover and clarify the nature and dynamic of the implicate order that resources the ministries. Second, to follow that dynamic as it informs the actual economy of ministry. The supposition here is that the transcendent source of order and novelty is immanent to the system exercising a whole–part influence *from within*. This source of all order and 'the *principium ordinis ordinantis* ("principle of the order that orders") is not the totality of the natural world, but rather its transcendental ground'.[5] The condition for the possibility that the source of order can be both transcendent *and* immanent within the system; indeed, that it is precisely *through* immanence that the transcendent ground of order is constituted as such, is what has to be specified in the doctrine of God. God's own economy, that is, God's maximal way of being for and in the created order, is the transcendent ground for the world's order. But clearly this divine economy of order does not conform to a simple linear causation. Rather 'God is a dynamic structured relationality in whom there is an infinite possibility of life'.[6] The divine fullness of order, its richness and freedom, which is irreducible, intrinsic and interdependent, is what is continually conferred upon the created order. This is the form of God's order that constitutes the possibilities for the expansive and perfecting order of the world.

The coordinates for uncovering the form and character of this implicate order of creation are elusive and resistant to full thematisation. The fundamental clues to this economy of divine ordering can be traced in the interrelation of the narrative of the life of the incarnate Logos and the vitalities of the Spirit (e.g., 1 Cor. 15:45). A question necessarily arises: How, in the economy of the divine being, is it possible that the world revealed in, for example, the modern sciences finds a deep consonance with the story of Jesus and the life of the Spirit? One possible response is to say that these twin coordinates embody the energetic order of the divine life. As such they confer life, order, and new possibilities for transformed existence upon the whole of creation.

The ministries of the ecclesia of this God are called to recognise and call attention to the trace of God's energetic and holy order. As the ministries of the church serve this implicit divine order they enable the church to realise itself as the embodiment and witness to the reality of God in the world. But the ministries cannot do this if they are not properly coordinated as instantiations of God's own

---

5 Kuhn, 'The Case for Order', p. 457.

6 Hardy, *God's Ways with the World*, p. 81.

ordering, that is, intrinsically related in a 'mode of togetherness' such that they raise each other to the fullness of the ministry of each. As the ministries are so interrelated they become participants in God's own energetic ordering of the Church for the world. To this extent the ministry and the ministries can be genuine mediations of God's own holy order.

Ministries 'One of Another': Listening to Scripture

A question inevitably arises: how helpful is the forgoing somewhat general and formal conceptual framework for understanding the ministries of the Christian Church? For example, what insight does it offer for the Pauline conception of the body of Christ as 'members, one of another' (Rom. 12:5)? How, at the local level, is it possible for 'members one of another' to share in *ministries* 'one of another'? How might it inform many of the internal tensions, for example, between ordained and lay ministry within particular churches? Could such an approach provide a fresh basis for dialogue across divided communions concerning the recognition of ministries? The value of a general theory is that it ought to be serviceable across a range of issues offering conceptual tools for analysis and hopefully be a catalyst for new approaches. A general theory does not immediately solve intractable problems nor is it a cure-all. But it might have healing properties if properly administered. In the present case a general theory of collaborative ministry ought to be able to show how the churches in their internal and ecumenical life can find deeper reconciliation through renewed common ordering of the ministries.

Ministries 'One of Another': A New Twist on the Body Metaphor

An interesting example of the way the above approach to ministry finds resonance with contemporary reading of Scripture is offered by the Oxford ethicist, Bernard Wannenwetsch in his politico-ecclesial reading of Romans 12:1–8. Wannenwetsch explores 'the deconstructive potential of the politics of God as enacted in the life of the Church' for the reshaping of secular ethics.[7] He does this through a careful examination of an 'in-house' text of the Christian community of Rome, which has traditionally been recognised as beginning the ethical part of Paul's letter and which he argues has a decided political ethic. He focuses on the idea of representation. This concept is a key to the apostle's understanding of the ministries of the ecclesia and is also 'central to any account of political authority'. The supposition is that the dynamics of representation in the community of faith might offer clues for the way political authority might be reconceived and practised in the secular realm. What is of particular interest for my purposes is the dynamic between the ministries uncovered by Wannenwetsch. In the opening verses of Romans 12, Paul outlines the way in which the different members of the one body serve the body through the

[7] Wannenwetsch, 'Members of One Another', p. 197.

gifts God has given. 'Having gifts that differ according to the grace given to us, let us use them: if prophecy, in proportion to our faith' (Rom. 12:6). The intention is not so much ranking or weighing the gifts (in proportion to a quantum of faith) but acknowledging that the charismata are diverse and distributed through faith.[8]

However, the key text for my purposes is the preceding one: 'so we, though many, are one body in Christ, and individually members of one another [*kath hei allelon mele*]' (Rom. 12:5). What James Dunn calls 'a slightly odd variation of the body metaphor', Wannenwetsch suggests is a 'transgression of its natural logic' for while 'we can imagine what it is to be members of the same body, to be a member *of someone else*, as Paul phrases it, can hardly be understood within the logic of the body metaphor'.[9] Thus we miss the point if we simply hear the apostle 'summoning the Christians to actively play their part, to accept their assigned role and fulfil their ministry'.[10] The thrust of the passage moves in another direction 'as it aims at the recognition of the ministry of *others*'. Yet even here the emphasis is not simply one of 'allowing others to be part of the community, to have a task, role and place in their own right. He goes much further in ascribing to them the dignity of becoming part of ourselves: "members of one another".'[11] For Wannenwetsch this is a 'description of the political existence of the body of Christ that is as intriguing as it is radical'.[12] It is equally intriguing and radical for the doctrine of ministry per se.

The relational dynamics here are important. At one level accepting the *charism* of another is more difficult than to accept another's weakness for the latter case gives opportunity for the expression of strength, whereas the former case can easily degenerate into a competition as to whose *charism* is more important. Yet Paul moves beyond merely acknowledging another's charisma to one of delight (following Luther) in 'accepting the ministry of the other *towards* myself'.[13] This is a radical challenge that goes beyond our 'natural human instinct to protect ourselves from each other' precisely because it appears to undermine the baptismal equality of the Christian community in asserting that some are to be prophets, teachers and so on in ways in which others are not. This might work well enough in a culture of the 'expert' where differentiation and specialization means that people express their capacities in different ways. Though the underside of this is an unwillingness to accept the authority of another if it touches on my own expertise. Yet in the Christian community the baptismal equality of all does not negate the importance and necessity of the exercise by particular persons of special ministries such as teachers and prophets. The 'claim that there should be special ministries (offices) and representations is not self-evident in a community where *the* ministry belongs

8 Ibid., p. 209.

9 Ibid., p. 210.

10 Ibid.

11 Ibid.

12 Ibid.

13 Ibid.

to the whole body as a whole'.[14] In the light of the fundamentally inclusive nature of ministry (e.g., 1 Cor. 14:29, 31) 'it is not an easy lesson to learn that there should be still "some" to represent it, some who are given a specific authority over the others in a particular sphere'.[15] Yet for the Pauline charismatic communities this is precisely the lesson to be learnt: 'the political life of the church is not solely built on charisma or 'natural authority'. Besides charisma there is 'pure' political authority which calls forth 'the acceptance of the special ministry or office of others'.[16] Yet all share in the ministries and are ultimately 'collaborators' in the joy of ministry (2 Cor. 1:24). Wannenwetsch concludes that 'it is exactly this acceptance of mutual representation that allows the church to become the community of discernment that probes and explores God's will (Rom. 12:2)'.[17]

The emphasis is thus *not* on the 'membership of *the other* in the body' – for example, whether we like them or not or have regard for their gifts – but something more radical. What is at stake, following John Chrysostom, is a question of amputating ourselves from the body by our pride. Thus by the denial of the principle of mutual representation we jeopardise our very own possession and share in the body. Wannenwetsch draws attention to the reflexive nature of representation whereby it 'denotes a presentation of something which is already there'.[18] Thus 'ministry does not create order but presupposes it'. In this sense the ministry is called forth by something given – the order present through God's primary forming of the community. Extending this argument we can say that the ministry called forth in turn re-presents this in order to enrich and bring the implicate order of God's life to be the marks whereby the Church lives. Yet representation does not mean 'exclusive ownership'; rather 'the individual minister is but a personal reference to the presence of the charisma of the whole body'.[19] The lie to any individualistic understanding of the ministries is exposed, for if the individual were 'the only one to have a particular charisma she could not *re*-present it' since there 'would be no "re-" no presence to refer to apart from her own personal gift'.[20] This means that the one exercising a '*charisma* to others' is 'exactly witnessing to the commonality of the charisma'. Hence the 'specific unfolding of the ministry into several offices is not a function of the specific *charismata* of the individuals'.[21]

14 Ibid., p. 211.

15 Ibid.

16 Ibid.

17 Ibid.

18 Ibid., p. 212.

19 Ibid.

20 Ibid., p. 213.

21 Ibid. Wannenwetsch gives an example: 'The office of a teacher is not established because one member or a few members of the congregation happen to be just so pedagogically gifted. Rather, God has established "teaching", the particular praxis of making the rationality of the Christian faith intelligible to one another because grace is, among other things, instructive grace; thus, the ministry of teaching is a *charis*, a gift of

Accordingly the charismata 'are not the property of the ministers as officeholders but the possession of the Church, a possession which makes it into a society'.[22] Finally, we note that representative ministry is directed beyond the maintenance of the Church to the Lordship of Christ.

Towards a General Theory of Collaborative Ministry: Preliminary Observations

Ministries One of Another

The above account of the inner relations of the ministries 'one of another' is a particular example of the argument developed above for ministries as a set of dynamically ordered relations. The ministries of the body are not vicarious but properly re-presentative; they are co-present to each other; each ministry is received by others as a ministry which is a part of the other. The ministries subsist within the body; they are re-presented to and for the body that it might become what it is; they are thus expressive of the being of the whole body but yet are brought to be by that body. The basis for genuinely collaborative and interdependent ministry is grounded in the *charis* of God expressed in interrelated but differentiated forms.

The dynamic that makes ministries 'one of another' operates at both micro (highly localised) and macro levels of the Church. The social evolution of the Church is generative of increasingly complex networks and levels of ministry. A differentiated representative ministry does then constitute novelty at higher levels of complexity. Its reach and ambit introduces new emergent properties of order. The 'order that orders' that emerges at more complex levels of ecclesial organization evidences both continuity with the diverse ministries and also embodies new possibilities for the Church to realise its mission. The emergent 'order that orders' does not imply diminution of the relational dynamic identified in the ministries 'one of another'. Rather, this dynamic adapts itself in such a way that all the ministries can endure, expand and enrich the being and witness of the Church to the gospel. In other words, higher levels of complexity ought to generate even richer forms of relation and interdependent ministries. Ministries remain 'one of another' throughout the fluctuations and disturbances of the ecclesial world; indeed, it is only as the ministries are dynamically ordered as outlined above that the resilience and freedom of the Church to bear its marks (one, holy, catholic and apostolic) can occur.

The implications of the foregoing for the inner coherence and vitalities of the ministries of particular churches, local communities of faith and the exercise

---

God to the whole body and which awakens different charismata in different members, often but not always by ordaining natural talents to serve the *oikodome* of the whole body' (ibid., p. 213).

22 Ibid.

of common ministries across the ecclesial divides ought not be underestimated. Ministries as dynamically ordered relations; representative ministries as emergent from the wider charismata yet influencing the ordering of less complexly ordered ministries; all ministries interdependent and irreducible; acting upon one another as if *each were not their own*; not self-constituting but constituted both *from* and *toward* another; indeed bent towards the other to release their outward directed energy; such features of properly ordered ministries are a necessary corollary of the nature of the transcendent ground of order which is nothing less than the economy of God in the world.

The dynamic of order uncovered in the biological and social worlds offers genuine insight into the way of order in the ecclesial world precisely because such interlocking realities are modes and means through which the economy of God's order is manifest. This, at least, is the fundamental theological axiom undergirding a Trinitarian doctrine of creation. The coordinates for this way of God in the world are rich and transformative, energetic and ordered, personal and universal. The Christian community has glimpses of this 'bright mystery'[23] of God in the face of Jesus Christ and the life-giving presence of the Spirit. As the ordered ministries of the ecclesia of God are shaped and directed by these coordinates they too bear witness to a highly complex and specific form of participation in God's active work bringing all things to their fulfilment in the kingdom of the triune God (1 Cor. 15:24–8). Indeed, from this perspective ecclesial ministries have a remarkable reach and sphere of influence. Yet the Church has barely begun to scratch the surface of the possibilities embedded in its very life. Ministries that serve the gospel of God represent a witness not merely to the ends of the earth (extensive) but richly into every domain of the created order (intensive).

Ministries that Bring Each Other To Be

How then, from a practical point of view, do such ministries belong to one another in such a way that they can be said to 'bring each other to be'? The dynamic identified in this chapter suggests quite simply that, for example, the wider ministries of the whole people of God bring the ministries of the more 'complex' orders (traditional offices) to be in so far as they fulfil their own calling and purposes within the ecclesia in relation to the 'order that orders'. It is not a question of encouraging the bishop, priest or deacon in their job, supporting, praying and so on. These may be all worthy and important activities. But the ministries of the people do not *do things for* ordained ministries in order to strengthen and raise these orders to their full stature in Christ. Rather, as parts of the whole ecclesia, they bring the orders to be as they *fulfil* their own ministries. In this way the ministries of the corporate priesthood *confirm* the ministries of oversight, teaching and gathering. This confirming is a rich bestowal of grace and strength for those ministries that facilitate and coordinate the work of the people of God. This aspect needs to be

23 Hardy, *God's Ways with the World*, pp. 17–19.

stressed because the usual emphasis is on how the ordained ministry enhances and facilitates the wider ministries of the Church. But the ministerial dynamic is *fully* relational and it is intrinsic to this kind of 'mode of togetherness' that neither ordained nor other ecclesial ministries can be what they are or shall be *without the other*. Ministry as a collaborative and coordinating activity of the Church is a condition of it being a ministry ordered according to the gospel. This is the inner logic of my earlier reflections. It implies an inclination or bending of each towards the other as a mode of recognition of the ministerial bond in Christ.

Ecumenical Implications

At the ecumenical level this suggests that the churches across the ecclesial spectrum will make little progress as long as they remain locked in paradigms for the recognition of ministries that reflect static ontologies, sharp boundaries and a fundamental inability to grasp the secret of their own inner life in the gospel that calls forth a richly differentiated and interdependent ministry. The general theory of ministry outlined above may provide some conceptual tools for the reconciliation of the ministries at all levels of the Church's life. For example, it may radically change the kind of criteria invoked in ecumenical dialogues concerning the recognition of ministries. It may become less a question of ministerial validity and purity of pedigree and more a question of faithfulness to the deeper dynamics of the ministries both *intra* and *inter* Church.

This suggests some different questions for the churches. How might the various churches give an account of the ministries as dynamically ordered relations within their own communion? What corrections and modifications might they first need to attend to before making judgements in respect to their dialogue partners? On the much vexed question of 'universal primacy' the above discussion suggests that an emergent primacy *may* be 'a gift to be shared',[24] but it would be a gift that looks very different from anything that presently obtains. Appeals to synodality and collegiality cannot deliver a new kind of primatial authority without a major re-ordering of the life of a communion (new wine cannot go into old wineskins; Matt. 9:17). Within a dynamically emergent ecclesial system the gift of authority would involve a radical 'relational primacy'. The churches are light years away from such a polity. Moves in such a direction will only come as the religious life of Christian communities undergo significant theological and ecclesial reconstitution.

The foregoing ought to provide a common basis for a deeper reconciliation of the ministries, in which the ecclesial spectrum, from Pentecostal to Catholic, may discover a richer framework for their common ministries which remain fundamentally incomplete without the other.

---

[24] See *The Gift of Authority: Authority in the Church 111*. An Agreed Statement by the Anglican–Roman Catholic International Commission (London and New York: Catholic Truth Society and Church Publishing, 1998), par. 60.

Sharing ministries 'one of another' takes us into the deepest reaches of the economy of God whose remarkable ordering and transforming order in Christ and the Spirit beckons the Church to new places for the sake of the gospel. How such a general theory of collaborative ministry might unfold in the context of traditional orders of ministry and the wider mission of the Church is the subject of Parts IV and V.

PART IV
Reforming Orders

Chapter 10
A Relational Ontology of Orders: Some Implications for Practice

Introduction: The Collaborative Order

Christian ministry takes its cue from the gospel of Jesus Christ through the power of the Spirit. These twin coordinates for a doctrine of ministry provide a theological basis for a fully relational and interdependent theory of ministry within the body of Christ. However, our brief excursion into the recent history of the development of ministry (Part II) has also revealed tensions and trends that continue in the present period. More often, as observed in Part I, these tensions can be traced to different emphases; either the doctrine of Christ (Christology) or the Spirit (Pneumatology). An over-ordered, 'stand alone' ministry is characteristically associated with a strong emphasis on Christology. Where Pneumatology undergirds ministry an open-ended and undifferentiated ministry is more common. The quest for an integrative account of the ministries of the Church has remained difficult to achieve, indeed elusive (Chapter 7).

However, our discussion showed that a genuinely relational and interdependent theology of ministry is a feature of a dynamic Trinitarianism informed by both Christology and pneumatology. This latter approach provides the foundations for a truly collaborative theory of ministry. Moreover, a certain consonance was discovered between such a theory of ministry and the dynamic of order located within creation as such (Chapter 8 and 9). The science of emergence provided an important clue to establish this correspondence between the redemptive ministry of the Church and the dynamic of order operating within the world. The relations between the ministries – the forms of complex order between the ministries and their interdependence – found a resonance in the science of emergence in the natural and social world.

Christian ministry may be focused on redemption but its dynamic is founded in the work of God's Spirit in creation. The reason is that the Spirit that gives life, form and structure to a complex world – as evidenced in the ways in which, at micro- and macro-levels life is intrinsically interconnected and differentiated – is the same Spirit at work in the generation of energetic social structure in the ecclesia of God. Collaborative structuring of life is inbuilt into the system as such. Its ecclesial form is a particular instance of the sociality that necessarily inheres in God's creation. On this account a collaborative theory of ministry is inherent in the character of the triune God present in creation and redemption. This is the inner logic of our earlier reflections.

An important conclusion of the above discussion was that the ministry of the Church is intrinsically collaborative if it embodies the *missio Dei* in the world in both its originative and redemptive moments. What this means practically is that neither ordained nor other ecclesial ministries can be what they are *without the other*. Ministry as a collaborative and coordinating activity of the Church of Jesus Christ is a condition of it being a ministry ordered according to the gospel. This may be an unsurprising conclusion. However, the course of Church history and many of the contemporary confusions of the Church regarding its ministries point to a poorly conceived notion of collaboration, usually invoked for pragmatic reasons but lacking strong theological foundations.

A question arises for a theology of Holy Orders in relation to the above more general theory of collaborative ministry. What implications flow from such a theory of ministry for a theology of Holy Orders? The chapters that follow (Chapters 10, 11 and 12) explore this question first, in relation to a theology of orders; second, in relation to the episcopate of the Church; and third, in relation to an ecumenical theology of the episcopate. At the heart of these reflections is what might be termed a relational ontology of orders that can be traced in both contemporary Trinitarianism and the science of emergence.

The task of reforming orders is both a theological and practical task and they are closely related. The doctrine of orders requires reforming in the light of an ontology of order developed so far. As this doctrine of orders is embodied in practice the orders of the Church will prove to be a truly reforming and renewing element in the mission of God. This chapter examines a number of issues involved in a relational theology of orders and explores some of the implications for ecclesial practice.[1]

Set Apart or Set in Place? The Dangers of a Theological Mistake

An Australian Anglican Ordinal Peculiarity

There is an important prayer in the Australian Anglican Ordinal: 'Send down the Holy Spirit upon your servant N, whom we set apart by the laying on of our hands, for the office and work of a priest in your Church.'[2] From one point of view there is nothing particularly remarkable about this prayer. Forms of it appear in most services of ordination throughout the Christian Church. In the Anglican ordinal it is an episcopal utterance: 'Here the Bishop with the priests present lay their hands on the head of each ordinand, and the Bishop says ...'.

---

1 This chapter is a significantly revised version of an earlier essay, 'Orders of Praise: Ordination, Mission and the *Missio Dei*', in William Emilsen and John Squires (eds.), *Prayer and Thanksgiving: Essays in Honour of the Revd Dr. Graham Hughes* (Sydney: UTC, 2003), pp. 87–100.

2 *A Prayer Book for Australia* (Sydney: Broughton Books, 1995), p. 796.

However, there is a slight change in the wording compared to the previous *Australian Prayer Book* of 1978.[3] A phrase has been inserted that, to the best of my knowledge, appears nowhere else in the Anglican Communion nor, for that matter, in any other ordination rite: 'Whom we set apart'. It is an intriguing insertion which, on the face of it, looks quite benign.[4] How should we interpret the notion of being 'set apart'? In the act of 'the laying on of our hands' clearly someone is being, in some sense, 'set apart'. The intention is clear: this person and not another is being singled out. But the prayer is the prayer of ordination and in that moment of recognition of the ordinand the notion of being 'set apart' is troublesome. Have we not here an unintentional example of clericalism, that most pervasive of all problems that has beset the Church, particularly in the modern period. Is it the case that in ordination the Church through its agents under God 'set apart' people? Perhaps we have here a sign of a deeper anxiety concerning the place and significance of traditional 'orders' within the life of the people of God. Clerical inflation is a well-attested strategy in times of pressure and doubt concerning identity and function. And within the framework of a prevailing clericalism there are quite significant issues concerning the divide between lay and ordained, perceptions of mission and ultimately theological issues concerning ontology, philosophy of the individual and the doctrine of God. Some of the issues surrounding this were canvassed in Chapters 2 and 3. In this chapter I hope to touch on some of these issues and inquire how the traditional 'orders' of ministry might contribute to the Church's life of praise.

In Chapter 2, I referred to the fate of 'Holy Orders' in the modern period. In that chapter and in Parts II and III, I noted that the emergence of the ministries of the whole people of God has raised fundamental issues concerning the purpose and function of those in traditional orders. Ordination and the life in 'Holy Orders' is very much a puzzle for many in the Church. Is it not time for them to be clearly 'set apart' as a means to recover and affirm their identity and relevance in a new context. This is attractive to many and has some able exponents.[5] But in this chapter I will argue that such a proposal introduces significant distortion into the theology of orders. But what help can we receive from the tradition regarding the purpose for orders? Can a return to the traditional rationale for orders in both the

---

3 *An Australian Prayer Book* (Sydney: AIO Press, 1978), p. 613.

4 The reason(s) for the insertion are not clear. In the General Synod papers the phrase first appears in a proof for the service of ordination for deacons sometime after mid-June 1994. By October 1994 the form of wording including 'whom we set apart by the laying on of our hands', had been agreed for deacons, priests and bishops (minutes of executive, 19 Oct. 1994). Subsequently the phrase appears in the ordinal services as agreed at the Anglican General Synod in 1995. The issue seems to revolve around the action of the bishop. Perhaps it is not so much a case of unintentional clericalism but rather heightened episcopal self-consciousness.

5 See Peter Carnley, *The Yellow Wallpaper and Other Sermons* (Sydney: HarperCollins, 2001), pp. 199–206.

Protestant and Catholic version assist in the recovery of the integrity of ministerial orders? The argument of this chapter is that the fate of Holy orders may be at root a theological problem that is tied up with the very tradition in which the orders are located.

Orders, Ontology and Function

In the Western Church two emphases – function and ontology – can be discerned in approaching questions of ministry and orders in particular.[6] At the more Catholic wing of the Church there continues a strong tradition of orders bearing ontological significance. Thus in ordination there is a change in the being of the one ordained. Henceforth such a person is different in their very person. The priesthood to which they have been called and ordained bears the sanction of the divine imprimatur and they embody in their being and life the mark of God's priest. Sacramentally this finds its focus in the priest who presides *in persona Christi* at the Eucharist.[7] Ordination in this tradition has powerful ontological weight.

At the other end of the spectrum is the highly functionalist approach that regards ordination as a commissioning in the Church (albeit under God) for the carrying out of certain important tasks in the Church. This is not construed as ontologically significant but essentially a practical matter to do with functions and distribution of ecclesial responsibilities. The notion of indelibility of orders is not nearly as important in this context and it is not unusual for people to move in and out of such functional arrangements.

Both emphases have strengths worth preserving. The more Catholic wing recognise that orders cannot be reduced to mere functionality, that those ordained are, in fact, different as a result of accepting and receiving their commission, however it may be described. Accordingly it is appropriate and necessary that the true ontological weight corresponding to God's presence and action in those

---

[6] For discussion see William J. Rademacher, *Lay Ministry: A Theological, Spiritual & Pastoral Handbook* (New York: Crossroad, 1992), pp. 91–5.

[7] *The Decree on the Ministry and Life of Priests* (*Presbyterorum Ordinis*), 7 Dec. 1965 states: 'Through that sacrament [ordination] priests by the anointing of the Holy Spirit are signed with a special character and so are configured to Christ the priest in such a way that they are able to act in the person of Christ the head' (p. 865). See Flannery (gen. ed.), *Documents of Vatican 2*, pp. 863–902. It is interesting to recall that this strong doctrine of identity of the priest with Christ has its counterpart in the Reformed tradition of Calvin in relation to the preacher who stands in the place of Christ as the Word is preached. Thus Paul Avis, quoting from Calvin's commentary on Acts (Acts 2:39) states that 'according to Calvin, God has appointed pastors and ministers "in his place, to speak as if out of his mouth"' (Avis, *The Church in the Theology of the Reformers*, p. 89. In the same vein the Second Helvitic Confession (1566), ch. 1 states: 'The Preaching of the Word of God is the Word of God'. This is a Protestant form of a full-blown ontology regarding the ministerial office.

admitted to Holy Orders be recognised and affirmed. On this view orders not only have divine sanction at a practical level it gives confidence and strength to those ordained and the people they serve.

The Protestant emphasis on function is a healthy reminder that, at the end of the day, there are jobs to be done for the good ordering of the community of faith. Furthermore, such jobs need to be properly distributed in the Church and there are some tasks and functions that are so essential that certain properly accredited persons are 'set apart' to perform them. It is not a question of ontology but of action and service pertaining to different, albeit important functions.

However, it is difficult to deny that orders concern both matters of ontology and function, of being and doing. This is the view of the Roman Catholic theologian, Walter Kasper. He argues that function and ontology (mission and character) are not genuine alternatives. He states that:

> [It is] precisely when one understands function … not (as) being an external function quality but (as) something that draws a person completely into service and seizes him [*sic*], that one can see how it stamps a person in his very nature and how it is an ontological determination of that person, and does not exist *in addition* to that person's essential relations and functions but rather *in* them. As soon as one frees oneself from a purely substantialist and 'heavy handed' ontology, which was certainly not the ontology of the great theologians of the high Middle Ages, alternatives like that between ontological and functional disappear of themselves.[8]

Kasper's view is not simply of theoretical import but has support at the level of praxis. From within Protestantism there is a veritable plethora of material these days exhorting clergy to recover the spiritual heart of their ministry through exercises and disciplines that have to do not so much with action plans, programs and fulfilment of vital tasks in the community but rather to do with contemplation, nourishing the vocation, meaningful encounter, retreat and discernment; in short, things to do with 'being' as such. Thus, whatever the official rhetoric, the fact is that at the ground the interwoven-ness of being and doing, ontology and function are relevant across the ecumenical divides regardless of the different assessments of the validity or otherwise of one another's orders.

Beyond Ontology and Function

However there are some deeper problems that have an impact upon the present state of Holy Orders in the Church of God. The first and most obvious one concerns the enduring significance of the above typology: Catholic ontology and Protestant function. Its persistence within the ecclesiastical world in an uncritical manner is remarkable. I have suggested that from a *practical* point of view the distinction

[8] Quoted in Nichols, *Holy Order*, p. 79.

may be far less relevant than commonly thought. Part of the reason for this may be the influence of a highly functionalist culture in which questions of ontology are regarded as irrelevant.

However, at an official and theological level the dualism does present difficulties regarding questions within the Church concerning mutual recognition of ministries. When this matter is pressed it is not uncommon to discover deeply ingrained views regarding the perceived deficiencies of the orders of another communion and the perceived superiority of one's own orders. This can be observed within communions as well. Thus the doctrine of apostolic succession is a point of debate and certainly difference *within* the Anglican Church. This affects how different sections of the Anglican Church regard the orders of other communions, for example, Lutheran and Roman Catholic Church.[9] Often the issue appears as simply one of judgements and disagreements concerning a communion's fidelity to historic unbroken apostolic succession. However more often the real issue concerns differing perceptions of what a priest becomes in ordination at the hands of a bishop. The ontological substrata has a magnetic-like effect on the deliberations at the surface. This may help to explain the persistence of the controversies over recognition of orders after the critical work has taken place over matters of historical continuity and apostolic succession. From the other side there is a continuing Protestant suspicion of orders within the Catholic tradition which are perceived to claim far too much ontological weight and insufficient emphasis on the ministry of the whole people of God. The unhappy dualism persists and is deep seated, practically, officially and theologically. It is for very good reason that the most problematic and unresolved area of modern ecumenical work relates to the nature of ministry and the question of orders.

A second difficulty that comes as part of the baggage of the above dualism is the pervasive and persistent problem of clericalism. Debates over Catholic ontology and Protestant function in relation to orders largely operates on the premise of the clerical paradigm, notwithstanding the developments in lay ministry. Even the notion of 'lay' ministry suggests a 'non-lay' ministry, that is, traditional orders which are the focus for the investment of the Church in training and preparation. This may be well and good though the reality is that almost all of the Church's funding for ministry education and training, and the arena for many of its continual debates, goes to those preparing for orders in the Church. It is highly problematic whether and to what extent the churches have moved beyond the clerical paradigm regarding ministry. Orders are the focus yet the conflictual nature of orders between the churches and the confusions about the nature of orders per se persist. Clericalism is the context for most of the debate. I simply note here that clericalism has a Catholic and a corresponding Protestant form. This has deep historical and theological roots but is readily apparent in the

---

[9] See *Apostolicity and Succession*. Underlying the stated ecumenical intent of this paper lies the equally significant aim of finding consensus *within* the Anglican Church's understanding of the topic.

way power operates within the traditional conception of orders. Thus the Catholic position can generate a 'Father knows best' approach and the Protestant CEO model is generative of a centralist power base.[10] In both cases other ministries have strong relations to the centre and weaker relations to each other. Collaboration is not intrinsic to either of these approaches and efforts to move in this direction encounter systemic difficulties as well as practical resistances.

A third and more systemic problem with the traditional construal of orders is not so much the fault of a poor theology but rather results from the pervasive influence of the philosophy of the individual within modern Western thought and social life. The traditional doctrines of orders are infected with this problem. Thus when it is a question of ontology and orders the individual is the focus. It is the being of the one ordained that undergoes change. Within the Protestant functionalist paradigm the emphasis is upon particular individuals who are charged to undertake certain responsibilities and tasks. All well and good, yet fundamentally in ordination the brief is for particular individuals who all too readily accept the challenge. The emergence of the charismatic leader and the consequent centralist individualist ethos of Church life is of a piece with its Catholic counterpart. Both traditions (and the varying locations along the spectrum) illustrate the all pervading effects of the philosophy of the individual. The matter is put sharply by John Zizioulas: 'ministry and ordination are not basically approached from the angle of the *concrete ecclesial community* but of the individual person (his [*sic*] "ontology" or his "function")'.[11] In our prevailing culture this generates a fundamental narcissism that exercises a latent and powerful force in the discernment of vocation for orders. Here an individual's sense of call becomes the focus and the testing of vocation is often resisted in many artful ways. Vocational affirmation becomes the critical issue rather than a considered examination of the form of a person's life and their fitness for a public ministry within the ecclesia of God. From this perspective it is the philosophy of individualism and what has been termed elsewhere as the 'acommunal bias'[12] of our society that has been

---

[10] The very energy that some have to invest in trying to devolve power and responsibility is a sign of the enduring significance of the centralist model for leadership. The dynamics of this are very interestingly uncovered in Exodus 18, which presents a case study on devolution of power and the principal of subsidiarity.

[11] Zizioulas, *Being as Communion*, p. 209. Zizioulas relates this problem more to issues to do with the separation of ministry from Christology and Trinitarian theology and the difficulty of relating the Church's ministry to that of Christ's. These theological and ecclesial issues are important and the weakness identified by Zizioulas makes the tradition far more vulnerable to the influence of the prevailing cultural of individualism.

[12] The term was used in the 1994 report *Ordination and Ministry in the Uniting Church*, p. 14 n. 3: 'By "acommunal bias" is meant the prevailing ethos of modern culture that favours individualism, competitiveness, and personal independence. What is presupposed is that the individual unit is self-contained and self- determining. In such a context, community is seen as necessary for the satisfaction of the individual, who is considered to be completely autonomous. Community is necessary but not intrinsic to being.'

and continues to be the most serious impediment to the development of a richer theology of orders in the Church of Jesus Christ.

A fourth and related problem with the traditional construal of orders concerns the dynamics of mission. When orders operate out of a clerical and individualistic paradigm, harbouring traditional historical conflicts and confusions about the present rational for their existence things do not bode well for the mission of the Church. Too much energy is consumed defending old positions, undertaking new programmes for engagement, or retreating into safe and irrelevant ecclesiastical havens. How the orders belong to the life of mission and more especially to God's mission is a moot point. What is the purpose of orders within the ecology of mission? Here is a question that is hardly ever asked let alone discussed in the Church. When it is considered the vision of mission to which orders are usually related is somewhat shrunken in appearance and decidedly ecclesiastical. How might we reconceive a theology of 'Holy Orders' that takes some of the above difficulties into account? Is there a way of mediating between traditional emphases on ontology and function, and challenges the philosophy of individualism and clericalism? Minimally, a theology of 'Holy Orders' will have to take these issues on board.

Orders within the Community of Faith: A Relational Ontology of Orders

'Send your Holy Spirit upon your servant N, whom we set apart.' In ordination does the Church under God 'set apart' priests? A Catholic twist would suggest that setting apart has ontological weight and a Protestant interpretation would see the setting apart as a very important act for the sake of undertaking special and urgent tasks. However the notion of being set apart, notwithstanding the best intentions in the world, is precisely what ordination is not about.[13] Rather, in ordination a person is set in a new place, within a new set of relations within the community of faith. The 1994 Uniting Church in Australia Report on *Ordination and Ministry* begins to move in this direction:

> Ordination places the minister in a new relation to others in the community, as a designated leader. The person is given a new status in the community, not in terms of hierarchical advantage, but in its proper sense of a new 'standing place', in the same way in which marriage places two people into a new relationship with

[13] We might say that a person is being 'set apart' as a moment in a liturgical rite but it becomes problematic when that moment becomes enshrined in a form of words which point to a more enduring separation which is precisely the problem in the Anglican Ordinal. In the *Decree on the Ministry and Life of Priests*, it is recognised that priests 'by their vocation to ordination, set apart *in some way* in the midst of the people of God … [in order] that they should be completely consecrated to the task for which God chooses them' (p. 866, my italics).

> each other which will never be the same again. Similarly, ordination does not place a minister 'over' the rest of the community, but in a new status within it.[14]

The language of 'removal from', 'set apart' and 'distance' has never been far away from the traditional construals of those in orders. It generates a false dichotomy between those who inhabit orders and the people of God. To be in orders is to be in a particular place within the ecclesia; to be related to others in a particular and quite specific way.

But precisely what orders are we talking about? What if the fundamental ordering occurs through baptism? This is, as Zizioulas argues, the first order of the Church for 'there is no such thing as "non-ordained" persons in the Church'.[15] Thus unsurprisingly the rites of baptism and confirmation (which involve 'laying on of hands') are 'essentially an ordination'.[16] In this act the person 'does not simply become a "Christian", as we tend to think, but he [*sic*] becomes a *member of a particular "ordo"* in the eucharistic community'.[17] When this is forgotten the laity become the 'non-ordained' – unnecessary in the eucharistic community – and clericalism appears. The other alternative is to make the baptised person 'the basis for all other "orders", as if he were not himself a specifically defined order but a generic source or principle'.[18] As noted in Chapter 2 the former move associated with clericalism is more common in Catholicism whilst the latter development explains much of the contemporary confusion within Protestantism concerning the purpose of orders.

Within the wider context of the order of the laity it is possible to understand ordination as the establishment of a new set of relations that were not in existence beforehand within the body of Christ. Accordingly ordination has unmistakable ontological weight. The difference is that it is not simply the individual who undergoes change in this ecclesial act but the entire community of faith. Ordination is a transformative rite which changes the very being and life of the community through the establishment of new webs and networks of relations. Those in orders are different people after ordination by virtue of the new ways in which they will be called to exercise responsibilities and function in relation to the wider body of Christ. Ontology and function are both relevant but only in the context of the community as well as the individual admitted to orders. This discussion points to what may be termed a relational ontology of orders.[19]

Such a relational ontology is precisely what we should expect against the backdrop of developments in both Trinitarian thinking and the science of emergence over the course of the twentieth century. Chapter 8 showed how the

---

14 *Ordination and Ministry*, p. 16.

15 Zizioulas, *Being as Communion*, p. 216.

16 Ibid.

17 Ibid.

18 Ibid.

19 This is implied in *Ordination and Ministry in the Uniting Church*, but not explicitly stated or developed beyond the paragraph quoted above.

science of emergence reveals an ontology of order in creation and social evolution that admits of increasing complexity and richer ontologies. Bottom-up emergence necessarily relates all parts together though genuine novelty arises as the parts develop at more complex levels. Yet the whole is always more than the sum of the parts and the higher levels of complexity influence the direction and function of the parts. The science of emergence points to a transformative dynamic embedded in the action of God in the world. By analogy ordination represents a new level of complexity in the ordering of the ecclesia but this ordering is both reliant upon and constituted by the pre-existing ministries. Yet the new level of order is genuinely novel and influences the ministries from which it emerged. On this account ordination enriches the ontology of the whole community; those admitted to such orders belong to a new ontology of the community; the focus is simultaneously on both the transformation of the persons in orders and the community in which they now stand in a new relation. The science of emergence helps to explain the way a relational ontology operates.

Theologically this relational ontology of orders is under-girded by the Trinitarian dynamic of God. Yet what is remarkable is how little of the renaissance of Trinitarianism has filtered into the theology of orders. This is the case, notwithstanding the fact that there has been important work on ministry in relation to the doctrine of the Trinity and an evident concern to redevelop a theology of ministry and break the prevailing non-relational, excessively hierarchical patterns of ministry. However, this work has not served the theology of orders as well as it could.[20] They have remained, for the most part, out of the loop of inquiry: the implication being that as the wider area of ministry is attended to this will have an automatic knock-on effect into the question of orders. Yet without an explicit articulation of what is involved, all this will do is ensure that the question of orders is further neglected and marginalised. In other words, Trinitarianism has often operated under the prevailing mistrust of orders and has not been able to bring the fruits of its work to bear as such.

---

[20] Zizioulas, from the Orthodox tradition broke new ground with his *Being As Communion* and most discussions in the area of ministry, including the present one, are indebted to his work. The strength of his study is the recovery of the Trinitarian ontology as the foundation for personhood. This establishes a foundation for consideration of ministry. However his approach bolsters support for a very traditional hierarchical conception of orders populated by males. Greenwood's *Transforming Priesthood* was a concerted attempt to follow the implications of Trinitiarianism into ministry (see Chapter 7 above). The present study places more stress on the importance of the transformation of the community of faith through particular ordination.

Some Implications for Practice: Mission, Theological Education, Gender and Lay Presidency

There are a number of areas in which a relational ontology of orders might clarify other related issues usually discussed in relation to orders and ministry.

Orders 'Of' or 'In' the Church?

First, I note that a more accurate depiction of orders *in* relation to church is Holy Orders *of* the Church rather than in the Church.[21] It is not unusual to hear reference to the ministry(ies) of the church but far less common to hear the phrase 'orders *of* the church'. For the most part orders are viewed as being *in* the Church whilst ministry is perceived to operate beyond and out in the world. Within this framework orders remained locked within the orbit of the ecclesiastical world and are easily skewed inwards rather than directed outwards. This raises a fundamental issue concerning the purpose of orders. In this regard I proposed some years ago that 'the purpose of an ordained ministry is to energise and direct the church's praise of the triune God in the world'.[22] In this conception the fundamental orientation of orders is outwards rather than inwards and the particular task of orders concerns the directing of energy flow in a structured manner. Orders are concerned with the ordering of the ecclesia though the spin on this these days is usually in the direction of administration and political activity, both of which are important and unavoidable but hardly what orders per se are about. A relational ontology of orders necessarily involves a dynamic of leadership among the people of God that is constantly reconnecting them with ever widening circles of life beyond the Eucharistic community. The reason is that if orders are 'of the Church' and the Church is an eschatological concept then the trajectory of orders and their intent is always in the direction of the unfinished-ness of the ecclesia in the kingdom.

---

[21] Perhaps a small point but highly significant for the early seventeenth-century Anglican ecclesiologist Richard Field, whom few have heard of but a colleague of Richard Hooker. Field's magnum opus was a five-volume treatise of ecumenical theology entitled *Of the Church: Five Books* [1606–10]. 3rd edn in 3 vols. [1635] (repr. Cambridge: Cambridge University Press, 1847), vol. 1, bk. 1, chs. 8–10. He was careful not to fall into the quite common dualism of today which distinguishes between those who are *in* and those *out* of the Church. The subtle change of the preposition was in fact driven by Field's strong ecumenical concern, one of the first post reformation ecumenical ecclesiologies. Who is 'of the church' requires a very different answer from the question who is *in* or *out* of the church (see Bk. 1, chs. 8–10).

[22] See *Ordination and Ministry*, p. 9.

Participation in the missio Dei

The emphasis on the outer-directed and unfinished nature of orders in the life of the Church is associated with a second issue concerning the importance of mediation in a theology of orders. The issue here concerns how orders enable the Church to participate in the *missio Dei*. The question of orders having a quasi-sacramental quality has long been a point of contention between Catholic and Protestants. Within a relational ontology orders may be understood as forms of mediation of the gospel. From this perspective mediation does not operate in a conduit-like manner but rather those in orders stand in a place of wisdom in relation to the tradition and community of faith not in an exclusivist way but quite particular way. The dynamics of mediation are of a fluid kind in which energy flows are facilitated through the connecting of many networks of activity. Orders belong to this web of facilitation and provide focus for the imperatives of the gospel to be appropriated and expressed through lay vocation in the world.

Orders and Theological Education

Within a relational ontology theological education and preparation for Holy Orders is necessarily undertaken in relation to those preparing for the full variety of ministries of the Church. The traditional seminary environment which has contributed to the ecclesiastical introversion of the Church can be reformed on the basis of an understanding of orders that requires those who are so ordained to be self-consciously operating within a rich network of people in the community of faith. Set apartness for training and education is no more relevant than set apartness in the rite of ordination and in the future practice of ministry. This has major implications for theological training and education. It does raise quite acutely the notion of being set apart. Perhaps we need a new language at this point to speak about the particularity of the place in which those ordained are required to stand and in what sense they are called to relate to others in ways specific and peculiar to their life in orders. This is taken up in Chapter 13 in the discussion of the nature of ordination vows.

Orders and Gender

Does a relational ontology of orders have implications for issues of the gender of those in Holy Orders? This may be a fruitful line of inquiry, particularly for those communions of the world that do not admit women to the major orders. It is remarkable that in the creative and rich theology of personhood of John Zizioulas, the question of gender in orders is not even raised. When the emphasis is not on the individual as such but upon the matter of placement within the ecclesia it is hard to see how the question of gender can exercise any determinative force in deciding the gender of who should be ordained. In fact a full relational ontology of orders may actually require both women and men to share in orders to give expression to the fullness of the relational ontology relevant to orders. Whether this principle can be extended to cover the ecclesially sensitive area of homosexuality and orders is a matter that requires further theological work. This debate is far from over notwithstanding strong positions taken on both sides of the argument.

Lay Presidency

The question of who may preside at a Eucharistic gathering is another controversial area for many. From the perspective of a relational theology of orders the one who presides at the Eucharist cannot be disentangled from what the Eucharist is. In this holy meal the local community is re-membered in Christ by his living presence. It is also connected with those who have witnessed to the faith of Christ (in time) and around the globe (space). It is a local Eucharist with universal intent. This diachronic and synchronic unity with all in Christ is most appropriately symbolised in the local context by those whose order is recognised beyond the local. The order that is local in practice but universal in intent corresponds to the local Eucharist. The relational ontology of orders corresponds to the relational theology of the Eucharist. Locally authorised persons who do not embody that wider symbol of unity import a significant distortion internally between Eucharist and presider since they no longer participate in the same local/universal dialectic. As a consequence the authorised person cannot embody that relation to those in orders across time and space. Such presidency is truncated and distorted and not fully relational.

Orders within an Ecology of Praise

It is not immediately apparent how the Church's ministerial orders contribute to the Christian community's life of thanksgiving and praise to God. Indeed, orders may be viewed by some as inhibitors rather than enablers of praise. I have argued elsewhere that the fundamental calling of the community of faith is to live for the praise of God.[23] This is a brief that is quite particular to the Church and encompasses the whole of its life through celebration, reconciliation and service in the world. Within this framework the ordering of the life of the community is both a sociological necessity and a theological imperative. Such ordering is the way the community structures its life and mission. The structuring is directly related to the resources which feed the community's life and have to be in turn distributed justly in the wider society. This is a challenge, not merely because of the complexity of church life but because, from a theological point of view, the greatest problem facing the Church is how to cope with the abundance of God's

---

[23] See Stephen Pickard, *Liberating Evangelism* (Harrisburg: Trinity Press International, 1999), ch. 4.

presence.[24] A somewhat odd problem to have and one that usually goes completely unnoticed in the Church. Most of the time the Church seems preoccupied with the lack of resources – money, people, buildings.

But the most basic and irreplaceable resource is the gospel itself in the midst of the people of the world. When the Church is recalled to this reality then it is able to grasp the significance of its orders within the life of the community. The energy that is available in the gospel is never undirected and unstructured. Energy and structure are co-related. The ordering of energy to enable it to be rightly, efficiently and justly directed and distributed is the particular function of Holy Orders in the Church. Given that the primary sources of energy for the life of the community of faith are related to its rituals (and what happens there), witness and service in the world, it seems clear that the particularity of orders is that it is through such means that the energy available through God can be released in an orderly and structured manner in order that the *missio Dei* might be furthered in the world. Orders then belong to the intelligent structuring of the Church's thanksgiving and praise in worship, discipleship and witness.

But, as I have argued, the orders do not operate autonomously above or at some remove from the Church and its many ministries. In Chapter 9 we observed that the wider ministries of the whole people of God bring the ministries of the more 'complex' orders (traditional offices) to be in so far as they fulfil their own calling and purpose within the *missio Dei*. In this way the ministries of the corporate priesthood *confirm* the ministries of oversight, teaching and gathering. This is correlated to the work of those in orders who enhance and facilitate the wider ministries of the Church. The ministerial dynamic is *fully* relational and it is intrinsic to this kind of 'mode of togetherness' that neither ordained nor other ecclesial ministries can be what they are or shall be *without the other*. Such is the delicate ecology of order within the ecclesia. Where this works well the praise of God is released and its effect magnified in an outflow of witness and joy.

It is the special task and discernment of those in orders to know how to point the community to its fundamental energy and resource and how to facilitate the release of the *dunamis* of the Spirit of Christ in order that true praise of God may overflow in the world. This at least is the ideal and the deepest rationale for Holy Orders in the Christian community. So it is both a practical matter of organising life in relation to what is present as resource, and a deeply theological issue concerning the dynamics of the emergence of praise in faith and life.

Thus we can speak, and not unreasonably, of 'orders of praise'. Exactly what those in such orders are called upon to be and do is a critical issue. Minimally, they will have to have the grace and wisdom to enable the retrieval and release of God's energy among the people. This will necessarily require those in Holy Orders to stand in a particular place and set of relations that involve interpretation of the

---

[24] This suggestion is made by Daniel Hardy and David Ford in *Jubilate: Theology in Praise* (London: Darton Longman and Todd, 1984), p. 71.

Word of God, a rich sacramental ministry and oversight of pastoral care in the community. Word and sacrament are critical precisely because they mediate the primary sources of God's energy in the Christian community. The energy itself is holy and transformative and those who are so charged with the responsibility of mediating such energy of love are rightly identified as belonging to *Holy* Orders. Exactly what tasks, responsibilities and character is called for in order to undertake such a holy calling is crystallised in the exhortation, examination and promises associated with the rite of ordination. This matter is explored in Chapter 13.

Chapter 11
Episcopacy, Management and the Problem of Ecclesiology

Introduction: Re-Forming the Episcopate

This chapter explores some of the ecclesiological issues relevant to a re-formed episcopate in contemporary Anglicanism.[1] It is focused on a number of questions germane to this book: how might the episcopal order that calibrates the orders and ministries within the ecclesia of God operate in a truly collaborative manner? How might the episcopate move beyond an episcopal vitalism that behaves in a non-relational and disconnected way in relation to the other orders and ministries of the Church?

The notion of 're-form' is deliberate and points to a number of issues. First, even the briefest familiarity with the history of the episcopate in time and space would offer sufficient evidence that the episcopate has and continues to undergo constant re-forming.[2] As the environment in which episcopacy has been practiced changes over time so too this has an impact in various subtle and not so subtle ways upon the form and function of the episcopate within church and society.

---

1 This is an expanded version of an earlier article: 'The Travail of the Episcopate: Management, and the Diocese in an Age of Mission', in Bruce Kaye, Sarah Macneil and Heather Thomson (eds.), *'Wonderfully and Confessedly Strange': Australian Essays in Anglican Ecclesiology* (Adelaide: ATF Press, 2006), pp. 127–55.

2 A good example of this from my own Australian Anglicanism can be observed in the episcopate of the first and only 'bishop of Australia', William Broughton. Broughton, discovered that with the loss of his inherited framework of royal supremacy and church–state relationship he had to reappraise the kind of social leadership offered in Australian society. For a helpful discussion see Bruce Kaye, 'Bishops and Social Leadership: What We Might Learn from the First and Only Bishop of Australia', in Cadwallader (ed.), *Episcopacy*, pp. 91–108. Over the 170 years of the Anglican episcopate in Australia there have been many interesting changes. For a general overview of the changing 'art' of episcopacy in Australia, see Alan Cadwallader, 'Antipodean Descriptions of the Art of Episcopacy', in *Episcopacy*, pp. 1–21. The changing form and re-forming of episcopacy is an ambiguous occurrence for it is not necessarily evidence of the reformation dictum, *ecclesia semper reformanda*. When re-forming takes place in an uncritical manner, as it were by osmosis in response to changing environments and needs, or through canonical and legal apparatus of the Church with minimal reference to deeper theological impulses then conditions arise in which re-forming might simply fail the test of *episcope semper reformanda*.

There are two areas in which a re-forming of the episcopate has been taking place, often with little critical reflection, but usually with significant anxiety. We might identify the two areas as the Church in its *intensive* mode (its gathered life within the local ecclesia – for example, the diocese) and its *extensive* mode (its life in relation to the wider Christian Church, in particular inter-church dialogues).[3] The present chapter examines the former intensive mode whilst the following chapter considers the impact of ecumenism on the nature of the episcopate as an instance of the Church in its extensive mode.

In the first area (intensive mode) the major influence upon the episcopate arises because the Church, for better or worse, has been deeply influenced by prevailing management models of leadership associated with the emergence of the corporate life of modern Western institutions. In some respects this has been a question of survival and recovery of administrative efficiencies for the purpose of fulfilling the episcopal brief received at consecration. Ruling and caring for the body is 'big business', made even more urgent with declining resources and increasing needs. The deployment of management techniques is enmeshed within traditional hierarchical patterns of authority (tendencies to centric, 'top-down' decision-making and communication) within a diocesan structure carrying heavy burdens for administrative and legal oversight. What has happened to the shape and form of the episcopate within this mix of contemporary management culture drawn from a secular corporate environment, and inherited patterns of authority and ecclesial structure? How might the re-forming that has occurred be critically assessed in the light of the gospel and mission of God's Church? What would a theological assessment look like compared to an administrative stock-take of duties, or a management consultation designed to develop strategies for streamlining a diocese for mission? Or rather, how might the various approaches complement each other? And what inhibitors are operating at the systemic level: those unnoticed but powerful drivers of 'corporate life'? This discussion does not pretend to be able to answer these questions but hopefully it can begin to prise open some of the issues. This ought to provide a clearer understanding of why a critical re-forming of episcopacy is so difficult and yet so necessary.

The chapter first examines the significance of management as a reforming instrument of the episcopate. This leads to the identification of some systemic problems that thwart reform. The chapter concludes with a reflection on the diocese, territoriality, catholicity and baptism as a paradigm for the re-form of the episcopate. What emerges in the chapter is an argument for a 'grounded episcopate' with stronger links between the 'order that orders' and the ministries of the

---

[3] The terms 'intensive' and 'extensive' have been adapted from Daniel Hardy's notion of 'extensity' as the 'spread-out-ness' of the Christian faith *in situ* in the world and 'intensity' through the 'inner dynamic of the wisdom of God' which occurs particularly in worship and the living tradition of the Church. This dynamic between intensity and extensity is fundamental to the formation of Christian life and service. See Daniel Hardy, *Finding the Church: The Dynamic Truth of Anglicanism* (London: SCM, 2001), pp. 109–13.

baptised. Conditions are thus established for a more cooperative and collaborative exercise of episcope throughout the whole church. In this way the secret of the episcopal office is shown to be closely related to the flourishing of the ministries of the whole people of God.

Episcopacy and Managerial Culture

Managing Episcopal Vows

In the 'Exhortation and Examination' for the consecration of bishops in *A Prayer Book for Australia*:

> [A bishop] is called to maintain the Church's witness … to protect the purity of the gospel … to proclaim Jesus Christ … guard its [the Church's] faith, unity and discipline … promote mission … ensure God's word is faithfully proclaimed and sacraments administered … Church discipline applied justly, with mercy … to lead and guide priests and deacons … be faithful in choosing and ordaining of ministers … watch over, protect and serve the people of God … to teach and govern them and be hospitable … know and be known by them … and be a good example to all.

The exhortation ends: 'These are the duties of a bishop, and they are weighty. Are you willing to perform them?'[4]

In common with most ordinals there follows a series of questions in the form of an 'examination'. The promissory character of the responses – 'I will, with God's grace', is not uncommon – is a promise made not simply to the assembled congregation, nor immediately to the presiding bishop but given the gravity of the liturgical setting, the promises are made primarily to God. Episcopal vows, like other religious vows in the Christian tradition, are made in the sight of the God of Jesus Christ. And the promisor recognises that the fulfilment of the promises requires not only the support and encouragement of the people and those to whom the ordinand is immediately responsible but at the deepest reaches of the human spirit it is nothing less than the grace of a God who is faithful that empowers one for the making and keeping of the vows.

The matter of the promises will be discussed in Chapter 13 however for the moment my concern is a directly ecclesial one. Under what kinds of conditions is it possible for bishops to fulfil their promises at consecration. The chapter is thus an inquiry into the ecclesial conditions necessary for the vows to be effectual, take root and shape an episcopal life within the body of Christ. Why is such a question on the agenda? Consulting a bishop's daily, weekly, monthly and yearly diary might offer a clue. This would tell the story of remarkable business, crowded

---

4 *A Prayer Book for Australia*, p. 802.

days, few spare moments, rapid and constant travel between engagements, little space, time and peace for critical reflection, let alone writing, and immersion in a host of ecclesiastical and secular appointments. What is the relationship between the diary and the vow? That is the question that deserves examination. This is not only a practical issue of organising time: it is also an issue of priorities and more particularly orientation of life. What does it mean any longer for a bishop to 'see over' the people of God? Is it possible? Do the consecration vows make any sense practically. Is it a hit and miss approach to 'solemn vows'? How do the vows made before God and the people inform the shape and dynamic of episcopal life?

My hunch is that the vows are good, the intentions are honourable and true, but the appropriation and embodiment of the vows in a form of episcopal life is seriously at risk if not compromised. The reasons for this are probably many but it just might be possible that the vows are designed for a church that does not exist. The thesis of the chapter is that the problem with episcopal vows does not ultimately lie with the character of a particular bishop – as important as this is, for the church has 'good' and 'bad' bishops.[5] Rather, the problem with the vows is to be located in the nature of the Church in which they have to be fulfilled. The problem is not first episcopal but ecclesiological. The chapter argues that management culture – for all its positive effects – nevertheless functions to maintain the status quo of ecclesial structures and thwarts a more intentional restructuring of the polity of the Church. The point is that episcopal vows do not occur in a vacuum but have an environment within which they are made and fulfilled. The problem with vows is a problem of the ecclesial environment. Change here is extremely difficult and exacerbated by the appeal of management technique.

Who can undertake episcopal office in our present environment? The coverage of responsibilities is wide and the modern diocese is highly complex, requiring a high degree of management and financial care. There are significant pressures upon leaders, pressures generated from expectations within the Church and wider public as well as those inner demands felt by individuals, particularly given the increasing scrutiny leaders are under in our society. Leadership is under suspicion in all quarters and this only increases the claim felt by those in authority to offer visionary leadership: with charisma – in uncertain times the charismatic leader more often than not is what is sought and expected – administrative savvy – efficient and effective management of a diocese and its increasingly limited resources – pastoral genuineness – the common touch – and quality teaching and preaching – scholarly but well earthed. In many respects bishops are in no different position from a host of occupations these days that have a high public profile and concomitant accountability.

> [A bishop] is at the beck and call of unreasonable expectations: constant availability and divine competence to solve all problems and right every ill

[5] See Ephraim Radner, *Hope Among the Fragments: The Broken Church and It's Engagement of Scripture* (Grand Rapids: Brazos Press, 2004), ch. 10, 'Bad Bishops'.

> of society. If he [*sic*] seeks to be an efficient manager, he is told that his is a 'spiritual' role; if the diocese lacks cohesion and direction he is to blame. He may well reflect that 'giving lead in the Church of England is like trying to take the cat for a walk'.[6]

Given these realities and the wider ecclesial and social context for episcopal ministry the vows made at consecration can look overwhelming. Administration and management require significant time and energy and a focus on managerial theology is not to be despised.[7] Being efficient and effective in the business of the episcopate is critical *precisely* so that the ordination vows can be fulfilled with integrity, albeit never fully. It is at this point that the need for good quality management arises almost as a default move to streamline, repair, recover lost ground and upgrade the system and structures of the local diocese and wider Church. The influence of the management ethos upon Church life has been immense. 'Ethos' is probably the right word for there is a world of difference between an ethos and the skilled application of quality management practices – so-called 'best practice'.

There may be nothing wrong with the incorporation of management models into the life of a busy diocese and world. The bishop as CEO of the diocese may be resisted in theory but inevitable in practice. Few would deny that in our present environment, where the Church is big business,[8] Church leaders should avail themselves of the best management wisdom from the corporate sector. It is neither possible nor particularly Anglican to set one's face against the world. In any case the effort usually fails for Church and culture are always in creative interaction, either consciously and intentionally or subliminally and without critical assessment of the process. Re-evaluation of structures, communication networks, development of strategic plans and mission statements, change management, use of management consultants – for the ostensible purpose of releasing the people of God for mission in the world – are all things to which bishops and their councils have become accustomed. Indeed, it would be irresponsible of the Church and its bishops not to encourage the above; for how can the Church be a generous giver of its life to the world for which Christ died, if it cannot manage the resources (including its people) of its household. The management paradigm is almost a given of our ecclesial world and bishops are the primary focus for authority and sanction of the forms of life and witness of the Church. Drawing upon the best

---

[6] Ian Cundy and Justin Welby, 'Taking the Cat for a Walk: Can a Bishop Order a Diocese?', in G.R. Evans and M. Percy (eds.), *Managing the Church: Order and Organization in a Secular Age* (Sheffield: Sheffield Academic Press, 2000), p. 26.

[7] See the classic book on the subject, Peter F. Rudge, *Ministry and Management* (London: Tavistock, 1968).

[8] See the provocative recent discussion from the US context, M. Budde and R. Brimlow, *Christianity Incorporated: How Big Business is Buying the Church* (Grand Rapids: Brazos Press, 2002).

wisdom from management in the corporate sector and integrating it with the wisdom of the living tradition of the Church may be precisely what Christians are called to do, both intentionally and with a focus on excellence. The Anglican theologian, David Ford, puts a most apposite question:

> How can Anglicans … take account of the models and pressures of powerful modern forms of authority in corporate enterprises in such a way that *episkope* neither succumbs (as so often in the past and present) to patterns not adequately informed by the gospel, nor fails to learn from them where possible.[9]

Thus one answer to the question about management: 'Is it a good thing?' might be: 'Yes if it is undertaken wisely.' For bishops the stakes are high, nothing less than the vows of their office.[10]

Management as 'Power of the Keys'

However, a danger arises when managerialism is incorporated in an uncritical way.[11] The matter is the subject of a sustained critique by a British theologian, Richard Roberts, who argues that 'the assimilation of managerialism into an organisation whose leaders have been – and remain – in a state of prolonged identity crisis endangers the "care of souls"'.[12] By reference to care of souls Roberts intends 'the fostering of that delicate ecology of spiritual opportunity that constitutes the fabric of real human community, koinonia itself'.[13] Roberts offers a powerful analysis of the state of English Anglicanism as he explores the dynamics and tensions between 'a long-standing crisis of identity and authority within English Anglicanism and the legitimation and actualisation of power provided by the prerogatives of managerialsim and its employment as a means

---

[9] See Anglican-Lutheran Consultation, *Episcope in Relation to the Mission of the Church Today*, p. 148.

[10] This underlies the statement in the report on episcopal ministry in the Church of England: 'The presenting practical problem in Episcopal Churches has come to be the manner in which a bishop today can, or should, hold his [*sic*] office in 'totality'. That is, as a personal, collegial and communal office, where it is clearly an impossibility for a single individual to carry out all the traditional and modern functions of a bishop.' See *Episcopal Ministry: The Report of the Archbishop's Group on the Episcopate* (London: Church House, 1990), par. 423, pp. 189–90.

[11] This matter was the subject of a special edition of *Modern Theology* 9/4 (Oct. 1993), *Ecclesiology and the Culture of Management*.

[12] Richard Roberts, 'Ruling the Body: The Care of Souls in a Managerial Church', in Richard Roberts, *Religion, Theology and the Human Sciences* (Cambridge: Cambridge University Press, 2002), p. 164.

[13] Ibid.

of ecclesial restoration'.[14] He analyses the restoration in two stages. First, the 'reinauguration of the ecclesial vision of the manager's "right to manage" seen in the restructuring of an "executive Church"'. Second, 'the introduction and implementation of the culture of performance and appraisal which may consolidate the oversight of episcope into an ecclesial Panopticon other and self-administered surveillance'.[15] Roberts argues that such managerialism amounts to a betrayal of the ecclesia and his focus is very clearly on the power elites of Anglican hierarchy, including of course its bishops. Much of the critique involves a deconstruction of two documents produced in the mid-1990s: *Working as One Body*[16] and *Strategic Church Leadership*:[17] the latter co-authored by a former university vice-chancellor and the Anglican theologian and sociologist, Robin Gill. An important assessment of the tensions inherent in the 1990 report between management, problems of governance and administration of the 'organization' on the one hand and on the other the inherited traditions of order and 'ancient ecclesiological principles' is contained in the book of essays cited earlier *Managing the Church*: an invaluable resource for Anglicans everywhere. It may be somewhat consoling for Anglicans in other parts of the globe that Roberts's critique is directed to the English Church though it is hard to resist the view that the dangers of the rational management of the Church have become part of the wider ecclesial culture, certainly of the West.

Roberts has drawn attention to the problem of episcopal leadership in the Anglican Church. On the one hand the exercise of episcopal ministry belongs to an ancient inherited 'right to rule' based on divine sanctions and historical consolidation enshrined, for example, in the 'Fundamental Declarations of the Anglican Church of Australia'.[18] On the other hand there is a long-running identity crisis for those in Holy Orders from which bishops cannot escape.[19] How then might the episcopate re-invent itself for a modern and postmodern world whilst holding firmly to ancient vows and responsibilities? The managerial option, which in effect transfers the 'right to rule' into the 'right to manage' is almost irresistible

---

[14] Ibid.

[15] Ibid.

[16] *Working as One Body*. The Report of the Archbishop's Commission on the Organization of the Church of England (London: Church House, 1995).

[17] Robin Gill and Derek Burke, *Strategic Church Leadership* (London: SPCK, 1996).

[18] *The Constitution and Canons of the Anglican Church of Australia* (Sydney: General Synod Office, 1998), Pt. 1, ch. 1: 'Fundamental Declarations', par. 3: 'This Church will ever obey the commands of Christ, teach His doctrine, administer His sacraments of Holy Baptism and Holy Communion, follow and uphold His discipline and preserve the three orders of bishops, priests and deacons in the sacred ministry.' There is no flexibility here for following the lead of the Episcopal Church of the United States in making provision for a *temporary suspension* of the constitution, in regard to 'preserving' the orders to facilitate the concordate of union with the Lutheran Church.

[19] See Chapter 10.

within the managerial culture of Western society. The danger in efficacy and efficiency (and associated aims and objectives discourse)[20] is that it becomes another way in which real power is recovered for episcopal leadership. This is not to deny that power is irrelevant to the episcope of bishops.[21] But the danger is that it can easily occur at the expense of a more collaborative, negotiated and interdependent form of ecclesial life. This latter approach is made even more difficult for the narcissistic leader and those whose emotional intelligence for leadership is underdeveloped.[22] Roberts notes that the 'right to manage' is related to the 'other'. The 'other' in such a framework is constituted as the 'trusting followership'.[23] Institutional and organization efficiency becomes the overarching objective albeit for the sake of the mission of the Church. What falls out of view is pursuit of 'active prophetic imagination' and 'effective pastoral care'. These latter two aims require a significant degree of 'professional autonomy' and the 'exercise of much discernment'.

The basic need to gain efficiency in organizational life may seem reasonable enough but there are systemic problems that skew the whole venture in the direction of an archaic power structure. Roberts brings to his support the historian Edward Norman who has noted that it has been a defining characteristic of the episcopal elite in the Church of England to 'absorb and transmit the dominant ideology of its peer group'.[24] This peer group is now constituted by senior executives and managers who are the leaders of the managerial revolution. Roberts's concern is that this revolution hands over 'imagination, thought, agency and control to management' in this case bishops and loss of 'spontaneity and creativity from below'.[25] In the new learning organization simple command-obedience is inadequate; now it is more a matter of ownership of the new identity, generated from the top but in a manner (via management) that it is received and implemented from below. Management of the 'power of the keys' may singularly fail to facilitate

---

20 See Stephen Pattison, 'Some Objections to Aims and Objectives', in Evans and Percy (eds.), *Managing the Church*, pp. 128–52.

21 For a discussion, see *Bishops in Communion*. House of Bishops Occasional Paper (London: Church House, 2000), pp. 33–7. 'The words and actions of bishops have the power to affect the lives of many people, especially devout church people, and are experienced as either affirming or undermining, building confidence or destroying it' (p. 34).

22 See, for example, Michael Maccoby, 'Narcissisitic Leaders: The Incredible Pros, the Incredible Cons', *Harvard Business Review* (Nov.–Dec. 1998): 27–49; Daniel Goleman, 'What Makes a Leader?', *Harvard Business Review* (Nov.–Dec. 1998): 1-25. Goleman addresses the relative paucity of studies on the affective dimensions of leadership. See D. Goleman, R. Boyatzis and A. Mckee (eds.), *The New Leaders: Transforming the Art of Leadership into the Science of Results* (London: TimeWarner Paperbacks, 2003).

23 Roberts, 'Ruling the Body', p. 170.

24 Ibid, p. 172.

25 Ibid., p. 174–6.

the exercise of power among the baptised.[26] Motivation of the baptised within a postmodern environment might require patterns of relating quite inimical to the practices of management in a modernist framework.[27]

From Episcopacy to Ecclesiology: Systemic Problems

The Travail of the Episcopate

A number of issues arise from the above discussion. First, it is hard not to feel sympathy for episcopal leadership in our difficult and insecure times. There have been and continue to be many areas of poor management and waste of resources. The crisis of leadership identity is profound and does have an impact upon those in Holy Orders. The episcopate is charged with the 'care of the churches' and oversight of the mission of the Church. Proper accountability for those in leadership at all levels is needful and indeed urgent, especially in the light of such things as clergy abuse.[28] Second, it is inevitable that the Church will assimilate and imitate to some extent the managerial practices of the 'host' culture. This is not all loss though it is important to make some careful distinctions between management technique and bureaucracy; the latter being much maligned but in fact vital for the well being of any organization.[29] The real concern is an uncritical appropriation of management programs, models and techniques. Problems in these areas surface in such everyday activities such as intercession: a religious practice in which one's own powerless requires a certain habit and form of life very much at odds with the disciplines of management which are aimed at the efficient use of power.[30] However, as suggested above, there are some enduring systemic issues that cannot be exorcised by reflection and careful weaving together of best management

---

26 The centrality of the problem of power in relation to the episcopate, episcope and the ministry of the whole people of God has been recognised by Stephen Sykes. See *Unashamed Anglicanism*, pp. 178–98.

27 See J. Hassard and M. Parker (eds.), *Postmodernism and Organizations* (London: Sage, 1993), pp. 96–9.

28 Yet within a management culture surveillance, assessment and accountability are constant and wearing. One of the criticisms of the critique of management culture is that it fails to provide a means for accountability. See the robust and carefully argued response to this by Richard Roberts, 'The Quest for Appropriate Accountability: Stakeholders, Tradition and the Managerial Prerogative in Higher Education', *Studies in Christian Ethics* 17/1 (2004): 1–21.

29 See, for example, Paul de Gay, *In Praise of Bureacracy* (London: Sage, 2000).

30 Michael Hanby, 'Interceding: Giving Grief to Management', in S. Hauerwas and S. Wells (eds.), *The Blackwell Companion to Christian Ethics* (Oxford: Blackwell, 2004), pp. 237–49, esp. 246.

practice and gospel imperatives, though some degree of self-consciousness at this level is a minimum requirement for episcopal re-form.

The Episcopate and the Migration of the Sacred

There are two issues of a systemic kind that have a profound impact upon the form and function of the Church and its episcopate. Both issues are of an ecclesiological kind and press home to us the importance of the relation between ministry and ecclesiology in a discussion about management, leadership and the episcopate. The first concerns the purpose of the Church in the context of late-modern/postmodern society. Contrary to many popular perceptions religion is not dead nor in fact dying. As David Tracey has well documented, the search for 'primal spirituality' and the 'return of the religious' continues unabated.[31] It is the reason why, notes American theologian, Harvey Cox, Pentecostalism has exercised such a potent force throughout the world and, in its more domesticated forms, why the Charismatic movement and its offshoots provided such an important impetus for renewal in the late twentieth century.[32] How well will mainline Churches be able to connect people with the deep realities of human need expressed through such a 'primal spirituality'? It is a problem, for increasingly the traditional institutional embodiments for such religious searching are being jettisoned by the younger generations. Furthermore, as Philip Jenkins has recently convincingly argued the Christianity of the twenty-first century will be significantly influenced by the religious and spiritual impulses from the southern hemisphere.[33] Roberts contends that for the secular West the sacred has not been lost or abandoned so much as 'migrated'.[34] In this context the Church has to rediscover its significant resources as a 'form of life' through which it is possible to encounter a radical otherness beyond the 'sacralization of the self' and 'self-religion'.[35]

This discussion raises a fundamental question: management for what purpose? It can hardly do to speak glibly about the mission of God or the Church or the service of love and care, without understanding the environment in which such a mission occurs.[36] What do those who exercise episcope see on the horizon or in the depths? To what extent is the episcopal vision impaired by the demands of management and organization? Is it that one's sight can only penetrate to the

---

[31] David Tracey, *The Spirituality Revolution* (Sydney: HarperCollins, 2003), esp. ch. 8.

[32] Harvey Cox, *Fire From Heaven* (London: Cassell,1996).

[33] Philip Jenkins, *The Next Christendom: The Coming of Global Christianity* (Oxford: Oxford University Press, 2002).

[34] Roberts, 'Ruling the Body', pp. 178–9.

[35] Ibid, p. 178.

[36] A criticism of *Working as One Body* is that it fails to give any attention to the nature of the 'mission field' (a very different thing from 'the mission of the Church') and its significance for any restructured management of the Church.

strategic question of restructuring in terms of management paradigms. So the first issue is a systemic problem: the force and inevitability of the management paradigm systematically distorts the vision. If the theological blur is overcome – the primacy of the recovery of the sacred is beheld – it can only be momentary before the organizational brief returns. What we end up with is an episcopal ministry which is constantly in danger of losing its prophetic edge. Given the enduring search for 'primal spirituality', albeit in 'migrated' secular and quasi-religious forms, what is an appropriate 'form of life' for the episcopate to nurture through, teaching, preaching, pastoral care and government? This requires an 'outside-in' approach to management in the Church, allowing the presence of the 'other' on the outside to shape the management of the Church. It is thus an ecclesiological and missiological matter: regard for the Church in its extensive outward directed mode of life. To draw this to the attention of the ecclesia of God may be a prophetic episcopal responsibility.

The Function of Management: Masking the Ideology of the Diocese

Related to the above issue is a second of a systemic kind. Here the question about the 'form of life' of the ecclesia becomes critical. What is an appropriate form of ecclesial life that opens up and points toward the sacred and human longing? Actually it is not difficult to map out characteristics of a Church given over to the nurturing of such needs in the world. One of the key words here is 'community'. The Church is a *koinonia* – a communion of peoples joined in common life, worship and discipleship. Most mission statements of the Church 'organisation' will embody this vision of ecclesia somehow. We instinctively know what is required. We re-present a lost ideal and then struggle within our ecclesial structures to implement the plan.

Here we come face to face with the nature of the episcopal system as it is practised in Anglicanism. It is almost taken as read that the diocese – as the 'local church' – has quasi-sacred status in the episcopal system. But in the history of the Christian tradition the traditional diocesan structure came relatively late on the scene. The diocesan system owes its debt to Cyprian, bishop of Carthage. It became, in the course of the fourth century, associated with a strong jurisdictional emphasis. In this episcope the bishop is an *alter Petrus* expressing the unity and communion of the Church in space.[37] Such a bishop is a conciliar being connected to all other bishops. This offers the Church a cogent symbol of the bond of unity between the local church and all other local churches. The Cyprianic office can easily become an 'external administrative office'. This jurisdictional model is particularly associated with Roman Catholicism but is also a feature of

---

[37] John Erickson, 'Episkope and Episcopacy: Orthodox Perspectives', in P. Bouteneff and A. Falconer (eds.), *Episkope and Episcopacy and the Quest for Visible Unity*. Faith and Order Paper no. 183(Geneva: WCC, 1999), p. 82.

Anglicanism; the main difference being that in the latter conciliarity is not trumped by a jurisdictional primacy.

In the Irenaean form of episcope the bishop is the authoritative teacher – the *alter apostolos* and as such serves as a living link with the apostles through a historical continuing in time. This is a continuity not merely of structure (Cyprianic) but apostolic faith. Anglicanism is indebted to both Irenaean and Cyprianic forms of episcope and in this way preserves both a synchronic (across territories) and diachronic (through time) unity in faith and life.[38] However, it is clear that in these forms of episcopal structuring the local church was the diocese. This was the logic of a theology of episcopacy focused on the unity of the ecclesia with its bishop.

Yet the price of this kind of episcopal unity has been high. The theory of the bishop in the local church has been maintained by redefining what 'local' means. The result is that the diocese becomes a complex network of 'local community' churches (parishes) organised on a territorial basis to secure 'coverage'. This does ensure at least two things: first, the bishop becomes an administrative figure who has jurisdictional as well as pastoral oversight of the whole; and second, the consequent loss of a sense of an embedded episcope at the micro level of church life. The Anglican system deals with this through a theory of shared episcope through delegation of a bishop's oversight responsibilities to priests who thus perform a representative role on behalf of the bishop.

However, this conception conceals a systemic structural problem associated with the management paradigm for episcopal ministry. In such a context any counteractive and critical movement to re-form the episcopate is undermined by a systemic structural defect – the ideology of the diocese – supported by a theory of delegation and representation which appears unassailable, and an appeal to management technique as a means to neutralise the deeper problem. An uncritical acceptance of a particular diocesan ecclesiology usurps the best theological intentions for re-forming the episcopate. *The diocesan system requires the assimilation of the management revolution in the Church.* Without the recourse to management technique the system's dysfunction would become manifest, perhaps intolerable. Within the prevailing framework there are severely limited possibilities for an episcopate to model and exemplify that form of life appropriate for a community given over to the nurture of the sacred in the midst of the world. Of course 'others' might be able to do this in a representative manner, in lieu of the bishop. But what about the person of the bishop and the re-form of the episcopate? The question is inescapable: is the episcopate trapped in a 'steel-hard casing' of an inflexible ecclesiology.[39]

The power of the prevailing Cyprianic ecclesiology in Anglicanism ought not be underestimated. *The irony is that managerialism is a creative attempt to overcome the worst features of this ecclesial form.* But the problem is systemic

---

[38] For a succinct and insightful discussion of the Cyprianic, Irenaean and Ignatian models of episcope, see ibid.

[39] Roberts, 'Ruling the Body', p. 179, quoting Max Weber.

and structural and therefore the jurisdictional/administrative model of episcopacy is transferred into the new managerialism. In this context the capacity of bishops to fulfil their episcopal vows is seriously weakened and/or compromised. We may be guilty of espousing a doctrine of the episcopate that does not and cannot exist. The reason being that such an episcopate belongs to a differently ordered church from the prevailing model.

Two things may be offered in response at this stage. What kind of ecclesiology could generate an episcopal office that made sense of the ordinal and vows? The Orthodox Church has long focused on the Ignatian model of episcopacy. Here the bishop is the president of the local Eucharistic assembly gathering the diverse gifts of the local community into a unity. Such a bishop is the *alter Christus*, a living icon who constitutes 'the focus and visible centre of unity within the local church'; who expresses 'the fullness, unity and multiplicity of the eschatological community in each place'.[40] This theology of the episcopate belongs to a Eucharistic ecclesiology. Of course this episcopo-centrism can become an episcopo-monism. But it does put the bishop in the midst of the people. And this is appealing, though, as the Orthodox theologian and bishop, John Zizioulas has noted, the ancient Ignatian model has suffered the fate of diocesanisation. The bishop remained the bishop of the 'local' church (renamed diocese) but ceased to be the head of the Eucharistic community. From Zizioulas's point of view, the diocesan system (as an aggregate of many local Eucharistic communities) is a corruption from an episcopal model developed in relation to a Eucharistic ecclesiology centred around the bishop in the local church.[41] However, replicating the Ignatian structure in the context of a global village rather than the ancient *polis* may simply be a romantic ideal and only succeed in generating something very different from what Zizioulas has in mind.[42] Nonetheless, in terms of the present argument it may be important to explore how an Ignatian ecclesiology might be creatively deployed in the service of a modified diocesanism. Certainly the notion of re-placing bishops through diocesan downsizing has similarities and fundamental sympathies with the Orthodox approach and might say something to Anglicans about their long-standing affinities with Orthodoxy.

Recognition of the problem of a theory of episcopacy which harbours systemic problems undermining the exercise of true episcope in the local church ought (in principle at least) to open the episcopate to a re-form that includes the excluded other from its midst. Not only the 'other' of the 'mission field', to say nothing of the 'other' within (i.e., the laity) but also, and no less importantly, the 'collective other' who bear the name of Christ but with whom we do not yet share our bread. It is precisely at this ecumenical point that the re-forming of the Anglican episcopate becomes an imperative. Though it is precisely in such ecumenical dialogue that we uncover some of the deeply held commitments and theological positions that

---

40 Erikson, 'Episkope and Episcopacy', p. 81.

41 For a discussion of Zizioulas's position, see ibid.

42 Ibid., p. 85.

have hitherto funded a theology of the Anglican episcopate. This is a matter that needs more careful attention in Anglicanism and is examined in the chapter that follows.

A Grounded Episcopate for an Emerging Church

From Territoriality to Places-in-Relation

This chapter has argued that recovery and re-engagement with ecclesiology is critical for re-forming episcopacy in Anglicanism. The managerial paradigm pervades the practice of modern episcopacy. Its appeal is precisely as a foil to the loss of episcopal form and function in the contemporary Church. Efforts to re-form through such a strategy necessarily fail due to an unexamined ecclesiology in which the modern Anglican bishop is systemically skewed towards an administrative/jurisdictional manager. A re-formed episcopate is correlative to a re-formed ecclesial structure. An important conclusion to this inquiry is that *the integrity of the episcopal vows requires a differently structured church in which they may be fulfilled.*

The proposal to reduce the size of dioceses is hardly new nor unproblematic, as the Church of England report, *Episcopal Ministry* made clear in 1990.[43] Though on that occasion it appeared as a practical measure to deal with the multiplication of suffragan bishops, a development at odds with the traditional theology of one bishop in one place.[44] Tensions *within* the theology of episcopacy – relationship between diocesan bishop and suffragan bishop – were only indirectly related to difficulties in the supporting ecclesiology.

Diocesan downsizing which retained strong conciliar networks between dioceses would represent a move towards a more grounded episcopate with affinities to the ancient Ignatian Eucharistic ecclesiology whilst retaining the strengths of a wider episcopal collegiality. The result would be a modified territorial episcopacy in which the ideal of coverage of territory was more dynamically related to the kinds of groupings and cultures envisaged in, for example, Brent's 'cultural episcopacy'. The idea of a diocese would be formed in relation to an understanding of 'place' rather than the Western preoccupation with 'space' and its associated concerns with

---

43 *Episcopal Ministry*, pars. 428–34. It noted that 'such a development would represent a return to what is judged to be the primitive model', yet the 'theological purity' would be purchased at the expense of a number of practical disadvantages: fear of greater administrative load, disjunction with prevailing economic and social orderings of society, impact on mission. These so-called disadvantages may not hold up to scrutiny. The report appeared equivocal on the matter though it did finally state that 'our Group would like to see serious consideration of the possibility of reduction in size of some dioceses by the creation of more dioceses' (par. 432).

44 Ibid., pars. 423–69.

'occupation' and 'territory'.[45] Does this mean the traditional notion of territoriality must disappear? Not exactly. Geography remains relevant; coverage remains critical. But how is it to be conceived? The 'normal system is "the bishop with restraint", that is, a territorial diocese ruled by a bishop, and divided into territorial parishes each in charge of an incumbent'.[46] The great advantage is coverage. But 'although the territorial principle is valuable, it is not part of the theological structure of the Church *in the form we know it*'.[47] Whilst in theory each diocese constitutes a local church with its chief pastor, priest and teacher (the bishop) the tendency is to see the diocese as 'little more than a territorial subdivision of a larger unit'.

A different approach would first emphasise the universal Church, 'the whole fellowship of which Christ is head and king, and in which he has set the apostolic ministry, and then to ask ourselves what a local church is and should be'.[48] This prompts questions about the 'desirable size of a particular church' and whether every 'true local church' should have a bishop? Considered from a theological point of view there may be a number of possible answers. Territoriality does not have an absolute claim for the organization of the Church. As one theologian noted some years ago:

> One might imagine as a future development a Christian community of some five hundred members, committed Christians in an entirely secularised community, with a bishop as their chief pastor and a presbytery of perhaps a dozen priests functioning with the bishop as a corporate body, and perhaps the bishop as the only full-time minister, and all the rest earning their living in some ordinary occupation.[49]

These words, penned over three decades ago, certainly envisaged a more flexible approach to the organization of the Church. It has resonances with a much earlier 'minister model' with a strong orientation on mission and resourcing the people of God.

More recent developments point to a future 'mission-shaped Church' which will have to be responsive to new forms of community. The Church might have

---

45 For an illuminating discussion see the work of the Australian theologian Geoffrey Lilburne, *A Sense of Place: A Christian Theology of the Land* (Nashville: Abingdon, 1989), esp. ch. 4, 'The Poetics of Space: Place and Space in the Western Tradition'; see also John Inge, *Towards a Christian Theology of Place* (Aldershot: Ashgate, 2003).

46 I am indebted to a late friend and mentor R.P. McDermott for this discussion of territoriality. It was ahead of its time in the late 1960s; see his 'An Anglican's Reflections on Priesthood', in N. Lash and J. Rhymer (eds.), *The Christian Priesthood* (London: Darton, Longman and Todd, 1970), p. 158.

47 Ibid., p. 159, my italics.

48 Ibid.

49 Ibid.

a more 'liquid' feel with greater flexibility in its structuring and linkages within and across communities of faith. Minimally the idea of territoriality will have to be rethought in more dynamic terms. This might require a new sense of place for the Church in which geography, human interactions and mobility, and patterns of communication combine in diverse ways to redefine what 'local' in relation to universal Church actually looks like. The correlate of an emerging Church is an emerging episcopate able to faithfully fulfil its vows. It is difficult to conceive how this can occur without a more intentionally grounded episcopate that functions at less of a distance from the Church for which it provides an appropriate guardianship and oversight. The natural and/or optimal 'episcopal reach' may have to be thought out. The 'order that orders' has to have a more than purely formal relationship with the ministries of the baptised. Rather, the episcopal order has to be dynamically related to the 'ordered ministries'.

The theory of delegation of authority and ministry is fine in theory but delegation ought not be a means by which dysfunctional relations between the ministries are maintained. In other words episcopal oversight has to be real and concrete, that is, grounded, not presumed or simply imagined. In the future we might be able to talk about a 'natural episcopacy' related to a variety of factors and criteria, but undergirded by a priority on facilitation of face-to-face relations, high quality interpersonal life, and the embedding of episcope in the local church with an orientation and impulse that expands the interconnections between different locales. To effect this the episcopate may need to be re-placed.[50]

In the complexities of a postmodern environment in which the search for 'primal spirituality' continues unabated and the particular (bordering on tribalism) has priority over the universal, the life of the Church and its mission has to be reconstructed from 'below'. An ecclesiology from the ground up is not one that begins entirely new and without the impress of the past. Rather, out of that very inheritance such a Church begins to think again about its place and how the ancient ministries of word, sacrament and care might be reconstituted. This points to an ecclesiology of wholeness and its structural form looks very different from the modern Anglican diocese. In some respects no one knows exactly what may emerge – in this we are joined with Ignatius, Tertullian, Irenaeus, Clement (of Rome) and the early Church in a gnostic world. But it is critical for the well-being and wholeness of the community of faith that there is an episcope that is generous in its presence. In this way the dynamics of the episcopate can follow the generosity of the triune God's holy and faithful presence in Jesus and the Spirit.

An Old Chestnut: Parity of Orders

Parity of orders will need a rethinking of the relations between the traditional orders, particularly those between priest and bishop. The fact is that the office of

---

[50] See Jeffrey Driver and Stephen Pickard, 'Re-Placing Bishops: An Ecumenical and Trinitarian Approach to Episcopacy', *St Mark's Review* 169 (1997): 23–8.

a bishop is highly mobile and fluid with respect to territory covered, communities encountered, public spaces addressed. The 'apostolic' nature of episcopal life is a feature of the diocesan structure. Increasingly the bishop functions more like a 'visitor'.[51] This 'peripatetic' ministry of visitation, of encouraging existing communities, networking and reconnecting communities, assisting in the founding of new ones has a decidedly ancient and Celtic lineage. The idea of a 'missionary bishop' enriches the exercise of episcope and suggests that the more 'settled' episcope of the priest of a local church does have an inescapable episcopal dimension.

The traditional argument for delegation of such an episcope requires a more honest reappraisal. It is not simply a question of parity of orders or stratification. There is a dynamic relation between the two orders, as clearly evidenced from the long history of the tradition.[52] Smaller dioceses make for a more embedded episcopate within the life of the many Eucharistic communities. Yet a more open relation between priest and bishop, where the accent is on the exercise of mutual episcope – as a balance to delegation *of* and sharing *in* the bishop's episcope – can enrich and model a form of episcope for the whole people of God. It also addresses the overtones of romanticism underlying a desire to return to the ancient Ignatian model, wherein the bishop presided over the local Eucharistic community. In a modified territorial model (as discussed above), bishop is both apostolic visitor and overseer but this episcope is dynamically related to the episcope of the priest/presbyter of the micro-Eucharistic community. This form of relation and differentiation of functions makes for that generosity of presence so vital for the life of the Church.[53] It is not difficult to see how such an approach would orientate traditional orders to a genuinely collaborative ministry and represent organizationally a 'top-down' influence with positive effect for the ministries of the whole Church.

The great advantage of Anglicanism is that it already has a strong doctrine of the Church catholic and interconnectedness between the many local churches. An ecclesiology from below is one which reconceives territoriality in such a way that the particular and the universal continue to be held in dynamic interplay, but only as the ecclesia is nurtured from the micro-local. *The Church may be the one*

---

[51] Duncan Reid proposes a 'visitor' model for episcopacy as more culturally relevant in an Australian context suspicious of notions of 'oversight' and associated tones of authority. See Reid, 'Are Bishops an Ecumenical Problem?', pp. 302–3.

[52] See Chapter 12 for an extended discussion.

[53] It also lends strength to the ancient tradition of the parity of orders in which the critical differentiation was one of jurisdiction and associated authority to ordain. With the emphasis clearly on the shared episcope of the whole Church the 'parity' argument cannot be so easily dismissed. Compare *The Porvoo Common Statement*: 'The bishop gathers together those who are ordained to share the tasks of ministry and to represent the concerns of the community', par. 44, p. 25. Is it the case that in an episcopal system 'delegation' of episcope is the only way in which a shared episcope might be understood?

form of human community that can meet the postmodern on its own terms without being seduced by the lure of the tribe. Clearly in such a conception the communion of the churches appears fragile and embryonic, a work in progress from a new location. This increases the responsibility of the bishop as the symbol and sign of the Church's unity through time and space. But the sign is a fragile one and points the episcopate and the church to the priority of trusts given and received, lived out of and lived into. Trust is at the heart of the baptismal calling and the one thing needful in our fragmented times.[54]

Catholicity from Below

Such structural changes not only modify traditional approaches to space and territory, and relations between the orders, they also imply a reappraisal of the Church's catholicity. Concomitant to diocesan downsizing is a reconfiguring of catholicity from below. Rather than claim the 'guarantee' and security of catholicity through the episcopal sign, the Church can rediscover what the catholicity of the Church, symbolised through the episcopate, actually means for the local church. It not only means the unity Anglicanism has with the Church universal. It also involves recognition and experience of the wholeness of the Church in any particular place and the need for this to be expressed in the wholeness of an ordered ministry. Yet the episcopal sign is a fractured sign and has been so for centuries. Catholicity has been partial at best; it too is fractured. Downsizing offers an opportunity for recovery of the wholeness of the episcopal sign of catholicity.

It is not clear what the shape might be of a reconfigured catholicity. But it will certainly be an enriched catholicity because smaller diocesan communities provide the basis for much closer working relationship with other churches in a local community, whether we like it, tolerate it or despise it. This interdependence is never an end in itself but for serving the *missio Dei*. This entails the search for wisdom to discern the presence of the sacred and embody the gospel in faith and life in the God's midst. This is precisely the way in which the gains of recent decades in ecumenism might be furthered. For it is in the overlaps and intersections of different ministries of the churches that it is possible to recover a deeper sense of shared episcope for the Church of Jesus Christ. Overcoming distance between the churches through a re-formed catholicity (at the local level) might be the next stage for Anglican ecumenism and strengthen the episcopal sign in the midst of the churches. It may be part of the Anglican brief to re-build the episcopal sign of catholicity from and through the local church. In this way episcopacy may be able to make its own particular contribution to the nurture of a missionary ecclesiology combining strong roots in local communities and a global vision of the coming kingdom.

---

[54] See Anthony Giddens' discussion of trust in the modern world, *The Consequences of Modernity* (Cambridge: Polity Press, 1990), ch. 3.

Deeper into Baptism: The Mark of the Episcopate

It would be an understatement to suggest that re-form of the Church was difficult. Changing outlooks and changing structures have to be achieved against the backdrop of powerful 'attractors': those enduring stories of an organization that shape its present constitution and function negatively to thwart change.[55] Most organizations are in the grip of 'attractors' that skew the organization in certain predetermined directions, functions and forms. Attractors function as systemic sources of chaos in an organization. As such attractors orientate an organization back into repetitive patterns of behaviour and practices that block permissions and prevent healthy changes that arise through the embrace of creative developments. Personnel may come and go, reviews and reorganization may occur but creative change may prove elusive. 'Feedback loops' become fixed and unresponsive to new situations and 'iterations continue to flow throughout the system to support a set of fixed responses'.[56]

The secret powers of an organisation lie in the way attractors exert influence within the organization, most often at subliminal levels. This chapter has drawn attention to the operation of some 'attractors'; stories about episcopal identity formed through mechanical means – unbroken succession in the episcopate; stories that fund a self-constituting autonomy poorly related to the wider episcope of the Church; stories about previous experiences of ruptured identity and recovery based on exclusion. The problem with such attractors is that they thwart initiatives for change; all change becomes 'attracted' to the underlying organization history which serves to nullify change. Attractors contribute to significant organization dysfunction which may lead people to feel that the organization 'isn't going anywhere'. Because attractors operate at subliminal levels the chaotic system can never move into new forms of order and harmony. In such environments 'agents can appear as passive recipients caught in the endless stream of their heritage'.[57] The power of such attractors becomes evident in times of change and transition when there are emerging powers based on newly forming stories – shared episcope, collaborative ministry, cooperative ventures.

The above proposals require a significant change in attitudes towards the exercise of power. It is simplistic to claim that bishops have too much power; or that other more 'invisible' people or groups exert power or even that structural imbalances in power need attention. These claims may be conceded immediately; the circuits of power can be uncovered. Beyond this there is the power of the stories that we are unable to forget, of pasts that determine present dispositions. How is the power of such stories broken or exorcised? Re-forming episcopacy will involve a revisitation, a remembering of the identity shaping pasts that hold us.

---

55 See Peat, *From Certainty to Uncertainty*, pp. 146–9.

56 Ibid., p. 148.

57 R.C. Holb, *Jurgen Habermas: Critique in the Public Sphere* (New York: Routledge, 1991), p. 66.

Episcopal memory carries a host of stories that may need to be re-membered, put back together in another way; in short, allowed to die that they might be reconstituted.[58] What emerges will depend entirely upon where the gaze is set, its orientation and the company kept. The argument of this chapter is that re-membering has to generate a 'grounded episcopate' more closely woven into the pastoral and missionary dimensions of the ministries of the local church. This more collaborative form of episcopacy requires a giving up as well as a taking on of new challenges. But this kind of remembering involves *metanoia* and renewal. It is the baptismal gift and the more deeply the episcopate enters such waters the greater will be the communion of the whole body of Christ.[59] The possibility of fulfilling episcopal vows is rooted in Christian baptism, of giving up, being reconstituted and re-formed in Christ through the Spirit. Luther's statement is as relevant to the episcopate as to any Christian; 'we all crawl towards our baptism'. It is as relevant to the community of faith as it is to its office bearers. The reason is clear. It is only as the ecclesia as a whole reappropriates the baptismal gift through the development of new forms of polity that a re-formed episcopate can make its vows in trust to God.

---

[58] Duncan Reid concludes his examination of bishops as an ecumenical problem thus: 'Churches may be called to give up, in an act of Christlike self-emptying, something precious that has been received.' Importantly Reid notes that 'It is not necessarily the most obvious – in this case the historic episcopate.... It may be the administrative authority we tend to invest in bishops, which frequently stands in the way of their exploring the diaconal elements of their own Christian episcope. It is certainly the tunnel-vision that has prevented us in the past from seeing genuine episcope manifested in non-episcopal churches' (Reid, 'Are Bishops an Ecumenical Problem?', p. 305).

[59] See *Communion, Conflict and Hope*. The Kuala Lumpur Report of the Third Inter-Anglican Theological and Doctrinal Commission (London: Anglican Communion Office, 2008), 'Appendix 2: The Anglican Way: The Significance of the Episcopal Office for the Communion of the Church', pp. 57–66.

Chapter 12
Episcopacy from Below: The Ecumenical Gift

Introduction: The Church in Extensive Mode

The previous chapter argued for a more 'grounded episcopate' as the basis for higher grade cooperation and collaboration among bearers of the episcope of the Church. This entailed a modified territoriality and the development of an emergent catholicity 'from below' as a compliment to a 'top-down influence'. This would assist in generating strong networks of collegiality between different local churches. The re-form of the episcopate along such lines involved a recovery of the reciprocity between what was identified in Chapter 8 as an 'emergent' and 'whole–part influence': a feature of complex systems in nature and society. The recovery of such a complementarity frees the Church from appeal to 'episcopal vitalism', that is, the supposition that it is necessary to 'add' something from outside the system in order to secure the authority and influence of the 'order that orders'. When this occurs (for example, invoking of particular notions of 'apostolic succession' as a dogmatic principal) the potential for genuine collaboration between the ministries is thwarted by a false 'top-down causality'.

The critique and proposals for a re-form of the episcopate thus represents the outworking of a theory of collaborative ministry developed in Chapter 8 and 9. In those chapters more complex forms of social ordering extended over a wider reach than 'lower-level' ordering. Nonetheless the different levels of ordering remained vitally related, interdependent and influential in reciprocal ways. The problem with more usual forms of episcopal polity is one of excessive 'distance' between the ministries of episcope that are supposed to be interdependent, not independent. This is not overcome by formal arrangements such as delegation by licence as a way of others sharing in a diocesan bishop's episcope. This may be necessary but can never be in and of itself sufficient. To speak of a 'grounded episcopate' was intended to highlight the priority of ministry as a 'set of dynamically ordered relations' (Chapter 9). How this might be worked out in various concrete situations clearly requires further work.

The discussion in Chapter 11 focused on the Church in its intensive mode, that is, its internal organization and life. However, when we consider the Church in its extensive mode of being – its way of being in the world – we find that the dynamics of a 'grounded episcopate' makes a similar claim upon the life of the Church. This chapter examines more carefully the way in which the ecumenical dimension of the Church calls forth and is a catalyst for a re-form of the episcopate from the ground up.[1]

When Anglicanism reaches beyond itself it invariably discovers something more about its own identity and calling. This is the gift of the 'other' whether it is on a personal, communal or institutional level. No doubt as bishops act as representative figures for the Church in society they are continually reminded of the true weight and responsibility the episcopal office carries as a prophetic witness in the world. But this also occurs at the intra-church level. This dimension of the Church's extensive mode of being generates a degree of episcopal self-consciousness. This occurs because as Anglicans listen to those from other churches, and are called to give an account of their own identity and hopes, they are necessarily drawn to reflect on the integrity, viability and possibilities for their own church. In particular, the ecumenical stage offers each church time and space to encounter itself through the 'other'. This is an ecumenical gift which comes almost by the way in a larger and more intentional listening beyond the confines of one's own communion. It is quite possible for particular churches to misuse the ecumenical space as a means to engage in internal debate and political manoeuvring.[2] When this happens the gift is effectively spurned. What issues arise for Anglicans in ecumenical conversations in relation to the episcopate? What implicit theology of episcopacy becomes explicit through such ecumenical encounters? What necessary re-form of episcopal ministry emerges from such dialogue? How might the ecumenical dimension of ministry contribute to a more vital collaborative approach to the Church's common ministry in the gospel? These questions form the background to this discussion.

An *Episcopally* Ordered Church

Is Anglicanism an *episcopally* ordered church? Certainly Anglicans can point to the existence of the threefold order of bishops, priests and deacons as parts of its ancient inheritance. How is this ordering understood by other episcopally ordered churches? What integrity and validity adheres to Anglican episcopal ministry? These issues have been particularly important when Anglicans have

---

1 The emphasis in this chapter is on the ecumenical dimension of the Church as an example of its extensive mode of being. It recognises that there are a range of ways in which the Church's extensity is expressed.

2 This danger was alluded to indirectly by the then general secretary of the Anglican General Synod, Revd Dr. Bruce Kaye, in a press release of 25 Nov. 2002 following his address to the Faith and Unity Commission of the Uniting Church. He stated in part: 'It is important to recognise that such dialogues not only deal with relations between churches, they also provide an external focus for the internal divisions within each of the churches. It becomes therefore a question of the integrity for Anglicans that we bring our conversations together and relate them openly to the differences within our own church'.

been in conversation with the Roman Catholic and Orthodox churches. As an example I will briefly examine the ARCIC agreed statements on ministry that have become an ecumenical benchmark for Anglican self-understanding over the last 30 years. The 1973 statement on ministry noted that 'the full emergence of the threefold ministry' occurred in the second century in the post-apostolic age and thereafter 'this threefold structure became universal in the Church'.[3] Essential to the ordained ministry is 'oversight' (episcope), a ministry in which 'presbyters are joined with the Bishop' and in the ministry of 'the word and the sacraments'.[4] Deacons likewise 'are associated' with bishops and presbyters in these things.[5] The Eucharist is the central act of worship and, interestingly, the Ignatian practice of linking the ministry of oversight with Eucharistic presidency is affirmed.[6] The centrality of the Eucharist means that the 'essential nature of ministry' is expressed therein.[7] Sacrificial categories are appropriate, first in relation to the once-for-all offering of Christ then, by virtue of presiding at the 'memorial of the sacrifice of Christ, the minister 'is seen to stand in a sacramental relation to what Christ himself did'.[8]

Although 'Christian ministers' 'share through baptism in the priesthood of the people of God … nevertheless their ministry is not an extension of the common Christian priesthood but belongs to another realm of the gifts of the Spirit'.[9] In relation to this matter the 'Elucidations' (1979) noted that the priesthood of the people and that of the ordained ministry 'are two distinct realities which relate, each in its own way, to the priesthood of Christ … which is their source and model'.[10]

Those in orders enter by ordination into 'this apostolic and God-given ministry'.[11] Presbyters, by joining the bishop in the laying on of hands at the ordination of a presbyter 'thus signify the shared nature of the commission entrusted to them'.[12] Ordination signifies the unity of local churches in themselves and with one another and this finds symbolic expression when other bishops lay hands on a bishop: 'this new Bishop and his church are within the communion of churches'.[13] Their participation also 'ensures the historic continuity of this church

[3] Anglican–Roman Catholic International Commission, *Final Report*, par. 6.

[4] Ibid., par. 9.

[5] Ibid.

[6] Ibid., par. 12.

[7] Ibid., par. 13.

[8] Ibid.

[9] Ibid.

[10] See 'Elucidations 1979 (Ministry and Ordination)' in Anglican–Roman Catholic International Commission, *Final Report*, pp. 40–45 (this reference p. 41, par. 2).

[11] Ibid., par. 14.

[12] Ibid., par. 16.

[13] Ibid.

with the apostolic Church and of its Bishop with the original apostolic ministry'.[14] The 'Elucidations' noted that episcope was exercised in terms of the threefold form but that the commission purposely did not examine whether episcope could be 'realised' in any other form. However, it was stated that 'episcope *must*[15] be exercised by ministers ordained in the apostolic succession'.[16]

The ARCIC statements on ministry centred on the origin and nature of ordained ministry and would have given confidence to Anglicans concerning the ministerial integrity of their orders. Indeed, the *Elucidations* suggested that it was time for a 'reappraisal of the verdict on Anglican Orders in *Apostolicae Curae* (1896)'.[17]

However, over two decades later the status of Anglican episcopal orders appears no more secure than in 1896. Recent statements from official quarters of the Roman Church signify a serious retreat from ARCIC. It seems that the expression 'sister church' ('ever beloved sister') is an 'improper' designation for the Anglican Church for the reason that 'sister church' refers to particular churches that have preserved a valid episcopate and Eucharist.[18] The Anglican Church, as one of the 'separated ecclesial communities' of Vatican II is now deemed, along with other churches of the Reformation not to be a church 'in the proper sense'. This ecclesial downgrading evidently arises due to the 'lack of the sacrament of orders that have not preserved the genuine and total reality of the Eucharistic mystery'.[19] It is perfectly in keeping with this view that the nineteenth-century judgement on Anglican orders has been recently described by Rome as an 'infallible papal declaration'.[20]

This raises a number of issues. First, clearly the official pronouncements from the Vatican give little encouragement that the Church of Rome has moved beyond a fairly archaic mechanicalism when it comes to questions of apostolic succession. This can take two forms either (a) a strong form which presumes an unproblematic reading of the early sub- and post-apostolic period as regards historical links or (b) a softer approach which appeals to an evolutionary developmental process

[14] Ibid.

[15] My italics. The 'Elucidations' predate *Baptism, Eucharist and Ministry* on episcope by three years. What we now take for granted about the importance of episcope throughout the whole church is in fact a relatively new development.

[16] Anglican–Roman Catholic International Commission, *Final Report*, par. 4

[17] Ibid., par. 6

[18] Roman Catholic statements as referred to in Francis Sullivan, *From Apostles to Bishops* (New York: The Newman Press, 2001), p. 233.

[19] Ibid., p. 3.

[20] Ibid., p. 3. Cf. p. 237 n. 4, in which Sullivan refers to Joseph Ratzinger, 'Commentary on Profession of Faith's Concluding Paragraphs', *Origins* 28/8 (1998): 119 as a source. See further, Francis Sullivan, 'A New Obstacle to Anglican–Roman Catholic Dialogue', *America* 179/3 (1–8 August 1998): 6–7.

which claims a presumption in favour of the Catholic apostolic lineage.[21] Either way the 'divine institution' of the ordained ministry is asserted on dogmatic grounds; it becomes a statement of faith.[22] Rome, it seems, continues to determine the ecclesial status of Anglicanism (and other churches) on the basis of judgements concerning the retention of a valid apostolic ministry. As Anglicanism fails the 'ministry test' it is judged not a church 'in the proper sense'. Ministry matters are being decided without reference to ecclesiology.

Second, this highlights a fundamental issue concerning the reciprocity that obtains between ministry and church. The Roman Catholic ecumenist, Francis Sullivan has stated:

> The approach taken by the CDF [Congregation for the Doctrine of the Faith] in its recent documents moves on only one direction: from a negative assessment of the ordained ministry in the ecclesial communities to a negative conclusion about their ecclesial character. Because they lack the episcopate in the apostolic succession, they are 'not churches in the proper sense'.[23]

This leads to a further point. Dialogue with Rome is a two-edged sword for Anglicans. What is given with one hand seems to be withdrawn by the other. Officially at least Anglican bishops are not 'real' bishops. Managing episcopal identity in such an environment requires a high degree of inner composure regarding the character and quality of the episcopally ordered communion, *Ecclesia Anglicana*. This should be also a humbling reminder that when Anglicans enter into dialogue with *other* episcopal and non-episcopal churches they need to be careful not to commit the same error as Rome.

Sullivan's comment above is apposite. Lack of an ecclesial consciousness in matters of ministry generates significant deformity when it comes to handling episcopal identity. Issues concerning the status of orders cannot be secured in an historicist or dogmatic manner without reference to an accompanying ecclesiology.

---

21 But this latter is more akin to Newman's *homogenous* theory of development which has little capacity to deal with discontinuities. Innovations are incorporated and assimilated in such a way that the emerging organic system of Christianity remains faithful to the original. There can be no surprises as such. See Newman's discussion on the power of assimilation' in John Henry Newman, *An Essay on the Development of Doctrine* [1845], ed. and intro. J. Cameron (Harmondsworth: Penguin Books, 1974), ch. 1, sec. 3, sub. sec. 5. (p. 131).

22 The appeal to 'divine institution' continues even in softer forms which presume a providential developmental process for the emergence of episcopal government. The difficulty is that adherence to notions of 'institution' import significantly more warrants for the historically contingent pattern than are justified at the bar of history or in dogmatics per se.

23 Sullivan, *From Apostles to Bishops*, p. 235.

The Anglican/Orthodox dialogues seem to have a greater awareness of this.[24] So too, it seems does the Roman Church as evidenced by its response to *Baptism, Eucharist and Ministry* on the recognition of ordained ministries:

> The recognition of the ordained ministry and of the ecclesial character of a Christian community are indissolubly and mutually related. To the extent that it can be recognized that a communion now exits between the churches and ecclesial communities, however imperfect that communion may be, there is implied some recognition of the ecclesial reality of the other. The question that follows is what does this communion imply for the way in which we perceive the ministry of the other?[25]

This more enlightened method of reasoning offers clues to Anglicans about how they interpret and appeal to their own episcopal tradition in *intra*- and *inter*-church dialogue. The reciprocal relation between ministry and Church does suggest that the basis of both may be found in baptism as the primary sacramental sign of the common ecclesial and ministerial calling of the people of God. A baptismal ecclesiology may provide the basis for an Anglican and ecumenical theology of the episcopate.[26]

A Church in 'The Historic Episcopate'

Anglicanism is not merely an episcopally ordered church, it is one 'in the *historic* episcopate'. The phrase from the Chicago–Lambeth Quadrilateral 1868 is the fourth 'element'[27] in the Anglican vision for the reunion of the churches. Yet the phrase harbours a variety of meanings for Anglicans. Most obviously it draws attention to the fact that bishops in Anglicanism have an identity informed by

---

[24] See, for example, *The Moscow Agreed Statement: Anglican–Orthodox Dialogue* (London: SPCK, 1977), sec. 6, 'The Church and the Eucharistic Community'; *The Dublin Agreed Statement: Anglican–Orthodox Dialogue* (London: SPCK, 1984), sec. 1, 'The Mystery of the Church'. These statements locate the primary continuity of apostolicity in the Eucharistic life of the Christian community through its local embodiments in time and space. Matters of ministry and episcopal character and status are placed within this larger frame.

[25] Quoted in Sullivan, *From Apostles to Bishops*, p. 235.

[26] For the importance of a baptismal paradigm for Anglican ecclesiology see Avis, *Anglicanism and the Christian Church*, ch. 18.

[27] In more discussions the constituents of the Quadrilateral have been given a more dynamic and integrative interpretation as 'a correlative set of "institutions"' and a 'system of communication whose several parts presuppose and depend upon each other' (see Norris, 'Bishops, Succession and the Apostolicity of the Church', pp. 61–2).

reference to the past, in fact to a past that stretches back to the early apostolic church. This much was agreed in the ARCIC conversations.

But what kind of lineage is it? The Anglican historian, Richard Norris, notes that it is,difficult 'to speak of "apostolic succession" or of "succession from the apostles", if by these expressions one intends to assert either that "the apostles" instituted the episcopal office as we know (or even as Christians of the late second century knew it), or that one can trace a clear "chain" of succession from any given bishop at any given time in history back to one or more "apostles"'.[28]

The latter view finds earliest expression in Cyprian who espoused a theory of 'succession by consecration' or succession of episcopal authority handed down by means of ordination.[29] Cyprian's notion of the episcopal authority necessary for administrative governance has had an enduring influence on Western ecclesiology in particular.[30] It has continued to influence Anglicanism and became particularly popular through the Tractarian movement of the nineteenth century. The 'chain' theory of succession, as an interpretation of the 'historic episcopate' endures in the mind of some Anglicans even in ecumenical circles.[31] The problem is the theory runs into the sand in the Church of the second century. It begs the question, why stop in the second century? For it appears to be precisely this period in which ministry patterns were still in a relative state of flux and before this time in the post-apostolic period the situation is even more unclear.

The appeal to an 'unbroken succession' of bishops back to the apostles offers certainty but it disregards the results of historical inquiry. However, as we have seen above, it remains part of contemporary Roman apologetic, as a dogmatic proposition, at least in some circles. It should also be noted that now this apologetic does not serve the Christian Church's claim for legitimacy in relation to second century Gnostic sects, but in regard to inter Christian dispute about legitimacy *within* the ecclesia of God. Norris also reminds us that in the early Church the claim for unbroken succession was 'fragile', 'secondary and supportive' to the wisdom of the churches of the time to discern 'whose "inheritance" was more likely to represent the lineaments of the original kerygma'.[32]

The discussion about the 'historic episcopate' has been enriched by more recent Anglican reflection on the themes of apostolicity and succession in the light of

---

28 Ibid., p. 55.

29 Ibid., p. 28.

30 Richard P.C. Hanson, 'The Nature of the Anglican Episcopate', in Michael Ramsey (ed.), *Lambeth Essays on Ministry: Essays written for the Lambeth Conference 1968* (London: SPCK, 1969), p. 82.

31 For example, see the view of the Anglican ecumenist Colin Podmore in his debate with Thomas Ferguson (Colin Podmore, 'Historian's Debate: "The Moravian Episcopate and the Episcopal Church": A Personal Response'. *Anglican and Episcopal History* 72/3 [2003]: 365). The discussion centred on the Anglican–Moravian Dialogue and the interpretation of the *Porvoo Common Statement*.

32 Norris, 'Bishops, Succession', p. 55.

new dialogues between the Anglican Church in the United Kingdom and various episcopal and non-episcopal churches in Europe. Apostolicity is now understood to encompass the whole life of the Church and is 'exemplified' and 'embodied' in 'marks' or 'elements': canon of Scriptures, creeds, confessional writings, liturgies, activities of preaching, celebrating sacraments, exercising pastoral care and oversight, common life of the church, engagement in mission. Apostolicity thus encompasses faith, sacrament, ministry and service.[33]

The appeal to the 'historic episcopate' remains important for Anglicans in so far as the bishop's *office* can be said to succeed the apostles in the essential element of oversight or *episcope.*[34] It also points to the fact that appeal to a legitimate succession in the office of the episcopate does carry weight in relation to the diachronic unity of the church. However, within a new ecumenical vision of the apostolic life, the office of bishop becomes a genuine sign and symbol of the connectedness of apostolic faith and life through time and space. But it is a *sign among other signs* and is not a 'guarantee' of fidelity.[35] Rather, bishops 'serve, symbolise and guard' the continuity of faith and communion; a sign 'of assurance to the faithful that the Church remains in continuity with the apostles' teaching and mission', but no individual bishop can provide this assurance alone.[36] The result is an enriched catholicity and apostolicity that is concerned less with an unbroken succession of persons and more with the unbroken continuity of apostolic communities; the tradition familiar to the Orthodox Church.[37]

These fresh insights on apostolicity and episcopacy as sign find embodiment in the *Porvoo Common Statement.* In this dialogue it is noted that: 'To ordain a bishop in the historic succession (that is, in intended continuity from the apostles themselves) is also a sign [of the kingdom of God]' but 'does not of itself guarantee fidelity of a church to every aspect of the apostolic life and mission … nor the personal faithfulness of the Bishop'.[38] The *Porvoo Common Statement* breaks new ground in ecumenical dialogue when it states that, 'a church which has preserved the sign of historic Episcopal succession is free to acknowledge an authentic Episcopal ministry in a church which has preserved continuity in the Episcopal office by an occasional priestly/presbyteral ordination at the time of the Reformation'.[39] Importantly the statement goes on: 'The mutual acknowledgement of our churches and ministries is theologically prior to the use of the sign of the laying on of hands in the historic succession'.

---

33 See the important background document for many dialogues, *Apostolicity and Succession*, par. 36. The above quotation is said to resonate with the Chicago–Lambeth Quadrilateral – all 'parts of a single system of communication' (par. 39).

34 Norris, 'Bishops, Succession', p. 54.

35 *Apostolicity and Succession*, par. 60.

36 Ibid.

37 Ibid., par. 67.

38 See ref. in *Apostolicity and Succession*, par. 69, part D.

39 Ibid.

The developments signalled in Porvoo find echoes in other conversations with American Lutherans and the Moravians, both of whom retain the episcopal sign.[40] The broader ecclesiological foundation for understanding apostolicity is similarly critical for Anglicans in dialogue with non-episcopal churches. This is reflected in the Meissen agreement and in Anglican dialogues with the Lutheran and Uniting churches in Australia.[41] In these contexts the episcopate as sign and symbol is a challenge for all churches rather than a problem to be solved by the non-episcopal churches. This is particularly the case in the report of the recent dialogue in the United Kingdom between the Church of England and Methodist churches.[42] This report signals a clear statement of intention that both churches will work together to address the question of the sign of episcopacy, its form and function.

However, in these ecumenical contexts tensions and inconsistencies have emerged in the Anglican commitment to episcopacy. Might it be that episcopal succession is a 'practical dogma' for Anglicans? Is there not a tension between 'the developing Anglican tendency to recognize the existing apostolicity of a church without "the historic episcopate"' and the insistence 'on the need of its presence for full communion'?[43] Such questions can no longer be contained within Anglicanism but now have to be pursued in conversation with other churches. The danger in discussions about episcopacy is a tendency to default to forms of 'episcopal vitalism'. This phrase was used in Chapter 8 and 9 as an example of the addition of a vital ingredient from 'outside' the system. It is a way of protecting the ecclesial system from ministerial reductionism but it imports into an organic understanding of the Church serious dissonance. We observed this in Chapter 4 in the Anglo-Catholic Moberly's account of the divine institution of episcopacy as an instrument of unity from beyond and over against the Church.

Recovering Anglican episcopal identity is a task that has benefited greatly from the ecumenical endeavours of recent decades. The question of identity through history has been enriched through new appreciations of the apostolicity of the Church. This stronger and more intentional ecclesiological base opens up the possibility for Anglicans to offer a more generous appreciation and work more cooperatively with the ministries of other churches. It also has a reflexive impact upon Anglican assessments of its own episcopal sign. Episcopal identity is not shaped by the past rather narrowly construed (single line theory of office and/or of consecration), nor can simple appeals of a dogmatic kind to 'divine institution'

---

40 Ibid., pars. 72–4.

41 The Anglican–Uniting Church dialogue in Australia developed its own framework on the basis of Meissen as a model for conversations between episcopal and non-episcopal churches. See *For the Sake of the Gospel*, par. 3.5.

42 *Anglican–Methodist Covenant*, esp. par. 193.

43 See Geoffrey Wainwright, 'Is Episcopal Succession a Matter of Dogma for Anglicans? The Evidence of Some Recent Dialogues' in C. Podmore (ed.), *Community, Unity and Communion: Essays in Honour of Mary Tanner* (London: Church House, 1998), p. 175.

be sustained in the ecumenical environment. The 'historic episcopate' is a more dynamic sign and symbol than Anglicans may have hitherto appreciated. This is the ecumenical gift that makes possible a generous appreciation of the oversight embodied in other churches and a greater capacity for listening and re-forming of the character of the episcopate within the Anglicanism. It has become increasingly clear that the 'historic episcopate' is first of all a 'shared episcope'.

The Concept of a 'Shared Episcope'

The distinction between episcopacy and episcope has proven one of the most fruitful lines of exploration ecumenically alongside the notion of *koinonia*. The distinction opens up an ecumenical space for participants from many churches for episcope functions as an 'open textured concept'.[44] Building on *Baptism, Eucharist and Ministry*, recent reflections offer the possibility of episcopally ordered churches recognising some common bonds in ministry with non-episcopal churches on the basis that *episcope* takes many forms. But is this a distinction based on pragmatic grounds by eager ecumenists or does it also have a foundation in dogmatics as such? The matter has recently received attention from the Anglican theologian, John Webster.[45]

Webster argues that the Church's commission to bear witness to the gospel through proclamation, sacrament and service necessarily requires an ordered ministry: 'Because the church is a visible and enduring arena of common life and action, authorised to indicate the gospel, "official" patterns of ministry are required'.[46] Such 'office' does not usurp the work of Christ or the Spirit or the witness of the whole Church rather it facilitates and unifies the authenticity of the Church's apostolic life. For this reason the Church's 'office' is an essential part of the fabric of the Christian community's formation in Christ. 'In this sense episcope, oversight, is the basic ministry of the church'.[47] He continues, 'What orthodoxy is in the realm of reflection, episcope is in the realm of practice and order: an instrument through which the church is recalled to Christianness, to the appropriateness of its action and speech to the truth of the gospel'. Webster's remarks on episcope point to the centrality of this ministry of oversight in the Christian Church.

The distinction between such *episcope* and the particular forms in which it has historically been expressed in the churches has been a critical development in the ecumenical arena over the past two decades. *Baptism, Eucharist and Ministry*

44 See Brent, *Cultural Episcopacy*, p. 59.

45 John Webster, 'The Self-Organizing Power of the Gospel of Christ: Episcopacy and Community Formation', *International Journal of Systematic Theology* 3/1 (March 2001): 69–82.

46 Webster, 'The Self-Organizing Power of the Gospel', p. 77.

47 Ibid.

called attention to the relationship between the office of the episcopate and the ministry of *episcope*. In doing so it pointed to the three forms in which oversight (*episcope*) occurred: personal, collegial and communal. The challenge for the churches has been to understand more fully how their own communions participate in *episcope* in these three essential areas of ecclesial life.

These insights have flowed into many bilateral dialogues, in particular between Anglicans and non-episcopal churches. When *episcope* is understood within the whole life of the Church a foundation is established for approaching particular questions about the commensurability of ordained ministries between the churches. Anglicans are able to recognise the practice of *episcope* in non-episcopally ordered churches and at the same time are challenged to reassess the variety and relations between the ministries in their own episcopally ordered church. Non-episcopal dialogue partners are called to consider how they might adopt the sign of the 'historic episcopate' within their own communion as a means of restoring a fuller personal *episcope*. Anglicans are challenged to reconsider the way in which the episcopal office might more appropriately embody the personal dimension that it theoretically espouses. The failure to embody a truly personal episcope due to defects in ecclesial structure and reversion to management disciplines (Chapter 11) is one of the deep ironies of the Anglican episcopate. More work needs to be done in this area, however the focus on *episcope* has raised some important issues for the identity of Anglican episcopacy. This suggests that ecclesial and ministerial identity cannot be crafted in isolation from that wider *episcope* of the people of God. *Episcope is a shared activity with particular foci and complementary forms.* This is a cure for an unhealthy mono-episcopacy in Anglicanism and points to the importance of ecclesiology as a critical dialogue partner in all discussions on ministry within and between the churches.

The Parity of Orders Debate

The shared nature of *episcope* opens up an interesting and not unimportant long running issue concerning the parity of orders between episcopate and presbyterate briefly touched on in the previous chapter. Many Anglicans would be surprised to discover that the relation between these two orders of oversight has a long and contentious history.[48] In the modern period the Anglican scholar and bishop of Durham, J.B. Lightfoot, in a celebrated essay, *The Christian Ministry* (1868), examined the matter.[49] He came to the conclusion that in the New Testament through

---

48 For discussion of the leading Anglican divines in the debate see the scholarly and fair-minded assessments of the early twentieth-century scholar A.J. Mason, *The Church of England and Episcopacy* (Cambridge: Cambridge University Press,1914), ch. 2 and the appendices. For an important but less balanced view see T.G. Jalland, 'The Doctrine of the Parity of Ministers' in Kirk (ed.), *The Apostolic Ministry*, pp. 304–49. See Philip Hughes' introduction to Lightfoot's, *The Christian Ministry* for an excellent overview.

49 See Chapter 4.

to the early second century, presbyterate and episcopate were interchangeable terms and that the mono-episcopate emerged in the early second century via episcopal elevation from the presbyterate. Lightfoot was hardly alone in this view given its general acceptance in the Roman Catholic Church though his scholarship gave great weight to his conclusions.[50]

The alternative view was that the presbyterate evolved by delegation from the episcopate, the former being a position of honour rather than office. Some of this argument surfaced in our examination Moberly's *Ministerial Priesthood* in Chapter 4. The contemporary Anglican historian, J. Robert Wright, believes that this 'higher' view of the distinctiveness of the Episcopal office was accepted in the Church of England of the mid-seventeenth century.[51] He points to the reorganisation of the Scripture passages to be read at the rites for priesthood and episcopate as evidence of the elevation and distinctness of the episcopate.[52] It is embodied in the rite for episcopal ordination in the 1979 *Book of Common Prayer of the Episcopal Church*. That the matter has been contentious is evidenced by the fact that it was only in 1968 at Vatican II that the Roman Catholic Church moved from a parity of ministers position to the second view, that 'the episcopate is the primary order of ministry constituting the fullness of the sacrament of holy orders'.[53] Modern scholarship increasingly supports the position of Lightfoot and a clearly recognised stream in the Catholic tradition.[54] Furthermore recent scholarship also points to the sheer novelty of the terms *presbyter* and *episcopos* in relation to both Jewish roots and Hellenism.[55] The historian Robin Lane Fox (who does not share sympathies with Christianity) concludes that the bishop in the early Church represented an innovation within the socio-cultural world of the time.[56]

The discussion of *episcope* breaks open the same field (the relations between the ministries) from a different perspective. It is instructive for the purposes of this inquiry for it indicates that episcopal identity has to be re-formed in relation to other ministries of oversight and it is not sufficient to retreat to well worn paths in this process. Episcopal ministry is historically contingent and this has to be held in tension with the claim for 'divine institution' of the orders. There is a general consensus that in the early period of Christianity (a) the development of the ministries of oversight is unclear, (b) that evidence clearly suggests a multiplicity

---

[50] Edwin Hatch had distinguished the two maintaining an 'equivalence of rank'. See Josaitis, *Edwin Hatch and Early Church Order*, p. 48.

[51] J. Robert Wright, 'The Origins of the Episcopate and Episcopal Ministry in the Early Church' in Wright (ed.), *On Being a Bishop*, p. 21.

[52] Ibid., p. 22.

[53] Ibid., p. 24.

[54] See Benjamine Merkle, *The Elder and Overseer: One Office in the Early Church* (New York: Peter Lang, 2003). Merkle offers a careful and comprehensive assessment of the state of contemporary scholarship citing support from other scholars. See p. 63.

[55] Ibid.

[56] See, Robin Lane Fox, *Pagan and Christians*, ch. 10.

of patterns, and (c) ministries were interchangeable en route to a consolidated mono-episcopal form. The modern ecumenical movement has given a degree of legitimacy to the diverse forms of episcope that have evolved in the churches.

We have entered a period in which the flux of ministries in the sub- and post-apostolic periods has become an important dialogue partner for all the churches. If Anglicans are to continue with an episcopal ministry in its threefold form they will have to do so in the light of the historically contingent nature of their orders; the reality of conflict about those orders; the unsettled and creative space of contemporary ecumenism, and the new possibilities that arise for re-forming and re-relating the episcopate to the Church and its ministries of *episcope*.

This is particularly important in Anglicanism for, as we have already observed in the discussion of episcopate and the management revolution (Chapter 11), a central issue concerns the diocesan structure as an inhibitor of an embedded episcopal ministry in local Eucharistic communities. Given this systemic difficulty Anglicans have maintained the theory of episcopal order through delegation to the presbyterate that represents the bishop. But *de facto* the substantive *episcope* of the eucharistic community is embodied in the presbyterate as the local *episcopos*. The matter has been stated boldly by the Episcopalian priest Alvin Kimel:

> The modern parish pastor exercises all ministries that previously belonged to a second-century bishop. He or she is the centre of unity within the congregation, serving the congregation as preacher, teacher, care-giver, administrator, baptiser, and eucharistic president. The parish priest is in reality not a presbyter but a bishop. The exception to this claim is the privilege of ordination.[57]

Kimel's main ally in this is, perhaps not surprisingly, the Orthodox bishop John Zizioulas. Zizioulas laments the present implosion of the ministries into the presbyterate and argues, as we have seen in Chapter 11, for the restoration of the bishop in the local Eucharistic community. However, from an Anglican point of view a more dialectical and open-ended relation between priest and bishop based on a significant measure of commensurability between the two forms of oversight allows for a multi-layered episcope requiring genuine collaboration and reciprocity between the ministries. In a more 'grounded episcopate' this reciprocity would be exemplified in the relationship between priest and bishop.

In fact Anglicanism embodies in its theory and practice of *episcope* a debt to two complementary and legitimate traditions from the early Church. The tradition identified by Lightfoot of an emergent episcopacy from an earlier presbyterate became the basis for a later devolution of episcopal ministry to the presbyterate. This points to an original dynamic and mutual relation between the episcopate and presbyterate: emergent and devolutionary. This more integrative relation became problematic for Anglicans from the seventeenth century and the two traditions

---

[57] Alvin F. Kimel Jr., 'Who are the Bishops? Episkope and the Church', *Anglican Theological Review* 77/1 (Winter 1995): 70.

were often viewed over against one another, representative of different ecclesial traditions rather than subsisting within any one tradition. That the latter was in fact the case is clearly evidenced in the Roman Catholic tradition and the long-standing debate about whether priest and bishop belonged to one essential order. It would appear that there is a need both to make sense of our polity and practice both for internal integrity and ecumenical honesty.

Collaboration on the Ground: The Ecumenical Gift

This chapter has highlighted the importance and imperative of a collaborative approach to the practice of episcope in the Church. This has emerged in three areas. First, I noted that the episcopate is dynamically related to the nature of the Church. The tendency to develop the episcopate on a parallel track from the Church, has come under increasing pressure. The dynamic relation between ministry and church means it is no longer adequate to determine the validity of ministries independently from the nature of the ecclesial life in which they operate. At this level we have to take more seriously the fact that different nomenclature (superintendent, bishop, moderator), whilst not necessarily indicating one-to-one correspondence, nonetheless warrants careful attention. Episcopacy might not be ubiquitous but at higher levels of social complexity there are emergent orders that share commensurable tasks and responsibilities. Significant differences remain. However, these are differences within ecclesial systems that are differentiated, ordered and representative. Accordingly, there is a strong imperative for the divided parts of the body of Christ to offer a generous appraisal of each other's attempts to give expression to the demands of a representative ministry that sees over other ministries. This presses home when it is 'up close and personal', where shared contexts and common tasks confront the dismembered body of Christ.

A second area in which the ecumenical dimension of episcopacy has led to a more sympathetic listening and appreciation of other communions concerned the notion of the 'historic episcopate'. This has been for many years interpreted somewhat narrowly however the impact of the ecumenical movement has enriched our understanding of the notion of apostolicity. This resides primarily within the body of the Church rather than the preserve of a pure line of leadership. The broadening of the concept of apostolicity has re-contextualised the meaning of the 'historic episcopate' and 'apostolic succession'. The episcopate is *one* sign of apostolicity of the church, not *the* guarantee. Moreover, in a broken body of Christ the sign is fragile and partial though highly valued. Conditions have emerged for a much closer working relationship between the multi-layered ways in which the apostolicity of the Church is expressed both *within* particular churches and *between* churches. Ecumenism necessarily draws the ministries of oversight together.

Finally, I have noted the significance of the distinction between episcope and episcopate. Where episcope is a shared venture in the Church, the episcopate is necessarily brought into closer relation with the richer episcope of the Church.

This too is the fruit of a growing ecumenism. It is experienced at the local level where the ministries of the churches 'bump' into one another and join in common tasks.

In the above ways there has been a breakdown of older boundaries, an overcoming of distance and an increasing impatience with disjunctions between ministries and also between churches. Moreover as I have argued from the outset of this book *inter-church* divisions on ministry are in fact mirror images of *intra-church* fractures. Unreconciled ministries between the churches are more often mirrors of intra-church confusion. The *inter* and *intra* are correlated. This means that the integrity of ministry has a double aspect. Accordingly, changes and developments of a more integrative kind ought to be reflected throughout the system. The ecumenical world has disturbed established boundaries and opened up the particular churches to the presence of the 'other' both across the divides and within each church. The churches, under pressure of internal reordering and confronted by common challenges in regard to mission and witness require an ecumenical vision. A litmus test for this will be the way the new-found resonances and links between the churches and their ministries are reflected in a more genuine collaborative venture in mission and witness. The ecumenical gift includes a new practice of episcopacy that reflects shared episcope, within a broad based apostolic church, which values richly layered representative ministries. An episcopacy 'from below' is the logic of a cooperative approach to ministry; the discovery of common tasks and challenges on 'the ground' is generative of new forms of episcope and its relation to the episcopate of the Church.

Episcopal re-form requires a critical assessment of the theological foundations upon which the episcopate has been erected. Anglican dialogue with other churches directs our communion back to its own self-understanding as a necessary cathartic moment in the quest for greater unity. This, at least, is part of what is involved in recovering episcopal identity in the Anglican communion. It is undergirded by the recovery of the reciprocity between ministry and ecclesiology. 'Recognition of the ordained ministry and the ecclesial character of a Christian community are indissolubly and mutually related'.[58]

[58] W.G. Rusch, 'Introduction', in P. Bouteneff and A. Falconer (eds.), *Episkope and Episcopacy and the Quest for Visible Unity*, Faith and Order paper no. 183 (Geneva: WCC, 1999), p. 7.

PART V
Recovering Orientations

Chapter 13
'This Your Promise': The Vows, Formation and Ministerial Existence

The Promissory Character of Ministry

The Vowed Life

This chapter explores the notion of the vow or promise as a hermeneutic for the ministerial life of the Church.[1] One thing that marks out those whom a community admits to Holy Orders is the examination that requires the making of certain promises, and includes a declaration of belief and intent. This ancient Church practice belongs to a broader tradition of the making of sacred vows and promises and entering into binding covenants that is widespread in the history of religions.[2] This is reflected in the tradition of 'vow-taking' and 'vow-making' in Israelite religion. In the Hebrew Bible, 'one may swear to another person, but may vow only to God'.[3] A common element in vow-making is its link to the cult and liturgy. Accordingly those admitted to Holy Orders make certain promises before the congregation and God. What is the significance of this liturgical act? How does it bear upon the nature of ministerial existence, especially for those in Holy Orders?

The argument offered here is that the category of promise is a vital clue for the dynamics of human transformation. As such its embedded place within the liturgical rites of the Church, and its particular focus in baptism and ordination, says something about the nature of human life and the way the ministries of the people of God belong to each other and God even as they serve the mission of the Church in the world. In our time the Church of Christ has to chart its way

---

1 A shorter revised version of this chapter was published as 'This Your Promise: The Theologian as Priest' in Heather Thomson (ed.), *Embracing Grace: Being a Theologian in the 21st Century* (Canberra: Barton Books, 2009), pp. 7–20.

2 See articles on binding, covenant and vows and oaths in Mircea Eliade (ed.), *The Encyclopedia of Religion*, 15 vols. (London: Macmillan, 1987): 'Binding', 4:217–20; 'Covenant', 4:133–7; 'Vows and Oaths, 15:301–5.

3 Tony W. Cartledge, *Vows in the Hebrew Bible and the Ancient Near East*, Journal for the Study of the Old Testament, Supplement Series, 147 (Sheffield: Sheffield Academic Press, 1992), p. 12.

amidst the momentous changes taking place internally and in the wider world. In this context it has to begin to rethink the nature of ministerial existence and learn again how it lives by promise; learn again how its habits and engagements are promissory in character. Exactly what this might mean for the ministries and especially for those in holy orders will be explored below.

Such an inquiry has a particular significance for me having spent over two decades of ministry involved in theological education in Uniting Church and Anglican contexts. In my nine years as director of St Mark's National Theological Centre in Canberra I shared with colleagues in the responsibility for preparing deacons and priests for Anglican ministry for a number of dioceses in Australia.[4] During that time we developed an orders programme focused on the ordinal and in particular the ordination promises. The ordinal promises became the hermeneutical key for understanding the nature and identity of deaconal and priestly life. The reorientation of ministerial training around the ordinal and vows, and the emergence of deaconal and priestly character gave renewed prominence to the virtue ethics tradition as determinative for ministerial existence. The reason for this was that the vows identified questions of ecclesial character for deacons and priests, not simply a list of skills to become competent in.

However at a deeper level the formation programme in relation to the ordinal raised fundamental questions about the dynamics of human transformation and its relation to the life of promise. The promises contained in the ordinal no longer appeared as so many hoops to jump through but rather uncovered some of the most critical issues about what it means to be a human being in God's world. In the context of the formation programme this meant the vows were intertwined with difficult personal and ecclesial issues, concerns regarding ministerial character and apostolic witness. The vowed life led students and teachers alike into that triple bottom line for discipleship identified by the apostle Paul: 'to know him, the power of his resurrection and the fellowship of his sufferings' (Phil. 3:10). It became our firm conviction that a life shaped by promise may offer insight into the nature of ministerial existence; for lay people as well as ordained, for priests drawn into the theological task and theologians exercising a priestly ministry. This chapter is a preliminary inquiry into the nature of promise and its relevance for ministerial life in a time of change and uncertainty in the Church.

'This Your Promise': An Historical Perspective

From ancient times the Church has developed ways to test and examine those persons called to ministries of leadership in the community of faith. Over the course of time the examination of candidates for orders was incorporated into ordination

---

[4] The key people involved in the program were Richard Bowie, Elaine Farmer, Graeme Garrett and the late Bishop Owen Dowling.

liturgies.[5] The historical roots of the examination seem to lie in the questions put to a candidate for the episcopate who had travelled to Rome to be ordained by the pope in the early Middle Ages.[6] The pope obviously needed to assure himself of certain things about an unknown candidate before going ahead. The questions found their way into later medieval Western ordination rites for the episcopate (e.g., the Sarum rite).[7] At the Reformation the reformers wanted candidates to make public declarations of their reformed beliefs and their commitment to exercise a true evangelical ministry. As a result similar questions and answers modelled on the medieval episcopal rites appeared in various sixteenth-century ordination texts throughout Europe.[8] Most contemporary ordination rites continue this ancient practice.[9]

The English ordination rite of 1550 established the basic structure and pattern that has endured in the Anglican Communion. Given the importance of the Reformer Martin Bucer for the form of the English rite it is no surprise that there are significant similarities between the ordination rites of the churches of the Anglican Communion and the churches of Protestantism. The examination of candidates is no exception though the length and emphasis varies. The 1550 ordination rite for priests offers a clear expression of the promissory character of the examination of candidates. After the ordinand has taken the 'Oath concerning the King's Supremacy' the bishop addresses the candidates on the nature and character of the office of priest and concludes:

> And that this present congregation of Christ, here assembled, may also understand your minds and wills in these things: and that this your promise [*promissio*], shall more move you to do your duties, you shall answer plainly to these things, which we in the name of the congregation shall demand of you, touching the same.[10]

There follow eight questions to the ordinand, each of which requires a response. Seven of these include a specific declaration of intent in the form of 'I will' and

---

5 See Paul Bradshaw, *Ordination Rites of the Ancient Churches of East and West* (New York: Pueblo, 1990), esp. ch. 2.

6 Ibid., p. 20 and private correspondence with the author.

7 The medieval rites contained no examination for the ordination of priests or deacons; see Marion Hatchett, *Commentary on the American Prayer Book* (New York: Seabury Press, 1980), p. 521. Compare Brightman, *The English Rite*, 2:930–97 for the influences of the Sarum rite and Bucer on the English ordination rites of 1550, 1552 and 1662.

8 See Paul Bradshaw, 'Reformation Churches', in C. Jones G. Wainwright and E. Yarnold (eds.), *The Study of Liturgy* (London: SPCK, 1978), pp. 331–41.

9 See Paul Bradshaw, 'Recent Developments' in Jones, Wainwright and Yarnold (eds.), *The Study of Liturgy*, pp. 341–9.

10 See Brightman, *English Rite*, 2:984; NB: the old English has been amended.

reliance on God's grace to fulfil the promise. There are a number of features of the rite relevant for our present purposes.

Promissory Character of Priest's Rite

First, the public declarations or testimony have a decidedly promissory character. In this respect we note that the questions and answers constitute a *public* examination that extends and recapitulates the earlier private examination undertaken on behalf of the bishop by the archdeacon or other delegated representative. Upon presentation of the candidates to the bishop the archdeacon states: 'I have enquired of them, and also examined them.' Given this assurance the bishop addresses the people, noting that after 'due examination' 'that they be lawfully called to their function and ministry; and that they be persons meet for the same'. The people are then invited to come forth if they have any objection. Before the bishop concludes the charge to the ordinands and puts questions to the ordinands a number of critical steps have already taken place: a private examination, public testimony concerning this and public scrutiny by the people. The second examination (questions and answers) is more properly a public declaration of intent. The examination moves beyond mere affirmation or declaration of belief to an intent in relation to the substance and responsibilities of the ministerial office. The declaration has a decided promissory character recognised as such by the bishop's reference to 'this your promise'.

A Question about Deacons and Bishops

The second matter to note is the absence of explicit reference to the promissory character of the examination in relation to the ordination of deacons and bishops. In the case of deacons, immediately following the 'Oath of the Kings Supremacy' the bishop 'examines' the deacon through a series of questions followed by the laying on of hands. At the consecration of a bishop the examination is immediately preceded with the following: 'before I admit you to this Administration whereunto you are called, I will examine you in certain Articles, to the end that the Congregation present may have a trial, and bear witness, how you be minded to behave yourself in the Church of God.'

Here the accent is on examination as such, though the responses of the bishop, like the responses of the deacon, retain the promissory character throughout. The substance remains, but the promissory frame is either absent (deacon) or altered (bishop). This probably reflects the general medieval view that the fundamental order was that of priest: the deaconate being an 'inferior' order according to the *Book of Common Prayer* (1662) and the episcopate representing a jurisdictional elevation but not admittance to a different order as such. An interesting confirmation of this can be observed in the current ordination rites of the Episcopal Church of America (1979). Following the public examination of the bishop the following prayer is offered: 'N., *through these promises* you have committed yourself to God, to serve his Church in the office of bishop. We therefore call upon you, chosen to be a guardian of the Church's faith, to lead us in confessing that faith'.[11]

After the ordination the bishop is vested 'according to the order of bishops'. Following the lead of Vatican II, the Episcopal Church of America has made it unambiguously clear that the episcopate constitutes a distinct order and the promises made at such an ordination provide the frame for the ordination of priest and deacon. Accordingly the reference to 'promise' no longer appears in the ordination of the priest. Though of course the promissory character of the responses (in the form 'I will') of the three orders is unmistakable.

Promise to Whom?

A third feature relates to the referents of the promise. The promise is not made in a vacuum but is constituted by a complex of referents. Most obviously the promise is made to one who has asked the question and exercises immediate authority over the ordinand (the bishop). However, the promise is made in the context of public liturgy amidst those who have confirmed their acceptance of the ordinand as fit for the office and eagerly await the public declaration of intent to fulfil the responsibilities laid upon the ordinand. Promises are made in the public space invested with accountability and responsibility. But the liturgical reference necessarily includes a divine reference; the promises are made to a particular person in the presence of a people gathered in the name of the triune God. Indeed, in the history of the tradition the *vow* made by those taking religious orders was made in the first place to God: this is what differentiated the 'solemn vow' from promises made between people.[12] This is in keeping with the biblical tradition of vows always taking place within 'the context of prayer in an address to God'.[13] Who then are the hearers of the promises in the ordination rites? The answer is that there are multiple referents encompassing earth and heaven.

Basis of the Promise

Fourth, the significance of this complex reference becomes clear when we consider the basis of the promise. In all cases the promise is made on the express assumption that the capacity to fulfil the promise is ultimately derived from God. This is the one to whom the promisor looks for strength and help to undertake and fulfil the promises made. By invoking the aid of the one who calls and sustains ministerial

---

11 *The Book of Common Prayer: According to the Use of The Episcopal Church* (New York: The Seabury Press, 1979), p. 519; my italics.

12 See, for example, A. Vermeersch, 'Vows', in Charles Herbermann et al. (eds.), *The Catholic Encyclopedia*, 15 vols. (New York: The Encyclopedia Press, 1912), 15:511–14. Compare article on 'vow' in Karl Rahner et al. (eds), *Sacramentum Mundi*, 6 vols. (London: Burns and Oates, 1970), 6:350–52.

13 Cartledge, *Vows in the Hebrew Bible*, p. 12.

life the promisor is woven into the dynamic of God's ways with human beings. To promise before God and invoke divine help in the fulfilment of the promise suggests a theological anthropology undergirded by the dynamics of forgiveness, renewal and the possibility of a ministry increasingly full of promise. The promise, in short, is immersed in a life of faith and trust in divine agency and a healthy appreciation of the many sided aspects of human agency; folly and weakness, creativity and wisdom. This is not to discount the remarkable capacity of other people to support, encourage and sustain someone in their promises but simply to underscore the point that this is also a work of the Spirit of God.

Content of Promises

Fifth, the form and dynamics of promising are correlated to the content of the promises. This is critical for it is the content of the particular promises that differentiate those admitted to Holy Orders from the wider baptised body. The promises mark the point of difference, a critical transition akin to a rite of passage.[14] Those in orders make certain specific promises that are not made by others of the Church of Jesus Christ. Furthermore in the mainline traditions of Roman Catholicism, the Orthodox churches and Anglicanism the promises are cumulative. For example, an Anglican bishop will have made at least 27 such public promises. By contrast there are three baptismal promises relating to fundamental allegiance to Christ, turning from evil and intent to live a Godly life. Such discipleship promises provide the basic framework for all subsequent promises at ordination. However the ordination promises are only in a very general sense a further specification of the baptismal promises. The ecclesial context is now one of leadership in the community of faith. The promises are quite specific to the kind of leadership and priestly ministry required in the body of Christ. Such promises induct a person into an office which belongs, as we saw in chapter eight, to a different order of relations within the Church. This is reflected in the actual content of the promises.

The promises are made in relation to a range of responsibilities and undertakings that give priority to the interpretation of the Word of God, provision for the sacramental life of the people, and the care and witness of the community of faith. To fulfil such responsibilities the ordinand also makes promises regarding the nurture of the inner life and relations with others including those to whom he/she may be immediately responsible and under whose authority ministry is exercised. The promises identify a particular ecclesial character and in doing so they map out a comprehensive pattern of relations, indicate a direction for ministry, and point to the primary sources for sustenance and energy. In this way the form and content of the promises unfold a form of life and its placement within a larger set of relations;

[14] See van Gennep, *Rites of Passage*.

people, God and world. The question of content is a matter of such weight that it needs to be taken up in its own right.[15]

The Fate of Liturgical Promise in Ordination

A final matter that does not directly arise out of the 1550 rite concerns the fate of 'promise' in modern ordination services. With the exception above, in relation to the consecration of a bishop in the Episcopal Church of America, the explicit language of promise has disappeared or is at best muted in standard Anglican ordination rites. Certainly the actual responses of ordinands remain clearly couched in the language of promise ('I will') but the framework does not strike the same emphatic note of promise. *The Alternative Service Book* (1980) emphasises one's 'resolve'. 'In order that we may know your mind and purpose, and that you may be strengthened in your resolve to fulfil your ministry, you must make the declarations we now put to you.'[16] This is followed, for example, in the ordination rites for priests and bishops in the Anglican Church of Kenya.[17] In the Canadian *Book of Alternative Services*, at the conclusion of the examination of a bishop-elect, the archbishop says: 'N, through these promises you have committed yourself to God, to serve his Church in the office of bishop.'[18] It is of note that the responses for deacons, priests and bishops are in the form of a simple 'I will', though in three of the seven responses the bishop-elect refers separately to God's help, Spirit and grace as the means by which this intent will be fulfilled. *The New Zealand Prayer Book* (1989) simply says: 'We now ask you to declare your commitment to Christ in his Church.'[19]

In the case of *A Prayer Book for Australia* (1995) the examination for deacons and priests is introduced thus: 'And now in order that this congregation may understand your intention, and so that your public profession may strengthen your resolve, answer clearly these questions …'.[20] Strangely the form of words has been omitted altogether for the consecration of bishops.[21] The slippage is marked: from one's 'promise' as a means to fulfil the office to one's 'public profession'.

15 For a contemporary presentation of the range of promises made for deacons, priests and bishops in the Church of England, see *Common Worship*, pp. 143–9. Comparisons could usefully be made with other formularies from other churches, though in episcopally ordered churches a discernible pattern and content would be observed.

16 *The Alternative Service Book 1980* (London: Hodder & Stoughton, 1980), pp. 345, 358, 389.

17 See, *Our Modern Services*. Anglican Church of Kenya (Nairobi: Uzima Press, 2002), pp. 103, 124.

18 *The Book of Alternative Services of the Anglican Church of Canada* (Toronto: Anglican Book Centre, 1985), p. 637.

19 *A New Zealand Prayer Book* (Auckland: Collins, 1989), pp. 894, 905, 917.

20 *A Prayer Book for Australia*, pp. 786, 794.

21 Ibid., p. 802.

The most recent revised ordinal for the Church of England completes the break between the act of public declaration of a promise and the capacity to undertake such a ministry (i.e., the intention behind the original ordinal construction at this point).[22] The accent is now on the trust of those ordaining authorities that the candidate is 'fully determined, by the grace of God, to devote oneself ["give yourself"; deacon]' to the particular ministry. Whilst the revisors are clear that the declarations are promises[23] the function of the public liturgical act to bestow power to fulfil the promise appears to have been abandoned.

In all these cases the language of promise has been transposed into categories that lose the force of the original (for example, 'declare your commitment', 'your public profession') or evacuate it altogether ('that you may be strengthened' or simply omit any introduction and begin with 'The Questions'[24]). In the case of the services of ordination of the Baptist Union of Great Britain, a somewhat confused amalgam of commitments, public witness to beliefs, and promises – general and 'solemn' – appear.[25] In the ordination services for presbyters and deacons of the Methodist Church in England ordinands are asked at 'The Examination', 'to declare [their] lifelong commitment to this ministry'.[26] Generally, the responses to the examination are in the nature of declarations of intent or commitments, with the emphasis on public testimony with a mixture of responses involving more usually 'I will' though also frequently 'I do'.

These developments can also be observed in the ordination rites of the Roman Church where the traditional vow and/or 'promise' has become the ordinand's 'resolve'.[27] Thus deacons 'declare' before the people an 'intention to undertake this office' through a series of 'I am' responses to questions of the type: 'are you

---

22 *Common Worship: Ordination Services*, p. 143.

23 Ibid., p. 129.

24 See *An Anglican Prayer Book*. Church of the Province of South Africa (Claremont: Collins, 1989), pp. 584, 588, 598. But this is not unusual.

25 *Patterns and Prayers for Christian Worship*. Baptist Union of Great Britain (Oxford: Oxford University Press, Oxford, 1991), pp. 167–205. Thus in the first pattern of ordination the ordinand responds in a promissory, forward looking form ('I will') whilst in the second pattern it is a simple affirmation of belief and commitment ('I do', 'I am'). The corresponding patterns of induction are couched as 'Induction Promises' and in one case ask the ordinand is asked if they will 'promise to carry out this ministry with enthusiasm and dedication … to which the ordinand replies that 'Relying on God's help I make this solemn promise' (190–91). Later in respect to 'Ministry Beyond the Local Church' there appear a raft of 'Promises' for an 'Act of Induction' and 'An Affirmation of Call' in which the person is asked to 'publicly acknowledge your commitment' (195–6).

26 *The Methodist Worship Book* (Peterborough, UK: Methodist Publishing House, 1999), pp. 303, 317.

27 *The Roman Pontifical*. Revised by Decree of the Second Vatican Ecumenical Council and published by authority of Pope Paul VI (International Commission on English in the Liturgy: Washington, 1978).

resolved'.[28] Deacons and priests 'promise respect and obedience' to their ordinary. Bishops are reminded that 'an age-old custom of the Fathers decrees that a bishop-elect is to be questioned before the people on his *resolve* to uphold the faith and to discharge his duties faithfully',[29] and on one occasion the bishop-elect replies 'I am, with the help of God'.[30] However, for the blessing of an abbot or abbess, the bishop's examination elicits the stronger form of response, 'I will'.[31] Those being consecrated to a life of virginity and those being admitted to religious life follow the other orders in making their 'resolutions',[32] though it does seem that in these latter rites it is God who makes promises and the religious declare their resolve.[33]

Loss of the Liturgical Promissory Canopy

Overall the ordinals from different traditions evidence a weakening of the promissory character of the rites for ordination.[34] This is highlighted by a fluidity and lack of differentiation between the language of commitment, resolve, declaration, intent, profession and promise. Is this significant? It may be argued that sharp distinctions cannot be justified: that to express an 'intent' or 'commitment' or indicate a 'resolve' *implies* a promise. On this account to promise (e.g., 'I will') is to make *explicit* what may be implicit in an intent or resolve. Such an approach tends to smooth out discontinuities in language and finds support in modern legal theories of promising which do not find a fundamental distinction between a statement of intent and a promise, but rather regard the difference as one of degree along 'the same spectrum'.[35] However we should not forget that an earlier tradition maintained a critical distinction between a promise and a declaration or 'mere statement of intention'.[36] This natural law tradition (in contradistinction from the later utilitarian account of promising) regarded it as almost self-evident that the two (promise and intent) were not the same. A person who states an intention may meet with the response, 'but do you promise?', 'and that question would be meaningless if the statement of intent could itself amount to a promise'.[37] Such an approach finds support in those approaches to promising that regard it as a 'speech act'

---

[28] Ibid., pp. 180–81, 290–91.

[29] Ibid., p. 244, my italics.

[30] Ibid., p. 246.

[31] Ibid., pp. 263, 275.

[32] Ibid., pp. 295–6, 313–14.

[33] Ibid., p. 315.

[34] This was certainly the view of Paul Bradshaw who, in private correspondence, considered the promissory character of the examination 'dubious' preferring 'public witness' or 'testimony'.

[35] See the argument of P.S. Atiyah, *Promises, Morals, and Law* (Oxford: Clarendon Press, 1981), pp. 24–5, 50–51, 100–101, 165–9.

[36] Ibid, p. 25.

[37] Ibid, p. 50.

that, once performed correctly, has the effect of placing the promisor under an obligation that is necessarily binding.[38]

One thing is clear. The relationship between promising, declaration of intent, firm resolve and commitment is contested. The ordination traditions of the Church were forged in an environment that gave prominence to the promise as a performative act with intrinsic obligations. Promising had greater weight than mere declaration of intention. A more utilitarian approach loosens the claim upon the language of promise. Other language can do the same work (promise being implicit). The modern ordination rites embody both traditions in an unsynthesised manner. This is unfortunate and breeds an ambiguity precisely at that point in the sacred rite where clarity is demanded. To this extent the ordination rites reflect the contemporary puzzle over the status of the promise.

However, a deeper problem concerns the contraction of the promise to the private world of the self, notwithstanding the framing of the promise in communal and Godward terms. Hence, whilst most rites still retain, at least to some extent, the 'I will' response involving an intent with a future orientation (and congruent with the category of promise), this is not often supported by invocation of God's assistance. The promise is left suspended within the orbit of human affirmation. The examination responses are clearly made to the bishop but their promissory character before and to God, for the most part, remain muted or oblique. Part of the reason for this lies in the fact that a 'resolve' is essentially an inner personal determination. One resolves 'in oneself' but this falls far short of a promise to God in the sight of the congregation. To promise, from the Latin *promissum* (from *promittere* – to send forth) is a movement outward, a sending forth of the self. The word of promise is an embodied outer-directed movement of the self. This involves trust, risk and service to the other. The journey from 'resolve', 'public profession', 'commitment' to promise requires a move from self-centred to other-centred. The promissory character of the ordination rite has suffered an anthropological reduction. This loss or diminution of the liturgical canopy of promise may be a sign of the fate of promise in the modern period.[39] It is unclear how Christian ministry is truly 'full of promise' and imbued with the 'fullness of promise'. Ought this to be a cause for anxiety in the Church? What is forfeited when promise fades? Is it possible to live beyond or without promise?

---

[38] Atiyah, discusses this in relation to J.L. Austin and J.R. Searle (ibid., pp. 99–103).

[39] For a discussion of the nature of promise from the seventeenth century to the present see Atiyah, *Promises, Morals, and Law.* Atiyah examines the nature of promising in relation to utilitarianism and non-utilitarian philosophies and offers a contemporary interpretation from the perspective of a philosopher of law. In doing so the author highlights 'the wide gap' between a legal theory of promising and modern philosophical work on promising. The religious dimension of the promise does not figure in the author's discussion.

Promise, Personal Identity and the Worshipping Self

The Priority and Fragility of Promise: Arendt and Ricoeur

The fate of the promise in the modern world is closely tied up with the fate of the person and issues surrounding the identity of the self. The problem can be easily stated in the form of a question: Who is the one who makes a promise? Under conditions of late modernity the concept of a stable, identifiable and enduring self has become increasingly problematic.[40] When all has been deconstructed the last wall to crumble is the one protecting the individual: a fissure opens up from within, the solidity of selves as centres of personal meaning is disrupted. The philosophy of the individual eventually calls into question its own status as the personal organising centre for life and action. The crisis of personal identity is apparent in the loss of personal agency and responsibility such that 'actions are depersonalised and a consequent ambiguity is raised about personal accountability'.[41] Is it then possible to make a promise and keep one's word?

For the philosopher and social theorist Hannah Arendt, the capacity to make and keep promises constituted that faculty by which human beings could deal with 'unpredictability' and the 'chaotic uncertainty of the future'.[42] Whilst the capacity to promise offered a means to 'partially dispel' unpredictability, forgiveness overcame the power of irreversibility. Arendt argued that these two faculties circumscribed the human condition in its need to 'undo the deeds of the past' and 'bind oneself' to the future. Such was the price of freedom. The unpredictability that promising confronted arose from the 'darkness of the human heart'. This had a twofold nature: the 'basic unreliability' of human beings to 'guarantee today who they will be tomorrow' and the 'impossibility of foretelling the consequences of an act'. Thus at the heart of the human condition was a fundamental inability of human beings to 'have complete faith' or 'rely' upon oneself. The function of the faculty of promising was 'to master this twofold darkness of human affairs'. Arendt recovered the priority of promise in human affairs but in doing so raised a fundamental question: Wherein lies the power of promising in order to achieve mastery over the 'darkness of the human heart'?

Arendt did not develop the matter further. But the problem she identified in the life of promise, that is, the 'darkness of the human heart' that threatens human capacity to promise, was recognised in Paul Ricoeur's remarkable discussion on the nature of personal identity. For Ricoeur personal identity retains its permanence

---

40 For a helpful discussion of the postmodern self which deals with the issues of fragmentation and suspicion in the context of the promise, see Anthony Thiselton, *Interpreting God and the Postmodern Self: On Meaning, Manipulation and Promise* (Edinburgh: T&T Clark, 1995), pp. 159–63.

41 See Hughes, *Worship as Meaning*, p. 101.

42 Hannah Arendt, *The Human Condition* (Chicago: University of Chicago Press, 1958), p. 237 and more generally pp. 243–7.

through time through the twin coordinates of character and promise: 'keeping one's word in faithfulness to the word that has been given'.[43] Ricoeur differentiates between the 'perseverance' of character and the 'perseverance of faithfulness to a word that has been given'; between 'continuity of character' and 'constancy of friendship'.[44] In this model of continuing identity through time keeping one's word 'does indeed appear to stand as a challenge to time, a denial of change'.[45] Regardless of change in desire, opinion or inclination the promise, couched in the form 'I will hold firm', points to a permanence of personal identity through time.

This ethical notion of self-constancy is the manner in which each person conducts himself or herself 'so that others can *count on* that person'.[46] This also means that such a person is *accountable for* their actions before another. 'Counting on' and 'being accountable for' are united in the notion of responsibility which also includes 'a *response* to the question "Where are you?" asked by another who needs me'.[47] The responsive statement indicating self-constancy is in the form, 'Here I am!'. Ricoeur might have added 'for you'.

But what kind of self-constancy are we talking about? Ricoeur differentiates between the 'Stoic pride of rigid self-consistency' and the 'modesty of self-constancy' appropriate for the self in the light of it's own fragility and 'nakedness' of being.[48] The one promising is painfully aware of the fragility of the self that promises so much. The question becomes: 'Who am I, so inconstant, that *notwithstanding* you count on me?' Underlying this is the recognition that there is 'a secret break at the very heart of commitment'.[49] It is for this reason that the 'true life' has an appropriate 'modesty of self-constancy' rather than a 'rigid self-consistency'.

Arendt's 'darkness of the heart' has, in Ricoeur's analysis, become 'the secret break at the heart of commitment'. The true life of promise by which we are sustained as selves in relation to others remains forever under threat of dissolution. Yet to relinquish the promissory character of personal identity is to risk loss of personhood itself: to live in and through our promises belongs to the narrative of our lives. However it is equally clear that promise making and keeping is necessarily a risky and fraught business.

If the promise is so foundational for human flourishing, yet human beings suffer a 'secret break at the very heart of commitment', how is it possible to sustain promise in order that its fullness might be realised in the practice of life? What more might need to be said about the one who makes a promise?

---

43 Paul Ricoeur, *Oneself as Another*, trans. K. Blamey (Chicago and London: University of Chicago Press, 1992), p. 123.

44 Ibid.

45 Ibid., p. 124.

46 Ibid., p. 165

47 Ibid.

48 Ibid., p. 167.

49 Ibid., p. 168.

The Transformation of Promise: Ford on the Self as Worshipper

David Ford's interaction with Ricoeur leads him to a conception of the worshipping self.[50] In doing so he follows Ricoeur's suggestion 'that biblical faith might recapitulate the determinations of self in such a way as to intensify and transform them'.[51] This is signalled for Ford by the move from a concern with self identity signified by the question 'Who am I?' to a further question, 'Who worships?'[52] In this transposition the promising self is drawn into worship that celebrates a covenant relationship with God. 'For the Christian this is a baptised community in which one's word has been definitively given to God and to one's fellow members.'[53] This implies a quite radical shift in which the ethical thrust encapsulated in the 'Here I stand' becomes a matter of worship, 'Here I stand before God'.[54] In this community of the self-constant God worship is 'inspired through being loved and delighted in by God'.[55] As one is enabled to relax in the 'passivity of being recognised' new horizons of 'worship related practices' are opened: 'attentiveness, repentance, gratitude, delight, and prophetic discernment'.[56] This involves a 'pattern of exchange' in which esteem for self and others is 'taken up and transformed by the dynamics of worship in praise, covenant commitment, sacrifice or eucharist'.[57]

Ford (following Ricoeur's category of 'attestation') refers to 'testimony' as the central category gathering the multiple determinations of selfhood in worship. Such testimony emerges through 'thanks, praise, lament, confession of sin ... vows, memories ... and so on'.[58] In the Psalms such testimony is based on trust in God. It is also the case that the Psalms are 'shot through with suspicion (generated by enemies, by events and from within the worshipper) as contrary to testimony'.[59] Yet in the Psalms trust is greater than suspicion and gives overwhelming testimony to an 'economy of superabundance'.[60] This is the cause of the 'singing self' exemplified in the Psalms.[61] Though the self of the Psalms 'is most comprehensively constituted through the activity of God.... It is continually opening towards God in appeal, affirmation, commitment, anguish, promise, hope,

---

50 David Ford, *Self and Salvation: Being Transformed* (Cambridge: Cambridge University Press, 1999), pp. 97–104.

51 Ibid. Cf. Ricoeur, *Oneself as Another*, p. 25.

52 Ford, *Self and Salvation*, p. 99.

53 Ibid., p. 100.

54 Ibid.

55 Ibid.

56 Ibid.

57 Ibid.

58 Ibid., p. 101.

59 Ibid.

60 Ibid.

61 Ibid., pp. 120–22.

joy exclamation, blessing, reminiscence and thanks'.[62] Thus Ford concludes that the self 'has God intrinsic to its identity through worship: the one before whom it worships is the main clue to its selfhood'.[63] Because of this it is also the main clue to the capacity of the self to both make and keep its promises.

The new placement of the self in worship has far reaching consequences for the making and keeping of a promise. Most obviously to be 'before God' is to be before one whose self-constancy is neither rigidly determined nor fragile and unsure. Rather, it is a self-constancy that is wholly dependable and trustworthy. Covenant commitments, vows and promises can be risked precisely because the promise is enabled and sustained from beyond self but not in a way that excludes the self. Notwithstanding my inconstancy, I can be counted upon, because I am a promising self, constituted by the God of promise. The humble confidence of such a testimony – Ricoeur's 'modesty of self-constancy' – is appropriate, for beyond the 'secret break at the very heart of commitment' there is the ever-present possibility of a reconstitution of the promise through participation in the worshipping community. The worshipping self has a remarkably rich and largely uncharted capacity to make and keep a promise. Neither despair nor triumphalism is justified in respect to our promises. Both these conditions function outside the orbit of the self constituted by the 'God of promise' encountered in worship.[64]

In themes reminiscent of our reflections above Jurgen Moltmann referred to:

> [God's essence residing in] the faithfulness with which he reveals and identifies himself in the history of his promise as 'the same'. His divinity consists in the constancy of his faithfulness, which becomes credible in the contradiction of judgement and grace. The word that God reveals has thus fundamentally the character of promise and is therefore eschatological in kind.[65]

The dynamic by which God's promissory character is unfolded and actualised is narrated in the Christian tradition through the agency of Christ and the Spirit. This promissory character of God 'gives ground for hope and criticism, and expects us to endure in hope'.[66] If the one before whom the self worships is 'the main clue to its selfhood' and the identity of that divine referent is fundamentally promissory, the possibility of making and keeping promises is located in the interwoven-ness of self, others and God in the worshipping community.

---

62 Ibid., p. 128.

63 Ibid.

64 Jurgen Moltmann, *Theology of Hope* (London: SCM, 1967), p. 143.

65 Ibid.

66 Ibid.

Conclusion: Ministries Full of Promise

Ordination Promises as Justified Wager

Who can risk a promise? Following Ricoeur we have seen that the making and keeping of promises belongs to a 'true life'. To refuse or avoid the promise is to deny that very act by which personal agency exercises its appropriate responsibility and lives in freedom. To live is to promise. Keeping one's word is constitutive of personal identity. A modesty of self-constancy is intrinsic to the true life. Such a view is inimical to the 'postmodern' self because the act of promising presumes a self that is whole and grounded by trusts and loyalties offered and received. Beyond the suspicions and mistrusts of the postmodern self lies the far deeper crisis of the threat of disappearance and decomposition of the self. On this account the wholeness of self is mere chimera. The postmodern self cannot evidently make a promise for there is no personal agency as such, nor are there 'others' to whom one might so promise. Yet Ricoeur shows another way through the labyrinth of the postmodern. He charts a way between the despair that arises from the threat of nothingness – 'nakedness' is a very different thing – and the ungrounded triumphalism of the modern self. His proposal for a 'modesty of self constancy' is congruent with an analysis of the self that recognises that promise is intrinsic to human life and also acknowledges the 'secret break at the very heart of commitment'; that fundamental unreliability associated for Arendt with 'the darkness of the human heart' . On this account the act of promising has more of the character of a wager; a wager that to live a true life between despair and triumphalism I have to live by promise.

In ordination a person makes a wager encapsulated liturgically in the promise as the response to the 'examination'. At this moment no essays are submitted, no grades are awarded, no assessments are made, only testimony is given. The testimony (attestation) is that, notwithstanding who I am I can be counted on to keep my word: 'Here I stand before God'. The stakes are high for it is a public wager, before the assembled people and the leaders. And this community will confirm the wager through the people's 'Amen' and the laying on of hands. So the promise involves an exchange of trusts without qualification. The liturgical rites of ordination ought to give unambiguous and clear testimony to the promissory character of ordination. All should feel the weight being invested in the promise and trusts exchanged. Truly the ordination promises are 'solemn vows' that bind a whole community together and orientate it to the gospel for the sake of the world. The promise encapsulates the way of creation and salvation. It is much weightier than an 'inner resolve' made public. To whom does one make a resolve? To say 'I am so resolved' is half right but it requires completion; the resolve ought to lead into an explicit promise to another. And the public act of promising returns a gift to the promisor increasing personal capability to rise to the promise.

How then might such a wager be made? Following Ford we have observed the intensification of the promise through its transposition into the mode of worship.

The promisor is a worshipping self; the ordination promise is made and received 'before God'. The wager is thus incomplete unless the 'I will' is accompanied 'by God's grace'. Without this 'rider' – not a qualifier – the promise is doomed, Ricouer's 'break at the very heart of commitment' is mortally exposed, the promise will most assuredly fail, the nakedness of the self will become nothingness. The 'rider' encapsulates another promise made from 'the other side' so to speak. It is the promise of the modesty of self-constancy of God. This is the gospel of promise unfolded in the life of Israel, Jesus, the Spirit and the Church. Here we see a promise kept from the foundation of the world: a faithful messianic journey that has travelled into 'the break at the very heart of commitment'. Promise is here reconstituted from within the life of God and precisely because this divine wager has been made good, the ordinand can make a promise and keep a word, but only in the company of the risen Christ and the community that bears his name. The worshipping self does not guarantee the failsafe quality of the promise; that would be idolatry. But the worshipping self is the only self that can truly take the risk and make a justified wager.

The promises then are at the very nerve centre of those in 'Holy Orders'. The ambiguities of life; the 'breaks' that wound and the 'break's that open up new possibilities; the unavoidability of the life of promise: such matters are latent within the ordination promises. The exchange of trusts points the ordinand to the community that has pledged to travel in and with the promises. The promise locks the promisor into a web of relations, fields of accountability and expectations of sustenance. To make a promise is to confirm the reality and necessity of the community. The ordination promises bear an intensity that is paradigmatic of the way the true life works. As such the promises function as a hermeneutic of ministerial existence. The pattern and course of ministry is interpreted in the light of the form and content of the promises. This gives the liturgical renewal of ordination vows a critical and joyful significance in the life of those ordained. Orders are marked from beginning to end by the promise and thus are covered from beginning to end by the self-constancy of the faithful God.

Promise as Critical Transition

The promises mark the point of difference; a critical transition akin to a rite of passage. No one else makes such promises in the presence of the gathered community, before the leaders of the Church and publicly before God. The weight of the promises in content, form and place within the community of faith is unmistakable, yet by and large the Church has forgotten its import. Might it not be precisely the nature and content of the ordination vows that represent the particular and clear point of differentiation between those ordained in the Church of Christ and the wider community of the baptised? If so then it is clear that a candidate for ordination is undertaking many things in order to do one thing: to make some promises in such a way that the promises can be kept. The ordinand is preparing to be able to be a person whose 'modesty of self constancy' will be an example to the faithful. The ordinand is being prepared to undertake promises filled with content, weight and responsibility. The critical issue then revolves around the questions: 'Am I the sort of person who can make and keep a promise?' 'What do I have to do in order to be able to make such promises?' 'What areas in particular do I have to attend to "where the break at the very heart of my commitment" is most tender and vulnerable?' 'To whom do I have to make these promises and what responsibilities have I and they to share in my preparation?' 'How might the people of God keep me in my promises and bring them to their fullness?' These are a sample of questions and there are no doubt a raft of others that flow in consequence.

A focus on the vows clarifies the purpose of ministerial training for orders and has a flow on effect into the development of programmes for preparation. It clarifies the differentiation between those in orders and the baptised and their many ministries. The reason for this is not simply the fact of making a promise, which is common to many people but rather the weight attached to it, the public nature of the promise and critically the actual content of the promises. The symbiosis of promise, context and content mark the liturgical moment of the promise. Accordingly the preparation for ordination requires attention to the threefold dimension of the promise. This necessarily requires engagement with personal formation issues to do with the self as promise maker, the particular content of the promises and the public world in which they will be enacted. A focus on the vows also clarifies what needs to be attended to in post-ordination training. To minimise the promise is to undermine the relations between the ministries. To give due emphasis to the promise clarifies roles and functions and opens up new possibilities for collaborative ministry. It is a revolutionary old idea.

Chapter 14
'I Saw Satan Fall Like Lightning': A Sermon on Team Ministry for Mission

Introduction

There is a real sense in which this book has been an extended theological meditation on the apostle Paul's statement: 'We who are many are one body in Christ, and individually we are members one of another' (Rom. 12:5). Chapter 9 addressed the matter directly in its discussion of this particular Scripture text. However throughout the book I have tried to show how the collaborative impulse of Christian ministry continually draws us into the deepest mystery of the ecclesia of God that in Christ we are indeed 'one of another'. This is how we are constituted as human beings in God's world. So it ought not be surprising that this dynamic underpins our life together as the people of God. If we are in fact 'one of another' then this will be the mark of those ministries that serve the kingdom of Christ. The collaborative ecclesia is actualised in ministries that bear this same shape and character.

What might a sermon look like that embodied such a vision of ministry? Reading sermons is not my favourite pastime. For a start it can never be the same thing as the act of preaching itself and it may lose what impact (positive or negative) it may have had at the time. On the other hand it seemed to me that at the end of this book I owed it to the reader to at least give an example of how the collaborative theory espoused in the book might be transposed into sermon mode. I preached the sermon that follows on the occasion of the commissioning of the ministry team and the induction of the Revd Ian Palmer as team leader of the Queanbeyan and District Anglican Church, NSW, 29 October 2005. The Anglican Church in Queanbeyan is a multi-centred country parish undergoing change. One of the secrets of its life has to do with the way the different centres – both older established country areas and newly developing suburbs – share their lives and work together in ministry for the sake of the gospel. The new rector was being commissioned at a critical stage in the life of the parish in which cooperation, mutual ministry and outreach to newer unchurched people was paramount. It was clear that this was not a single person ministry – it never had been. On what basis would the parish move forward? What theological protein could the preacher offer to sustain the collaborative venture? The title of the sermon arose out of a conviction that the powers and principalities of this world are rendered impotent to the extent that the church of Jesus Christ commits itself to genuine team ministry.

A Sermon

'I saw Satan fall like lightning': Team Ministry for Mission

If there is one complaint I hear more than any other from the baptised of the Church concerning those in Holy Orders, it is that they do not know how to work in teams. For a good part of our history it has looked like a one-man band. And in more recent years it can look like a one-women band as well. But who can blame them? Everything about the Anglican system or polity seems to encourage the single leader approach. We have so much to learn.

But others say, We need a leader! And not just anyone, but preferably someone with youth and vitality, wisdom beyond years, great preacher and teacher, adept at organising and seasoned counsellor, respectful of tradition but innovative and able to make things happen – but not too fast.

We all have experienced working in teams is tiresome. It slows creative thinkers and strategists down. There are always difficult people and they consume the energy of the team. The saying is true: '10 per cent of the people consume 80 per cent of the time'. How much more could have Jesus achieved if he had not had to rely on a team. 'How long am I to bear with you' (Mark 9:19). I bet he said that more then once!

But sometimes teamwork is the very secret of achieving a goal. 'I saw Satan fall like lightning' (Luke10:17–18). This was Jesus' response when the mission teams returned. The experience of all pulling together in one direction, hanging in there through doubt and conflict. Now that breeds confidence in Christ and change in the kingdom of God. Moreover teamwork has that remarkable effect of more than doubling the energy of a group. It is empowering.

So what's the truth of the matter? Teams or not teams? Single leaders or many leaders? In times of crisis we prefer one leader; a messiah figure who will show the way. Look at our present troubles in the Western world. The need for a clear and unambiguous voice to listen to and follow. We crave it. And then just as quickly we despise it.

We then invoke the language of teamwork. It must be the egalitarian way to go. It would be, in the words of a former Prime Minister, most un-Australian not be a team player. But beware the team that is nothing but a shop front for manipulation. Power from the bottom up. This is the new democratic way of managing the people. It looks far more acceptable than the authoritarian top-down model.

And this problem is a real difficulty for the Church today. Why? Because the Church is wedded to a strong hierarchical pattern of authority and ministry. This is an ancient way and it is presupposed in so much of our life together. But it is unfashionable and difficult to sustain in our society. So we are caught between a rock and a hard place. We belong to an ancient structure of authority that is very much a top-down approach. But this way has been crumbling during the modern period. We mistrust it. Too many bad examples. And so we search around for a new way in leadership. We try to be collaborative and work in teams but often we can't make it work or there are resistances.

Can clergy be team players? Can the people of God be team players? What about this church? Can this people and this clergy of Queanbeyan? What do you make of this verse from the apostle Paul? 'So in Christ we who are many form one body, and individually members of one another'. Here in Chapter 12 of the apostle Paul's letter to the church at Rome, about 55 CE, he recommends a team approach to ministry and mission. Was there a problem? Why did he have to make a comment? Most of the apostle's letters are about conflict between people on the team. They are into one-upmanship, jealousy, self-promotion – I am of Apollos, I am of Peter, I am of Paul (see 1 Cor. 1:12). And after all, why would the apostle write at length to the church at Rome about shared ministry and the diversity of gifts for ministry and mission if there was no problem; if there were no difficulties in the body of Christ with respect to collaboration, team work and the work of the gospel.

So the romantic and rose-coloured glasses should be dispensed with. The Church has always aspired to a truly collaborative approach to its mission and its best theology has undergirded it. But the painful reality has been that teamwork has been a matter we have struggled with. Grace and forgiveness seem to be the essential prerequisites. And a good dose of longsuffering and occasional bouts of prophetic activity.

Shared power and collaborative practice seems like a gospel imperative. The Holy Spirit is the baptiser endowing the Church with gifts and power for ministry. This Spirit is no respecter of position or privilege. Yet the clerical spirit inhabits many churches. Given this state of affairs it seems fairly obvious that the rhetoric of the churches will be laced with the language of collaboration and the theology of collaboration is embedded in Anglicanism and our *Prayer Book* encapsulated in Cranmer's 1549 Good Friday Collect. This prayer stresses the vocation and ministry of all the faithful:

> Almighty and everlasting God, by whose Spirit the whole body of the Church is governed and sanctified; Receive our supplications and prayers, which we offer before thee for all estates of men [*sic*] in thy holy Church, that *every member* of the same, in his [*sic*] *vocation and ministry*, may truly serve thee; through our Lord and Saviour Jesus Christ, who liveth and reigneth with thee, and in the unity of the same Spirit, ever one God, world without end. Amen (my italics).

This Collect presumes that all members of the Church have a vocation and ministry. It points to a profound mutuality in ministry wherein each ministry bestows life and energy on other ministries. This theology of ministry is the background to the apostle's words: 'So in Christ we who are many from one body, and individually members of one another' (Rom. 12:1–8).

We have heard it before. In the opening verses of Romans 12 Paul outlines the way in which the different members of the one body serve the body through the gifts God has given. 'Having gifts that differ according to the grace given to us, let us use them: if prophecy, in proportion to our faith' (Rom. 12:6). The intention is not so much ranking or weighing the gifts (in proportion to a quantum of faith) but acknowledging that the charismata are diverse and distributed through the body. However, the key text for our purposes is the preceding one: 'so we, though many, are one body in Christ, and individually members of one another'. This is strange is it not?

We can imagine what it is to be members of the same body. We belong to families, networks of friends, work associates. And in the Christian community we talk much of being the body of Christ and embrace the organic image of the apostle. Just as a body has arms and legs, eyes and mouth, so in the body of Christ there are diverse parts, different gifts and we share the common charismata of the Spirit. None of us owns our gifts; they are gifts! God is the giver. For this same reason everyone ought to act in faith and embrace the God who gives gifts and calls us to break the tapes of yesterday – whether the 'I can't do it', 'I'm not good enough', or 'leave it to me you fools, or 'I'll show them how to do it' or 'they might have a gift but mine is more important and they'll just have to learn that the hard way'. We need a conversion to enter into the meaning of the metaphor of the body of Christ and shared ministry for mission.

This much we may in our graced moments say yes to. But what about this strange bit that the apostle has tacked on: 'and you are individually members of one another'. How can I be a member *of someone else*? The apostle's metaphor of the body breaks down. How do we hear this? As a summons for the people and leaders of the Anglican Church of Qeanbeyan to actively play their part? For everyone here to accept their assigned role and fulfil their ministry? Well in one sense I hope so. But isn't it more? Is it allowing others to be part of the community, to have a task, role and place in their own right. You know, the every member ministry argument. Sure, why not. And woe-betide a church that does not go that far. That pulls up short. That cuts ministry of the baptised off at the knees. And woe betide the person who says 'Lord here I am, please leave me alone and get someone else to do the ministry'. This is to think wrong thoughts. It is to reject one's baptism.

But the apostle goes much further. He is saying that we as individuals in the body are a member of someone else. How can we be members of someone else? Certainly his intention is not just everyone has a part to play – terrific, first base. Certainly he is saying we all have an assigned role and gifts to go with it – terrific, second base. Certainly he is saying 'and by the way we have to be willing to have the grace to see that others have to share in the ministry – not be jealous and desirous of the limelight – terrific, third base. But there's more as the man says.

The apostle's main burden is to convince the Church that its members need to learn to recognise the ministry of others. Even the ministries we exercise are to be bent towards the ministries of others. Indeed we belong to the other. This is startling and is it not a little intrusive? The apostle is ascribing to others the dignity of becoming part of ourselves: 'each member belongs to all the others'. Here is a radical doctrine of ministry for mission. In the world wide Anglican communion we have lost sight of this truth that we belong to each other. We prefer to keep it locked up in a local congregation. On the grand scale we do as we please, or so it seems.

Learning to accept the ministry of the other *towards* myself. This is dangerous. Not only am I to see myself as belonging to someone else; my ministry belongs to and bends towards another. In this way the other has a claim upon me.

The emphasis is thus *not* on the 'membership of *the other person* in the body' – for example, whether we like them or not or have regard for their gifts – but something more radical. Rather our ministry is tied up with the ministry of another's. The ministries are bound together. The ministries we exercise can only be gospel ministries as they are in relation to others. It is as if the ministries give life to each other. They animate each other. Furthermore the ministry I exercise only has life as it belongs to others. Not ownership of ministries but truly shared visions of ministry for the common good. And this includes representative leadership.

How does this strike those of us who have ministered in Holy Orders for a number of years? Has it been like that? What have been the best times? Usually when we have been part of a venture with others, collaborators together. Here are the joy filled times. The worst times are often the lonely and isolated experiences in ministry. We will have both, but the apostle's words ring true: through it all 'we belong to each other'.

And those baptised of the Church, commissioned to be witnesses to the gospel in ordinary time 168 hours of the week, not just Sundays. What are the times that have been most memorable for you? I'll wager that they are the satisfactions from joining with others in common tasks and visions, completing a project, knowing the bond we have in Christ.

Teamwork isn't something invented by management gurus. It is the way human community flourishes even amidst the pain and conflict. It is no easy street but it is the street upon which the church has to travel with Christ.

My ministry is called forth by the ministries of others. The ministries animate each other. There are no autonomous and self-perpetuating ministries. Our life is not only hid in Christ, our ministries are hid in Christ and in each other.

The ministries of Christ Church Queanbeyan are hid in the ministries of St Matthews, Karabar and St Thomas' Michelago and St Paul's Burru, the Community of the Celebration and the congregation that meets in the community hall at Jerrabomberra. These centres may feel more or less important than the other. But the truth is that each ministry centre belongs to the others. Each ministry team in each centre is to bend their life to the other. Christ Church may be older but its ministry is to be bent toward the newer places. Those new centres like Jerabombra do not go it alone but are intertwined with their fellow members of the body of Christ in the other centres.

Sounds simple, but to live as if this was the imperative of the gospel, that's the hard thing. Your new team leader comes with a great deal of wisdom and experience in such a ministry and a passion for mission. The task of the church here is to be an exegesis of the sacred text – 'each belongs to the other'.

The ministries of the centres belong to the rest of the body. The team leaders: Ian, Michael, David, Mary and those who share this responsibility with them belong to each other. We dare not amputate ourselves off from the body of Christ by failing to see the ministries we exercise as part of each other, of belonging to each other. The calling is clear. You are to live in ministry and mission as if this text from the apostle was written to you. That's why we hear it read in the body tonight.

An image springs to my mind – a body image not human but from the world of flora. In the courtyard of the library at St Mark's are some wonderful ferns perhaps 3 or 4 metres high. With all the recent rain the ferns are flourishing. At the outer edge the older fronds are brown in parts and losing lustre and strength. Closer to the centre the strong fronds are in full bloom. And from the very heart of the fern, surrounded by the other fronds are many new fronds – still curled up – full of potential. They too will unfold and continue the life of the fern; feeding off the nutrients of the older fronds. So too in the body of Christ there are the older ministries, the mature ministries and the emergent ministries. They belong together. Under the right conditions the life of the body continues.

And in the body of Christ all the ministries are interdependent. All act upon one another as if *each were not their own*; not self constituting but constituted both *from* and *toward* another. Such features of properly ordered ministries belong to a collaborative ethos and practise. The emergent ministries come from the centre protected and nurtured by the nutrients of the body. Their unfolding brings joy in the Church and is a sign of new life in mission.

There is no doubt that ministry as a collaborative and coordinating activity of the church is a condition of it being a ministry ordered according to the gospel. Sharing ministries 'one of another' takes us into the deepest reaches of the life of God whose remarkable ordering and transforming order in Christ and the Spirit beckons the Church to new places for the sake of the gospel.

Tonight as we hear this ancient sacred text from the apostle and missioner to the gentiles – of which we are a part – let us take heed, let us take heart, let us be collaborators in the gospel of Jesus Christ in this place. Herein lies the deepest joys of our life in Christ. We ask God's richest blessings for the people of God in this parish, its leaders and all who witness to faith in Jesus Christ.

Chapter 15
Conclusion: The Collaborative World

Recapitulation: Ministry in the Context of Creation and Redemption

In this book I have tried to develop a theory of collaborative ministry that takes its cue from a Pauline theology of the body of Christ in which members are 'one of another' (Rom. 12:5). This radical conception of communal interrelatedness arose out of redemptive life in Christ, but was nothing less than an actualising of a primal relatedness given in creation. As such the theory of collaborative ministry developed in this book provided an instance of the relationship between the doctrines of creation and redemption. This was a preoccupation of the central chapters of the book (Part III). The focus in these chapters was on the collaborative order as such, as a foundation for the specific practice of collaborative ministry. Collaboration as a 'mode of togetherness' was in fact the way a complex and highly differentiated creation actually worked. The cooperative venture entailed in ministerial practices of the whole people of God was accordingly a particular and special instance of God's activity in creation. From this perspective collaborative ministry as we know it ought to be 'second nature' so to speak. Indeed it is properly speaking 'first nature'. The remarkable collaborative order that stretches from Genesis through the story of redemption to the final consummation of all things is the work of God: creator, redeemer and sanctifier. The logic of this argument was that the Church of Jesus Christ is rooted in God's creating and re-creative activity through Word and Spirit. Much more could have been said about this and perhaps that matter can be taken up more intentionally on another occasion.

What this conception does mean is that collaborative practices in ministry actualise the collaborative ecclesial order. The community formed by God through the Spirit of Jesus is not an alien sociality imposed on the world but rather represents the true form of the social world given in and with creation as such. The story of the Church is, from this perspective the constant retrieval, renewal and ever expanding 'mode of togetherness' encoded into the world of the triune God. But of course the story of the reforming of community is never a seamless activity but occurs through inner disruption, fragmentation, failure and human sinfulness. The collaborative order given in creation and instanced in the life of the Church is indeed a fragile, broken and contingent order always under threat of dissolution and suffering its own sin. As a result it always lives by the re-creative and redeeming Word of God and the Spirit who is the Lord and giver of life. At any rate such a conception has been as a red thread running through the weave of this book.

One thing ought to be clear from the above; 'To collaborate or not to collaborate' is never a question in pastoral ministry. To ask the question is to lose sight of the fundamental reality of what the Church is and who we are formed to be in the purposes of God. Rather the Church is called repeatedly to actualise in its life collaborative practices that bear witness to its life in the triune God.

The opening chapters of the book tried to map out the fortunes of the doctrine(s) of ministry in the contemporary scene and gave considerable attention to some of the perennial difficulties encountered in ministry within and between the churches. In particular I drew attention to the long-standing war of attrition between clerical and laity on the matter of ministry. It was clear that the Church has more often failed to grasp the secret of its own life as a community of faith and accordingly showed little awareness of the intricate and necessary relationship between the many and varied ministries of the body of Christ. This was highlighted by the fact that rarely if ever had any consideration been given to how the ministries of the laity contributed to the identity, establishment and nurture of those ministries for which the churches have traditionally ordained certain persons. This pointed to a need to (a) clarify the relations between the ministries and (b) provide a theory of truly collaborative practice whereby all ministries were enhanced rather than some always being diminished in relation to others; a problem observed in the recent history of ministry (Part II).

As noted above Part III of this book formed the critical theoretical section. Here the logic of a collaborative order and the interrelations between the ministries of the people of God were displayed. It was tested against Scripture using Paul's reference in his letter to the Romans (12:5) where he referred to the members of the body of Christ being 'one of another'. Here in embryo was the deep reality of the collaborative order of the body of Christ. The argument developed in these chapters provided a rationale for a fully fledged ministerial order for the Christian Church. Such an order was not antithetical to an episcopal polity. Indeed the discussion clarified why the traditional orders of the Church and episcopal polity per se belonged to a mature and dynamic collaborative order. This also gave rise to a relational ontology of orders which had practical implications as well as indicating what a re-formed and ecumenical episcopate might look like (Part IV). Two final chapters (13 and 14) rounded out the inquiry with a reflection on the nature of ministerial existence from the perspective of ordination vows and team ministry.

'No longer servants but friends': A Collaborative Ideal?

It seems that a collaborative approach to Christian ministry is not only a useful practical way of getting things done to advance the kingdom of God but ultimately arises out of the nature of the gospel to which the Church bears witness. Collaborative ministry is 'first nature', the most natural pattern of practice for the ministries of the body of Christ. I began this book with a quote from a colleague who remarked that what I have described as a natural ministerial practice in fact required a high level of spiritual maturity. I end this book with a brief epilogue, as it were, to this opening remark.

Recently I attended a local country church's centenary. The people's warden read from the minutes concerning the original building of the church and significant events in the life of the parish. At one point she read from the minutes of a 1940 parish vestry meeting at which the then warden (her father) indicated he was resigning to leave for service in the war. He did not know if he would return. In the course of his farewell he gave thanks for the parish priest's help to him over the years and he ended with these words: 'you have not only been my priest but also my friend'. The words 'but also my friend' continued to echo in my mind for two reasons. First, that it seemed to be a friend in ministry took the relationship to a deeper level and was the occasion of a great deal of thankfulness. Second the 'but also' was suggestive of a dissonance between being a priest and being a friend. Clearly in this particular case the relationship between priest and parishioner had transcended the divide.

The incident raised many questions for me which, on reflection, I saw echoed in the book I had been writing. Can those charged with exercising authority in the community of faith and within the wider structures of the churches also be friends with those among whom they minister? This issue is not a new one nor is it a settled one from my observations and experience as a lay person and someone in Holy Orders. I know many of my mentors from an earlier generation have been careful to differentiate between their priestly work and the friendships they form. The dangers of compromising their capacity to minister without favour have been frequently signalled as the reason to maintain a certain distance when it comes to friendship per se. And there is some wisdom in this advice because it is simply not true that in church life we are all pals and all the same and all exercise the same authority. So on balance friendship has not been a theme that has had much mileage in discussions of Christian ministry, at least in my experience.

However as discussed in Chapters 3 and 4 there are certain emphases in a theology of ministry that feed such an approach. Thus where the foundation for formal ministry has a strong Christological focus the 'stand alone' nature of ordained ministry more easily generates a natural 'pastoral distancing' from the people of God. In this case friendship is hardly a category that commends itself. For some it is a matter of more formal distancing as a matter of principal while for others I have heard it said that friendship is a fragile thing and not a sound basis for the work of the gospel which requires 'partnership'! I felt this told me more about that particular leader than it did about fragile friendship.

In those ministries that owe more to an emphasis upon the Spirit the category of friendship may seem more congenial though often the idea of 'everyone a friend' can mask other dynamics to do with the misuse of power.

So can or ought friendship function as a paradigm for collaborative ministry? Should we heed the wisdom of those who see the dangers of also being a friend or those who dismiss friendship as too fragile to bear the weight of gospel ministry? There are some serious problems in too ready a dismissal of the category of friendship for ministry. Most obviously friendship would seem one of the most natural and important ingredients for a truly collaborative ministry. If the truth of our lives in Christ is that we are inescapably 'one of another' then friendship is encoded into our life together. Indeed friendship is the form of our 'mode of togetherness' or the 'we-mode cooperation'. All those well-loved phrases about interdependence and mutuality require high quality relations. Often we professionalise the relationships – sometimes for very good reason – but often this simply masks our failure to appreciate how to be a friend within relationships of unequal power relations. This raises some questions about different kinds of friendship; different kinds of relationships in which friendship occurs.

Perhaps the first reason why friendship cannot be easily dismissed from the discussion of collaborative ministry is because friendship seems to be intrinsic to ministry shaped and informed by the gospel. Precisely because the ministry I am speaking of is *Christian* and is intended to serve the gospel of the kingdom we cannot escape the fact that being a friend is exactly what Jesus seemed to encourage among the first disciples. Indeed in Jesus' farewell discourses he no longer calls his disciples servants but friends (John 15:15). This descriptor is associated with living in the joy of ministry (John 15:11). Jurgen Moltmann has captured the dynamic well: 'Through the death of their friend the disciples become his friends forever. On their side they remain in the circle of his friendship when they keep his commandments and become friends *of one another*'(my italics).[1] In this dying for the disciples 'out of divine joy' and 'for those who are his … the relationship of servants to God, the Lord, comes to an end. Through the friendship of Jesus the disciples become the free friends of God'.[2] Although it is not strictly speaking an equal relationship nonetheless it is one of mutuality.

The note of friendship among disciples of Christ has resonated throughout the Christian tradition. Well known theologian and ethicist, Stanley Hauerwas picks up this same theme:

> What's been constant with me is the importance of friendship. I think that's why God gave us Christ, to make us friends with God, and friends with each other, so that our relationships are nourishing and not so alone in this world. Loneliness is the besetting pathology for Americans. It's a part of the human condition, but Americans are worse because we don't want to have to depend upon anyone. Learning to be vulnerable again is crucial.
>
> So I continue to praise God for the people who claim me as a friend. That's what the Church makes possible. In the Gospel of John, at the end of Jesus' ministry, he said that before I called you disciple, but now I call you friend.[3]

---

[1] Jurgen Moltmann, *The Church in the Power of the Spirit* (London: SCM, 1977), p. 117.

[2] Ibid., p. 118.

[3] *Resident Aliens: A Conversation with Stanley Hauerwas*, 21 November 2006 http://www.everythingchristian.org/News/psalms_n4.ihtml?nid=2558&catid=2.

As indicated in Moltmann's discussion of Jesus and the disciples in John 15, friendship is not a simple matter. Friendship can be genuine and mutual notwithstanding the differences between people regarding authority and responsibilities. Friendship is not friendship if one person controls, dominates or sublimates themselves to the other. Furthermore the more intimate the friendship the more each person begins to recognise the remarkable otherness and mystery of the other; what one theologian has aptly termed the 'unreachable height' of the other.[4] This occurs in a shared and collaborative ministry precisely because it is based on trust and true friendship.

This means that the real art and challenge of collaborative ministry is to live as 'one of another' in friendship within differing levels of formal and public authority. This is what requires the kind of spiritual maturity recognised by my colleague at the outset of this book. Within a differentiated structure of authority friendship takes new and demanding forms but it is not for that reason something to be avoided. The reason is clear; it is an imperative of the gospel of Jesus. It points to the fact that friendship as well as grace is a costly thing involving humility and respect for others particularly those who have less authority and power than oneself.

From this perspective it is not difficult to see why the language of servant leadership became so important and popular in the final quarter of the twentieth century. I have wondered if servant leadership discourse is a more acceptable way of depicting collaborative ministry. It certainly appears more humble and self-effacing and seems to avoid some of the dangers observed in the appeal to friendship. And there is no doubt that the New Testament in general, and Jesus' ministry in particular, was deeply informed by the servant/slave paradigm. Yet the servant leader approach to ministry, linked as it often is to self-emptying and diminishment, can produce unhealthy consequences, particularly for women and marginalised groups, and perpetuate a servant/master dichotomy.[5]

Apostolic life is not exhausted by the category of servant and, as we have observed above, Jesus called his disciples 'friends.' He said this precisely because he had become fully and sacrificially one with them. He was truly the one who made it possible for disciples to be 'one of another'. The category of friendship is thus not an optional extra but theologically encoded into any ministry that actualises the gospel of Christ. Ministry as friendship means 'being fully engaged with God, others, and one's self'.[6]

---

[4] See the discussion in Daniel Hardy, 'Christian Affirmation and the Structure of Personal Life', in Thomas F. Torrance (ed.), *Belief in Science and Christian Life: The Relevance of Michael Polanyi's Thought for Christian Faith and Life* (Edinburgh: The Handsel Press, 1980), p. 87.

[5] See for example the critique of the servant paradigm by Edward Zaragoza, *No Longer Servants but Friends: A Theology of Ordained Ministry* (Nashville: Abingdon Press, 1999), pp. 32–7.

[6] Ibid., p. 83.

Perhaps friendship and servanthood are companion categories for ministry and leadership. As such they are given in and with each other. They are not simply different options that present themselves for appropriation. Nor are they simply complementary forms of ministry. Rather they inhere in each other; they too are 'one of another'. Together friendship and servanthood make collaborative ministry what it is and inform the manner in which it is undertaken. This means collaborative ministry is forever a fragile and suffering ministry that lives by trust and joy. It is the way in which Christian disciples learn how much indeed they are 'one of another' faithfully following the pioneer ministry of Jesus Christ.

Bibliography

All Are Called: Towards a Theology of the Laity. General Synod, Board of Education. (London: Church House, 1985).

The Alternative Service Book (London: Hodder & Stoughton, 1980).

Anglican–Lutheran Consultation. *Episcope in Relation to the Mission of the Church Today* (Geneva: Anglican Consultative Council and The Lutheran World Federation, 1988).

Anglican–Lutheran Dialogue. Report of the Anglican–Lutheran European Regional Commission, Helsinki (London: SPCK, 1982).

An Anglican–Methodist Covenant. Common Statement of the Formal Conversations between the Methodist Church of Great Britain and the Church of England, GS 1409. (London: Church House, 2001).

An Anglican Prayer Book. Church of the Province of South Africa (Claremont: Collins, 1989).

Anglican–Roman Catholic International Commission. *The Final Report* (London: SPCK, 1982).

Apostolicity and Succession. House of Bishops Occasional paper (London: Church House, 1994).

Arendt, Hannah. *The Human Condition* (Chicago: University of Chicago Press, 1958).

Atiyah, P.S. *Promises, Morals, and Law* (Oxford: Clarendon Press, 1981).

An Australian Prayer Book (Sydney: AIO Press, 1978).

Avis, Paul. *The Church in the Theology of the Reformers* (London: Marshall Morgan and Scott, 1981).

——. *Anglicanism and the Christian Church* (Edinburgh: T&T Clarke, 1988).

Baptism, Eucharist and Ministry. Faith and Order Paper no. 111 (Geneva: WCC, 1982).

Barth, Karl, *Church Dogmatics*. Trans. G.W. Bromiley and T.F. Torrance. 14 vols. (Edinburgh: T&T Clark, 2nd edn, 1975).

Bellah, Robert, et al. *Habits of the Heart: Individualism and Commitment in American Life* (New York: Harper & Row, 1985).

Bishops in Communion. House of Bishops Occasional Paper (London: Church House, 2000).

The Book of Alternative Services of the Anglican Church of Canada (Toronto: Anglican Book Centre, 1985).

The Book of Common Prayer: According to the Use of The Episcopal Church (New York: The Seabury Press, 1979).

Bradshaw, Paul. 'Recent Developments', in C. Jones, G. Wainwright and E. Yarnold (eds.), *The Study of Liturgy* (London: SPCK, 1979), pp. 331–41.

——.'Reformation Churches', in C. Jones, G. Wainwright and E. Yarnold (eds.), *The Study of Liturgy* (London: SPCK, 1979), pp. 341–9.

——. *Ordination Rites of the Ancient Churches of East and West* (New York: Pueblo, 1990).

Brent, Alan. *Cultural Episcopacy and Ecumenism: Representative Ministry in Church History from the Age of Ignatius of Antioch to the Reformation with special reference to Contemporary Ecumenism.* (Leiden: E.J. Brill, 1992).

Brightman, F.E. *The English Rite: Being a Synopsis of Sources and Revisions of the Book of Common Prayer*. 2 vols. (London: Rivingtons, 1915).

Buchanan, Colin. 'Anglican Orders and Unity', in David R. Holeton (ed.), *Anglican Orders and Ordinations*. Liturgical Studies, 39 (Cambridge: Grove Books, 1997), pp. 16–28.

Budde, M., and R. Brimlow, *Christianity Incorporated: How Big Business is Buying the Church* (Grand Rapids: Brazos Press, 2002).

Bulley, Colin. *The Priesthood of Some Believers* (Carlisle: Paternoster Press, 2000).

Burkhard, John. *Apostolicity Then and Now: An Ecumenical Church in a Postmodern World* (Collegeville: Liturgical Press, 2004).

Buxton, Graham, *The Trinity, Creation and Pastoral Ministry: Imaging the Perichoretic God* (Milton Keynes: Paternoster Press, 2005).

Cadwallader, Alan, 'Antipodean Descriptions of the Art of Episcopacy', in Alan Cadwallader (ed.), *Episcopacy: Views from the Antipode* (Adelaide: Anglican Board of Christian Education, 1994), pp. 1–21.

Campbell, Alistair. *The Elders: Seniority within Earliest Christianity* (Edinburgh: T&T Clark, 1994).

Cannistraci, David. *Apostles and the Emerging Apostolic Movement* (Ventura: Renew Books, 1996).

Carey, George. 'Reflections upon the Nature of Ministry and Priesthood in the Light of the Lima Report', *Anvil* 3/1 (1986): 19–31.

Carnley, Peter. *The Yellow Wallpaper and Other Sermons* (Sydney: HarperCollins, 2001).

——. *Reflections in Glass* (Sydney: HarperCollins, 2004).

Cartledge, Tony W. *Vows in the Hebrew Bible and the Ancient Near East*. Journal for the Study of the Old Testament Supplement Series, 147 (Sheffield: Sheffield Academic Press, 1992).

Charles Herbermann et al. (eds.). *The Catholic Encyclopedia*. 15 vols. (New York: The Encyclopedia Press, 1912).

Christensen, Torben. *The Divine Order: A Study in F.D. Mauice's Theology* (Leiden: E.J. Brill, 1973).

'The Church as Koinonia: Gift and Calling', in Michael Kinnamon (ed.), *Signs of the Spirit: Official report of the Seventh Assembly of the World Council of Churches* (Geneva: WCC; Grand Rapids: Eerdmans, 1991), pp. 172–4.

Clarifications of Certain Aspects of the Agreed Statements on Eucharist and Ministry of the First Anglican-Roman Catholic International Commission:

Together with a Letter from Cardinal Edward Idris Cassidy, President, Pontifical Council for Promoting Christian Unity (London: Church House and Catholic Truth Society for the Anglican Consultative Council and the Pontifical Council for Promoting Christian Unity, 1994).

Cocksworth, Christopher, and Rosalind Brown. *Being a Priest Today* (Norwich: Canterbury Press, 2002).

Collins, John. *Diakonia: Re-Interpreting the Ancient Sources* (Oxford: Oxford University Press, 1990).

——. *Deacons and the Church: Making Connections between Old and New* (Leominster: Gracewing, 2002).

Common Worship: Ordination Services (London: Church House, study edn, 2007).

Communion, Conflict and Hope. The Kuala Lumpur Report of the Third Inter-Anglican Theological and Doctrinal Commission (London: Anglican Communion Office, 2008).

Congar, Yves. *Lay People in the Church: A Study for a Theology of Laity* (Westminster: Newman, 1957).

The Constitution and Canons of the Anglican Church of Australia (Sydney: General Synod Office, 1998).

Countryman, L. William. *Living on the Border of the Holy: Renewing the Priesthood of All* (Harrisburg: Morehouse, 1999).

Cox, Harvey. *Fire From Heaven* (London: Cassell,1996).

Croft, Stephen. *Ministry in Three Dimensions: Ordination and Leadership in the Local Church* (London: Darton, Longman & Todd, 1999).

Csordas, Thomas. *Language, Charisma and Creativity: The Ritual Life of a Religious Movement* (Berkley: University of California Press, 1997).

Cundy, Ian, and Justin Welby. 'Taking the Cat for a Walk: Can a Bishop Order a Diocese?', in G.R. Evans and M. Percy (eds.), *Managing the Church: Order and Organization in a Secular Age* (Sheffield: Sheffield Academic Press, 2000), pp. 25–48.

Dawswell, Andrew. 'A Biblical and Theological Basis for Collaborative Ministry and Leadership', *Anvil* 21/3 (2004): 165–78.

The Decree on the Ministry and Life of Priests (*Presbyterorum Ordinis*). 7 Dec. 1965. In Austin Flannery (ed.), *Documents of Vatican II* (Dublin: Dominican Publications, 1975), pp. 863–902.

De Gay, Paul. *In Praise of Bureacracy* (London: Sage, 2000).

The Doctrine Commission of the Church of England. *We Believe in the Holy Spirit* (London: Church House, 1991).

Driver, Jeffrey, and Stephen Pickard. 'Re-Placing Bishops: An Ecumenical and Trinitarian Approach to Episcopacy', *St Mark's Review* 169 (1997): 23–8.

The Dublin Agreed Statement: Anglican–Orthodox Dialogue (London: SPCK, 1984).

Dunn, James D.G. 'Ministry and the Ministry: The Charismatic Renewal's Challenge to Traditional Ecclesiology', in James D.G. Dunn (ed.), *The*

Christ and The Spirit, vol. 2, *Pneumatology* (Edinburgh: T&T Clark, 1998), pp. 291–310.

Ecclesiology and the Culture of Management (Special edition of *Modern Theology* 9/4 [Oct. 1993]).

Education for the Church's Ministry. Report of the Working Party on Assessment of the Committee for Theological Education, Advisory Council for the Church's Ministry Occasional Paper no. 22 (London: ACCM, 1987).

Eliade, Mircea (ed.). *The Encyclopedia of Religion*. 15 vols. (London: Macmillan, 1987).

Episcopal Ministry: The Report of the Archbishop's Group on the Episcopate (London: Church House, 1990).

Erickson, John. 'Episkope and Episcopacy: Orthodox Perspectives', in P. Bouteneff and A. Falconer (eds.), *Episkope and Episcopacy and the Quest for Visible Unity.* Faith and Order paper no. 183 (Geneva: WCC, 1999), pp. 80–92.

Eucharistic Presidency. A Theological Statement by the House of Bishops of the General Synod, GS 1248 (London: Church House, 1997).

Faivre, Alexandre. *The Emergence of the Laity in the Early Church*, trans. David Smith (New York: Paulist Press, 1990).

Farrar, Austin. 'The Ministry in the New Testament', in Kenneth Kirk (ed.), *The Apostolic Ministry: Essays on the History and Doctrine of Episcopacy* (London: Hodder & Stoughton, 1946), pp. 113–82.

Field, Richard, *Of the Church: Five Books* [1606–10]. 3rd edn in 3 vols. [1635] (repr. Cambridge: Cambridge University Press, 1847).

Fishburn, Ross. 'Michael Ramsey's Pashcal Ecclesiology' (unpublished PhD thesis: Melbourne College of Divinity, Melbourne University, 2008).

Ford, David. *Self and Salvation: Being Transformed* (Cambridge: Cambridge University Press, 1999).

For such a time as this: *A Renewed Diaconate in the Church of England.* Report to the General Synod of the Church of England of a Working Party of the House of Bishops, GS1407 (London: Church House, 2001).

For the Sake of the Gospel: Mutual Recognition of Ordained Ministries in the Anglican and Uniting Churches in Australia. Report of the Anglican and Uniting Church National Dialogue, Australia (Sydney: Anglican General Synod Office, 2001).

Fox, Zeni. *New Ecclesial Ministries: Lay Professionals Serving the Church* (Franklin: Sheed and Ward, 2002).

Franklin, R. William (ed.). *Anglican Orders: Essays on the Centenary of Apostolicae Curae 1896–1996* (London: Mowbray, 1996).

Fries, H., and K. Rahner. *Unity of the Churches: An Actual Possibility* (Philadelphia: Fortress Press, 1983).

Gidden, Anthony. *The Consequences of Modernity* (Cambridge: Polity Press, 1990).

The Gift of Authority: Authority in the Church 111. An Agreed Statement by the Anglican–Roman Catholic International Commission (London and New York: Catholic Truth Society and Church Publishing, 1998).

Giles, Richard. *Always Open: Being an Anglican Today* (Cambridge, MA: Cowley, 2004).

Gill, Robin, and Derek Burke. *Strategic Church Leadership* (London: SPCK, 1996).

God's Reign and Our Unity. Anglican-Reformed Dialogue. (London: SPCK, 1984).

Goleman, Daniel. 'What Makes a Leader?', *Harvard Business Review* (Nov.–Dec. 1998): 1–25.

——, R. Boyatzis and A. Mckee. *The New Leaders: Transforming the Art of Leadership into the Science of Results* (London: Time Warner Paperbacks, 2003).

Greenwood, Robin. *Transforming Priesthood: A New Theology of Mission and Ministry* (London: SPCK, 1994).

——. *Transforming Church: Liberating Structures for Ministry* (London: SPCK, 2002).

Grillmeier, Aloys. *Christ in the Christian Tradition*, vol. 1, *From the Apostolic Age to Chalcedon (451)*. Trans. John Bowden (Atlanta: John Knox Press, 2nd revd edn, 1975).

Gunton, Colin. 'The Church on Earth: The Roots of Community', in Colin Gunton and Daniel Hardy (eds.), *On Being the Church: Essays on the Christian Community* (Edinburgh: T&T Clark, 1989), pp. 48–80.

—— and Daniel Hardy (eds.). *On Being the Church: Essays on the Christian Community* (Edinburgh: T&T Clark, 1989).

——. *The One, the Three and the Many: God, Creation and the Culture of Modernity*. Bampton Lectures, 1992 (Cambridge: Cambridge University Press, 1993).

Hahnenberg, Edward. *Ministries: A Relational Approach* (New York: Crossroad, 2003).

Haire, James, and Gordon Watson. 'Authority and Integrity in the Ministry of the Church', *Phronema* 18 (2003): 29–53.

Hanby, Michael. 'Interceding: Giving Grief to Management', in S. Hauerwas and S. Wells (eds.), *The Blackwell Companion to Christian Ethics* (Oxford: Blackwell, 2004,) pp. 237–49.

Hannaford, Robert. 'Foundations for an Ecclesiology of Ministry', in Christina Hall and Robert Hannaford (eds.), *Ministry and Order* (Leominster: Gracewing, 1996).

Hanson, Anthony T. *The Pioneer Ministry* (London: SPCK, 1975 [1961]).

—— and Richard P.C. Hanson. *The Identity of the Church* (London: SCM, 1987).

Hanson, Richard P.C. 'The Nature of the Anglican Episcopate', in Michael Ramsey (ed.), *Lambeth Essays on Ministry: Essays written for the Lambeth Conference 1968* (London: SPCK, 1969), pp. 79–86.

——. *Christian Priesthood Examined* (London: Lutterworth Press, 1979).

Hardy, Daniel. 'Christian Affirmation and the Structure of Personal Life', in Thomas F. Torrance (ed.), *Belief in Science and Christian Life: The Relevance of Michael Polanyi's Thought for Christian Faith and Life* (Edinburgh: The Handsel Press, 1980), pp. 71–90.

—— and David Ford. *Jubilate: Theology in Praise* (London: Darton, Longman & Todd, 1984).

——. 'Created and Redeemed Sociality', in Colin Gunton and Daniel Hardy (eds.), *On Being the Church: Essays on the Christian Community* (Edinburgh: T&T Clark, 1989), pp. 21–47.

——. *God's Ways with the World: Thinking and Practising Christian Faith* (Edinburgh: T&T Clark, 1996).

——. *Finding the Church: The Dynamic Truth of Anglicanism* (London: SCM, 2001).

Harford, George, and Morley Stevenson (eds.). *The Prayer Book Dictionary* (London: Isaac Pitman and Sons, 1913).

Hassard, J., and M. Parker (eds.). *Postmodernism and Organizations* (London: Sage, 1993).

Hatch, Edwin. *The Organization of the Early Christian Churches*. Bampton Lectures, 1880 (London: Rivingtons, 1881).

Hatchett, Marion. *Commentary on the American Prayer Book* (New York: Seabury Press, 1980).

Hayes, Alan. 'Christian Ministry in Three Cities of the Western Empire', in Richard Longenecker (ed.), *Community Formation in the Early Church and in the Church Today* (Peabody: Hendrickson, 2002), pp. 129–56.

Hebert, Anthony. 'Ministerial Episcopacy', in Kenneth Kirk (ed.), *The Apostolic Ministry: Essays on the History and Doctrine of Episcopacy* (London: Hodder & Stoughton, 1946), pp. 493–534.

——. *Apostle and Bishop: A Study of the Gospel, the Ministry and the Church Community* (London: Faber & Faber, 1963).

Holb, R.C. *Jurgen Habermas: Critique in the Public Sphere* (New York: Routledge, 1991).

Hort, F.J.A. *The Christian Ecclesia* (New York: Macmillan, 1897).

Hughes, Graham. *Worship as Meaning: Liturgical Theology for Late-Modernity* (Cambridge: Cambridge University Press, 2003).

Inge, John. *Towards a Christian Theology of Place* (Aldershot: Ashgate, 2003).

Jalland, T.G. 'The Doctrine of the Parity of Ministers', in Kenneth Kirk (ed.), *The Apostolic Ministry: Essays on the History and Doctrine of Episcopacy* (London: Hodder & Stoughton, 1946), pp. 304–49.

Jeanrond, Werner. 'Community and Authority: The Nature and Implications of the Authority of the Christian Community', in Colin Gunton and Daniel Hardy (eds.), *On Being the Church: Essays on the Christian Community* (Edinburgh: T&T Clark, 1989).

Jeeves, Malcolm. 'Toward a Composite Portrait of Human Nature', in Malcolm Jeeves (ed.), *From Cells to Souls – and Beyond* (Grand Rapids: Eerdmans, 2004).

Jenkins, Philip. *The Next Christendom: The Coming of Global Christianity* (Oxford: Oxford University Press, 2002).

Josaitis, Norman F. *Edwin Hatch and Early Church Order* (Gembloux: J. Duculot, 1971).

Kauffman, Stuart. *The Origins of Order* (Oxford: Oxford University Press, 1993).

Kavanagh, Aidan. 'Christian Ministry and Ministries', *Anglican Theological Review* 66, Supplementary Series no. 9 (1964): 36–48.

Kaye, Bruce. 'Bishops and Social Leadership: What We Might Learn from the First and Only Bishop of Australia', in Alan Cadwallader (ed.), *Episcopacy: Views from the Antipode* (Adelaide: Anglican Board of Christian Education, 1994), pp. 91–108.

Kelly, Gerard. 'The Recognition of Ministries: A Shift in Ecumenical Thinking', *One in Christ* 30 (1994): 10–21.

Kimel, Alvin F. Jr. 'Who are the Bishops? Episkope and the Church', *Anglican Theological Review* 77/1 (Winter 1995): 58–75.

Kirk, Kenneth (ed.). *The Apostolic Ministry: Essays on the History and Doctrine of Episcopacy* (London: Hodder & Stoughton, 1946).

Kuhn, Helmut. 'The Case for Order in a Disordered Age', in Paul G. Kuntz (ed.), *The Concept of Order* (London: University of Washington Press, 1968), pp. 442–59.

Lane Fox, Robin. *Pagans and Christians* (London: Penguin Books, 1988).

Larive, Armand. *After Sunday: A Theology of Work* (New York: Continuum, 2004).

Lightfoot, J.B. *The Christian Ministry*, ed. and intro. Philip E. Hughes (London: Morehouse-Barlow 1983).

——. 'The Christian Ministry', in *St Paul's Epistle to the Philippians* [1868] (London: Macmillan, 1986), pp. 181–269.

Lilburne, Geoffrey. *A Sense of Place: A Christian Theology of the Land* (Nashville: Abingdon, 1989).

Lumen Gentium, Decree on Ecumenism and Decree on Ministry and Life of Priests. In Austin O'Flannery (gen. ed.), *Vatican Council II: The Conciliar and Post-Conciliar Documents* (New York: Costello Publishing Company, 1981), pp. 1–95.

Luther, Martin. 'An Appeal to the Ruling Class of German Nationality as to the Amelioration of the State of Christendom' [1520], in *Martin Luther: Selections from his Writings*, ed. John Dillenberger (New York: Doubleday, 1961), pp. 403–85.

Maccoby, Michael. 'Narcissisitic Leaders: The Incredible Pros, the Incredible Cons', *Harvard Business Review* (Nov.–Dec. 1998): 27–49.

McDermott, R.P. 'An Anglican's Reflections on Priesthood', in N. Lash and J. Rhymer (eds.), *The Christian Priesthood* (London: Darton, Longman & Todd, 1970), pp. 141–61.

Making Unity More Visible. Report of the Meissen Commission, 1997–2001 (London: Church House, 2002).

Martin, Francis. *The Feminist Question* (Grand Rapids: Eerdmans, 1994).

Mason, A.J. *The Church of England and Episcopacy* (Cambridge: Cambridge University Press,1914).

Mason, Kenneth. *Priesthood and Society* (Norwich: Canterbury Press, 1992).

Merkle, Benjamine. *The Elder and Overseer: One Office in the Early Church* (New York: Peter Lang, 2003).

The Methodist Worship Book (Peterborough: Methodist Publishing House, 1999).

Miller, Charles. 'The Theology of the Laity: Description and Construction with Reference to the American Book of Common Prayer', *Anglican Theological Review* 84/2 (Spring 2002): 219–38.

Moberly, R.C. *Ministerial Priesthood, Chapters (Preliminary to a Study of the Ordinal) on The Rationale of Ministry and the Meaning of Christian Priesthood* [1897] (London: SPCK, London, 1969).

Moltmann, Jurgen. *Theology of Hope* (London: SCM, 1967).

——. *The Church in the Power of the Spirit* (London: SCM, 1977).

The Moscow Agreed Statement: Anglican–Orthodox Dialogue (London: SPCK, 1977).

The New International Dictionary of New Testament Theology, ed. Colin Brown, 3 vols. (Exeter: Paternoster Press, 1978).

A New Zealand Prayer Book (Auckland: Collins, 1989).

Nichols, Aidan. *Holy Order: Apostolic Priesthood from the New Testament to the Second Vatican Council* (Dublin: Veritas, 1990).

Newbold Adams, Richard. *The Eighth Day: Social Evolution as the Self-Organization of Energy* (Austin: University of Texas Press, 1988).

Newman, John Henry. *An Essay on the Development of Doctrine* [1845]. Ed. and intro. J. Cameron (Harmondsworth: Penguin Books, 1974).

Norris, Richard. 'Bishops, Succession and the Apostolicity of the Church', in J. Robert Wright (ed.), *On Being a Bishop*. Papers on Episcopacy from the Moscow Consultation, 1992 (New York: Church Hymnal, 1992), pp. 52–62.

On the Way to Fuller Koinonia: Official Report of the Fifth World Conference on Faith and Order. Faith and Order Paper no. 166. Ed. Thomas Best and Gunther Gassmann (Geneva: WCC, 1994).

On the Way to Visible Unity [The Meissen Common Statement]. Board for Mission and Unity GS 843 (London: Church House, 1988).

Ordination and Ministry in the Uniting Church. Report from the Assembly Commission on Doctrine for study and comment. Uniting Church in Australia. (Sydney: National Assembly, 1994).

Our Modern Services. Anglican Church of Kenya (Nairobi: Uzima Press, 2002).

The Oxford Dictionary of the Christian Church. Ed. F.L. Cross (Oxford: Oxford University Press, 1974).

Patterns and Prayers for Christian Worship. Baptist Union of Great Britain (Oxford: Oxford University Press, 1991).

Pattison, Stephen. 'Some Objections to Aims and Objectives', in G.R. Evans and M. Percy (eds.), *Managing the Church: Order and Organization in a Secular Age* (Sheffield: Sheffield Academic Press, 2000).

Patzia, Arthur G. *The Emergence of the Church* (Downers Grove: InterVarsity Press, 2001).

Peacocke, Arthur. *God and the New Biology* (London: J.M. Dent & Sons, 1986).

——. *Theology for a Scientific Age* (London: SCM Press, 1993).

——. 'God's Interaction with the World: The Implications of Deterministic "Chaos" and of Interconnected and Interdependent Complexity', in Robert Russell, Nancy Murphy and Arthur Peacocke (eds.), *Chaos and Complexity: Scientific Perspectives on Divine Action* (Indiana: University of Notre Dame Press, 2nd edn, 1997), pp. 263–88.

Peat, David. *From Certainty to Uncertainty: The Story of Science and Ideas in the Twentieth Century* (Washington: Joseph Henry Press, 2002).

Pelikan, Jaroslav. *Christian Doctrine and Modern Culture (since 1700)* (Chicago: University of Chicago Press, 1989).

Pickard, Stephen. *Liberating Evangelism* (Harrisburg: Trinity Press International, 1999).

——. 'Orders of Praise: Ordination, Mission and the *Missio Dei'*, in William Emilsen and John Squires (eds.), *Prayer and Thanksgiving: Essays in Honour of the Revd Dr. Graham Hughes* (Sydney: UTC Publications, 2003), pp. 87–100.

——.'Healing the Wound: Collaborative Ministry for Mission', *St Mark's Review: A Journal of Christian Thought and Opinion* 199 (2005): 3–11; a revised version subsequently appeared in *Ecclesiology* 3.1 (2006): 81–101.

——. 'The Travail of the Episcopate: Management, and the Diocese in an Age of Mission', in Bruce Kaye, Sarah Macneil and Heather Thomson (eds.), *'Wonderfully and Confessedly Strange': Australian Essays in Anglican Ecclesiology* (Adelaide: ATF Press, 2006), pp. 127–55.

——. 'This Your Promise: The Theologian as Priest', in Heather Thomson (ed.), *Embracing Grace: Being a Theologian in the 21st Century* (Canberra: Barton Books, 2009), pp. 7–20.

Podmore, Colin. 'Historian's Debate: "The Moravian Episcopate and the Episcopal Church": A Personal Response', *Anglican and Episcopal History* 72/3 (2003): 351–84.

The Porvoo Common Statement. Conversations between the British and Irish Anglican Churches and Nordic and Baltic Lutheran Churches. The Council for Christian Unity of the General Synod of the Church of England Occasional Paper no. 3 (London: Church House, 1993).

A Prayer Book for Australia (Sydney: Broughton Books, 1995).

The Priesthood of the Ordained Ministry. Report of the Board for Mission and Unity of the General Synod of the Church of England (London: Church House, 1986).

Prigogine, Ilya, and Isabelle Stengers. *Order Out of Chaos: Man's New Dialogue with Nature* (New York and London: Bantam Books, 1984).

Rademacher, William J. *Lay Ministry: A Theological, Spiritual & Pastoral Handbook* (New York: Crossroad, 1992).

Radner, Ephraim. *Hope Among the Fragments: The Broken Church and Its Engagement of Scripture* (Grand Rapids: Brazos Press, 2004).

Rahner, Karl, et al. (eds), *Sacramentum Mundi*, 6 vols. (London: Burns and Oates, 1970)

Ramsey, Michael, *The Gospel and the Catholic Church* (London: SPCK, 1936).

Ratzinger, Joseph. 'Commentary on Profession of Faith's Concluding Paragraphs', *Origins* 28/8 (1998): 116–19.

Reid, Duncan. 'Are Bishops an Ecumenical Problem? Episcopacy and Episcope in Two Bilateral Conversation', in Alan Cadwallader (ed.), *Episcopacy: Views from the Antipode* (Adelaide: Anglican Board of Christian Education, 1994), pp. 289–305.

The Report of the Meissen Commission, 1991–1996. General Synod, GS Misc 490 (London: Church House, 1996).

Resident Aliens: A Conversation with Stanley Hauerwas, November 21, 2006 http://www.everythingchristian.org/News/psalms_n4.ihtml?nid=2558&catid=2.

Ricoeur, Paul. *Oneself as Another*, trans. K. Blamey (Chicago and London: University of Chicago Press, 1992).

Ritschl, Dietrich. *The Logic of Theology* (London: SCM, 1986).

Roberts, Richard. 'Ruling the Body: The Care of Souls in a Managerial Church', in *Religion, Theology and the Human Sciences* (Cambridge: Cambridge University Press, 2002), pp. 161–89.

——. 'The Quest for Appropriate Accountability: Stakeholders, Tradition and the Managerial Prerogative in Higher Education'. *Studies in Christian Ethics* 17/1 (2004): 1–21.

Robertson, David. *Collaborative Ministry* (Oxford: Bible Reading Fellowship, 2007).

Robinson, John. 'Kingdom, Church and Ministry', in K. Carey (ed.), *The Historic Episcopate* (Westminster: Dacre Press, 1954), pp. 11–22.

—— et al. (eds.). *Layman's Church* (London: Lutterworth Press, 1963).

The Roman Pontifical. Revised by Decree of the Second Vatican Ecumenical Council and published by authority of Pope Paul VI (International Commission on English in the Liturgy: Washington, 1978).

Rosato, Philip. 'Priesthood of the Baptised and Priesthood of the Ordained: Complimentary Approaches to their Relation', *Gregorianum* 68/1–2 (1987): 215–66.

Rudge, Peter F. *Ministry and Management* (London: Tavistock, 1968).

Rusch, W.G. 'Introduction', in P. Bouteneff and A. Falconer (eds.), *Episkope and Episcopacy and the Quest for Visible Unity.* Faith and Order paper no. 183 (Geneva: WCC, 1999), pp. 1–11.

Schillebeeckx. Edward. *The Church with a Human Face: A New and Expanded Theology of Ministry* (London: SCM, 1985).

Schleiermacher, Friedrich. *The Christian Faith* (Edinburgh: T&T Clark, 1968).

Schwobel, Christoph. 'The Creature of the Word: Recovering the Ecclesiology of the Reformers', in Colin Gunton and Daniel Hardy (eds.), *On Being the Church: Essays on the Christian Community* (Edinburgh: T&T Clark, 1989), pp. 110–55.

Stone, Darwell. *The Church: Its Ministry and Authority* (London: Rivingtons, 1908).

Sullivan, Francis. 'A New Obstacle to Anglican–Roman Catholic Dialogue', *America* 179/3 (1–8 Aug. 1998): 6–7.

——. *From Apostles to Bishops* (New York: The Newman Press, 2001).

Sykes, Stephen. *Unashamed Anglicanism* (London: Darton, Longman & Todd, 1995).

——. '"To the Intent that these Orders may be Continued": An Anglican Theology of Holy Orders', in R. William Franklin (ed.), *Anglican Orders: Essays on the Centenary of Apostolicae Curae 1896–1996* (London: Mowbray, 1996), pp. 48–63.

The Theology of Ordination. Report by the Faith and Order Advisory Group of the Board for Mission and Unity, GS 281, ND.

Thiselton, Anthony. *Interpreting God and the Postmodern Self: On Meaning, Manipulation and Promise* (Edinburgh: T & T Clark, 1995).

Thornton, Lionel. 'The Body of Christ in the New Testament', in Kenneth Kirk (ed.), *The Apostolic Ministry: Essays on the History and Doctrine of Episcopacy* (London: Hodder & Stoughton, 1946), pp. 53–112.

Thrall, Margaret. *The Second Epistle to the Corinthians*, 2 vols. (Edinburgh: T&T Clark, 1994).

Tracey, David. *The Spirituality Revolution* (Sydney: HarperCollins, 2003).

Towards Koinonia in Faith, Life and Witness. Discussion paper, Fifth World Conference on Faith and Order, Santiago de Compostela. Faith and Order Paper no. 161 (Geneva: WCC, 1993)

Tuomela, Raimo. *The Philosophy of Sociality: The Shared Point of View* (Oxford: Oxford University Press, 2007).

Van Gennep, Arnold. *The Rites of Passage.* Trans. M.B. Vizdom and G.L. Caffee (Chicago: University of Chicago Press, 1960).

Vermeersch, A. 'Vows', in Charles Herbermann et al (eds.), *The Catholic Encyclopedia* (New York: The Encyclopedia Press, 1912), 15:511–14.

Volf, Miroslav. *Work in the Spirit: Toward a Theology of Work* (New York: Oxford University Press, 1991).

Wainwright, Geoffrey. 'Is Episcopal Succession a Matter of Dogma for Anglicans? The Evidence of Some Recent Dialogues', in C. Podmore (ed.), *Community,*

Unity and Communion: Essays in Honour of Mary Tanner (London: Church House, 1998), pp. 164–79.

Wannenwetsch, Bernard. '"Members of One Another": *Charis*, Ministry and Representation: A Politic-Ecclesial Reading of Romans 12', in C. Bartholomew et al. (eds.), *.A Royal Priesthood: The Use of the Bible Ethically and Politically A Dialogue with Oliver O'Donovan*, vol. 3 (Carlisle: Paternoster Press; Grand Rapids: Zondervan, 2002), pp. 196–224.

Weber, Max. *The Theory of Social and Economic Organization*, trans. A.R. Henderson and T. Parsons; revd and ed. Talcott Parsons (London: William Hodge and Co., 1947).

Webster, John. 'The Self-Organizing Power of the Gospel of Christ: Episcopacy and Community Formation', *International Journal of Systematic Theology* 3/1 (March 2001): 69–82.

——. *Holiness* (London: SCM, 2003).

Wheatly, Margaret J. *Leadership and the New Science: Discovering Order in a Chaotic World* (San Francisco: Berret-Koehler, 1999).

Working as One Body. The Report of the Archbishop's Commission on the Organization of the Church of England (London: Church House Publishing, 1995).

Wright, David. F. 'Ministerial Priesthood: Further Reflections', *Anvil* 3/2 (1986): 195–207.

——. 'The Charismatic Movement: The Laicizing of Christianity?', in Deryck W. Lovegrove (ed.), *The Rise of the Laity in Evangelical Protestantism* (London and New York: Routledge, 2002), pp. 253–63.

Wright, J. Robert (ed.). *On Being a Bishop*. Papers on Episcopacy from the Moscow Consultation, 1992 (New York: Church Hymnal, 1992).

——. 'The Origins of the Episcopate and Episcopal Ministry in the Early Church', in J. Robert Wright (ed.), *On Being a Bishop*. Papers on Episcopacy from the Moscow Consultation, 1992 (New York: Church Hymnal, 1992), pp. 10–62.

Wrong, Dennis. *The Problem of Order* (London: Harvard University Press, 1994).

Young, Frances. 'Ministerial Forms and Functions in the Church Communities of the Greek Fathers', in Richard Longenecker (ed.), *Community Formation in the Early Church and in the Church Today* (Peabody: Hendrickson, 2002), pp. 157–76.

Zaragoza, Edward. *No Longer Servants but Friends: A Theology of Ordained Ministry* (Nashville: Abingdon Press, 1999).

Zizioulas, John. *Being as Communion: Studies in Personhood and the Church* (London: Darton, Longman & Todd, 1985).

Index